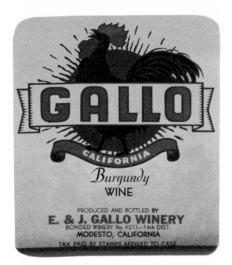

GALLO
CALIFORNIA
Burgundy
WINE

PRODUCED AND BOTTLED BY
E. & J. GALLO WINERY
BONDED WINERY No. 4213—14th DIST.
MODESTO, CALIFORNIA
TAX PAID BY STAMPS AFFIXED TO CASE

THE WINE CELLARS OF
ERNEST & JULIO GALLO

ERNEST & JULIO GALLO VINTED & CELLARED THIS
WINE & BOTTLED IT IN MODESTO, CALIF.
ALCOHOL 11.0% BY VOLUME

GALLO
CALIFORNIA
VIN ROSÉ

Light Pearls Wine
Fragrant-Provocative
Delicious

SERVE COLD, OR OVER ICE

GALLO
Spañada
GRAPE WINE & NATURAL FRUIT FLAVORS
MADE & BOTTLED BY GALLO VINEYARDS, MODESTO, CALIF. - ALC. 11% BY VOL.

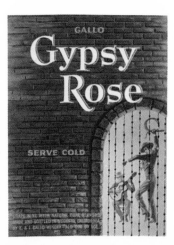

GALLO
Gypsy
Rose

SERVE COLD

BOTTLED AT OUR WINERY IN CALIFORNIA
PASTOSO   SCELTO
GALLO
Vintner's Stock
CALIFORNIA
BURGUNDY
ALCOHOL 13% BY VOLUME

MADE AND BOTTLED BY E. & J. GALLO WINERY

ERNEST AND JULIO

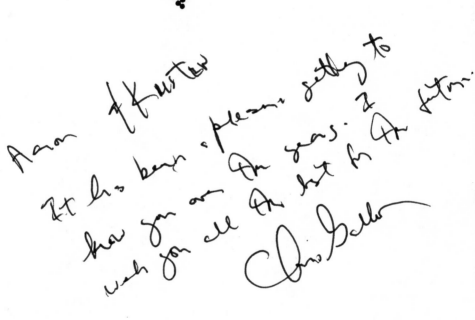

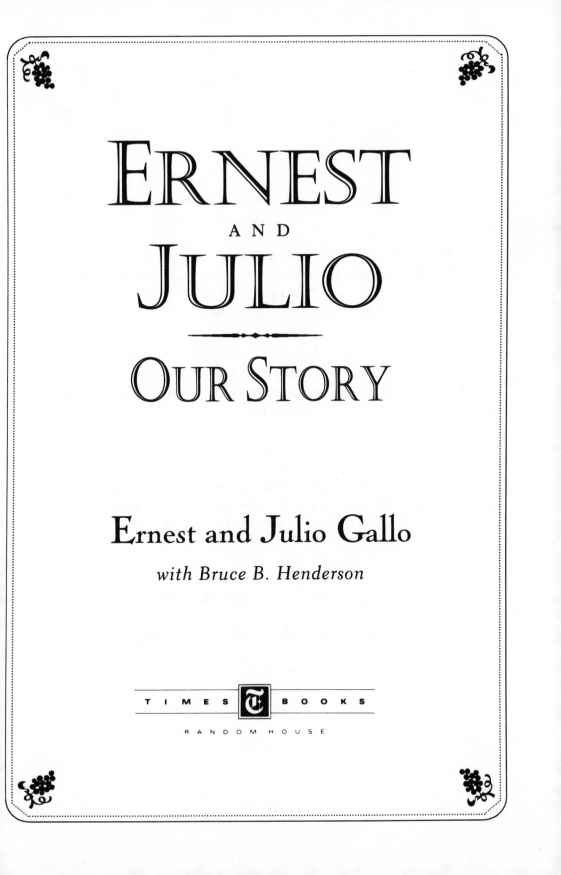

ERNEST
AND
JULIO
OUR STORY

Ernest and Julio Gallo

with Bruce B. Henderson

TIMES BOOKS

RANDOM HOUSE

All rights reserved under International and Pan-American Copyright
Conventions. Published in the United States by Times Books, a division
of Random House, Inc., New York, and simultaneously in Canada by
Random House of Canada, Limited, Toronto.

Library of Congress Cataloging-in-Publication Data
Gallo, Ernest.
Ernest and Julio: our story/by Ernest and Julio Gallo: with
Bruce B. Henderson.
p. cm.
Includes index.
ISBN 0-8129-2454-1
1. Gallo, Ernest. 2. Gallo, Julio. 3. Vintners—California—
Biography. 4. Wine and wine making—California—History.
I. Gallo, Julio. II. Henderson, Bruce B. III. Title.
TP547.G34A3 1994
641.2'2'0922794—dc20   94-10011

Book design by Anne Scatto/PIXEL PRESS

Manufactured in the United States of America

9 8 7 6 5 4 3 2

First Edition

For Amelia and Aileen

The winemaker is a warrior.
He has to fight the vagaries of nature, storms,
insects, disease, rot, hail and bad luck.
This is why every bottle is worthy of respect and
every glass must be drunk with the honor it deserves.
That soil, that man, that fight, are embodied in your glass.

—ANONYMOUS, FROM THE ITALIAN

CONTENTS

ERNEST AND JULIO

1

A LUG BOX FOR
A CRADLE

Ernest

One of my earliest memories is of a vineyard.

I must be only four or five years old. It is harvest time in California, probably around mid-August.

Grandfather and Grandmother Bianco—the only grandparents I ever knew because my paternal grandparents, the Gallos, never left Italy—and several helpers are in a vineyard picking grapes, filling up the lug boxes that will in turn be emptied into a horse-drawn wagon. It is back-breaking work. There is little for a child to do. When I tire of running up and down the rows, Grandmother makes a bed for me in a lug box, which she pushes into the shade under a canopy of vines. As she moves down the rows picking grapes, she drags me with her. The summer heat, the grapes and vines, my grandmother's smile, are all part of this memory.

I am now in my mid-eighties as I recall that time long ago. Forgive me if I recollect some events and facts better than others. Selective memory is a fascinating human trait, allowing us, in most cases, to remember many more of the good things that have happened in our lives than the bad. For that we should be grateful.

I never thought I would find myself doing a book about my life, though I had long been urged to do so by family and close friends. History has always fascinated me, but I have been so busy that I have rarely taken the time to reflect on my own past. As I watched my grand-children grow into adulthood, I realized that I wanted them to know the real story of the E. & J. Gallo Winery, the business that Julio and I spent our lives building. I also realized that it was a story that only Julio and I could tell.

Julio, a year my junior, had already come to similar conclusions.

But we confess to another motive as well.

This country is in very serious trouble economically. Throughout the years, Julio and I have fought hard to make the wine business in this country important, and even now, to keep it as an American indus-try. Doing so has never been easy, and today we find that it has never been more difficult. We have regretted seeing some of the very impor-tant American industries overshadowed and even surpassed by the in-dustries of other nations. To us, that is downright embarrassing. Julio and I long ago agreed that, as long as we lived, we would never permit foreigners to dominate or control the American wine industry. Other wine-producing countries often have the advantage of cheaper land and lower labor costs. Our challenge has been made even greater be-cause our government has been disposed to lowering import tariffs to assist other countries' economies at the expense of our own.

Since we started our winery in the summer of 1933—based on a tem-porary permit obtained three months before the end of the "noble ex-periment" known as Prohibition—it has always been our philosophy to do whatever was to the long-range benefit of our company, regardless of its effect on current profits. Our attitude is considered fairly unusual in this age of often overpaid managers of public companies, whose pri-mary interest is a favorable earnings comparison to the previous quarter or year in order to earn a current bonus, too often regardless of the long-range effect on the company. We have been able to maintain this philosophy because we have kept our business private, entirely in the family. We do not like to answer to anyone for our mistakes. (My advice recently to a group of young company presidents was this: "Keep your company private, and if it has already gone public, buy it back.")

Our message is that unremitting desire, commitment, hard work, striving for perfection, and the occasional good fortune that seems to travel with those attributes are what it takes to overcome the odds and rise from having so little to the top of a major industry.

Our story also illustrates that in the American system this seemingly impossible goal can be achieved within the short span of a lifetime by the offspring of immigrants who started from nowhere, with nothing.

Julio and I faced what must have seemed to others to be overwhelming odds when we set our course more than sixty years ago. I am glad that we were young, brash, and inexperienced. We brought to the effort a spirit and confidence that perhaps only youth can muster.

We wish for our story to show, particularly to the young, that our country's system *does* work for those who refuse to tolerate mediocrity and continually strive for perfection and success.

I WAS BORN ON MARCH 18, 1909, in Jackson, California. Here in the foothills on the western slope of the Sierra Nevada, my parents, Joe and Susie—born Giuseppe Gallo and Assunta Bianco in Italy—ran a small boardinghouse catering to Italian immigrant miners. But the gold rush was winding down, and as the big mines closed one by one, people began to move away. My parents soon relocated to Oakland, across the bay from San Francisco, where they operated another small boardinghouse. My mother did the cleaning and cooking, serving three meals a day to the boarders, while my father tended bar in his saloon on the ground floor.

I lived with my grandparents in the San Joaquin Valley town of Hanford from the time Julio was born until I was six. My mother, I was later told, could not handle her daily chores for the boarders and at the same time care for both me and the new baby, Julio, who was born one year and three days after me. So I was farmed out.

Behind my grandparents' home at 301 West Fourth Street in Hanford, my grandfather operated a small winery, probably with a capacity of no more than eight or nine thousand gallons. He and Grandmother owned a number of adjoining lots on their street, as well as a twenty-acre vineyard northwest of town. I would learn later that Grandfather had gone into partnership with a fellow Italian on a forty-acre vineyard, but soon the two men quarreled and decided to split. One half of the vineyard was in fine shape but the vines in the other half were marginal. The men argued, naturally, about who should get the best half. At an impasse, they agreed to play a game of cards, with the winner taking the best half. Grandfather won the game and the prime acreage.

My grandfather Battista Bianco had preceded his wife and children to America. He was thirty-two when he arrived at the U.S. Immigration Center at Ellis Island in New York Bay on May 2, 1892, as a steerage passenger aboard the S.S. *Werra*. After establishing himself in California and saving some money, he sent for his wife and children to join him in 1896. Grandmother came with their son and three daughters, including my mother, then eight years old. After a difficult Atlantic crossing, they too passed through Ellis Island, then boarded a train west.

In those early years with my grandparents, I grew especially close to my grandmother, a loving and nurturing woman whom I will always miss, no matter how old I live to be.

Like many Italian sons of his era, my grandfather learned to make homemade wine at the side of his father. They lived in the Piedmont region of northern Italy, where grape varieties like Dolcetto, Brachetto, Barbera, and Nebbiolo are grown and made into that country's robust Barberas and Barolos, and lighter Barbarescos. After settling in Han-

6

ford, then one of California's largest grape-growing regions, and pruning and harvesting for others, Grandpa eventually started pruning and harvesting his own grapes and crushing them to make a hearty wine that he sold to his neighbors who brought their own gallon jugs. His first and most loyal customers were Basque sheepherders from the surrounding hills. They came to town with their earthen jugs for him to fill for a nickel.

I have a second very clear early memory, and this one is of wine.

I was inside the little backyard shed that served as my grandfather's winery. The grapes, brought here by horse and wagon, were crushed and had been fermenting for several days. After the wine had been drawn from the tank, two workers were taking turns pushing a metal bar back and forth, pressing the pomace, or grape residue. On a break, the men filled a tin cup with new wine dripping from the press and each in turn drank some. I came over, curious. Picking up the cup, I tasted the few drops left. The pressed wine was sweet. The men laughed. I filled the cup again, drained it, and went back for more. I still remember the two workers laughing.

The next thing I knew, I was waking up in my grandmother's bed, feeling very ill, my head spinning. It was not necessary for her to deliver a lecture—the state of my head and stomach were ample punishment. At age five I had my first hangover. It was also my last.

Not long after that, I was brought back to live with my parents and brother in Oakland. With Grandpa suffering respiratory problems, my grandparents hoped a different climate would help and they moved to southern California. I am not clear when I would have returned to my parents' home, had it not been for my grandfather's health problems and their relocation. Grandma apparently hadn't wanted to give me back, and did so reluctantly.

Within months my grandparents were back in Hanford. The change of climate had not helped. When Grandfather's condition worsened, he was admitted to the Hanford Sanitarium. Four days later, while being prepared for surgery to drain a lung abscess, he was administered ether for anaesthesia. It caused a sudden paralysis of his weakened respiratory system and he stopped breathing. He died on the operating table. Grandpa was fifty-nine.

After rejoining my parents, I missed Grandma. I saw her only occasionally until her death at age sixty-four in 1927.

At the time of my grandfather's death, it had been twenty-four years since he had left Italy for the United States. His proudest day might well have been on March 31, 1902, when he stood in Kings County Superior Court, Hanford, beside an Austrian and an Englishman and joined them in taking the oath of citizenship.

On that day, my grandfather was the first in our family to become an American citizen.

IN 1917, when I was eight, we moved to a farm.

Prohibition had put my father out of the saloon business, and my parents closed up the boardinghouse as well. They bought a farm outside of Antioch, forty miles away.

The 120-acre farm had a tule swamp running diagonally through it. On either side of the slough were bluffs, which had previously been tilled and planted. There was also a 20-acre vineyard on the property.

My brother, Julio, and I were up every morning at dawn tending to chores, including milking a few cows. We worked after school and on weekends. Most days we stayed in the fields until coming in at dark to do our homework. My father had not been raised on a farm and had no aptitude for the work. He had to learn everything the hard way. He tried to plow in midsummer when the ground was dry and rock-hard instead of waiting for it to soften up after the rains. Since trucks were beginning to replace horses, he had gotten a good price on some giant dray horses. But the Clydesdales were too large and awkward for field work. Father succeeded only in repeatedly breaking the plow's moldboard. He soon traded the big horses for mules.

By the age of eight, I was driving a four-mule team through the fields behind a plow. The acres of tomatoes we planted near the slough areas did not grow, nor did the garlic we planted on the bluffs. We also tried potatoes, another normally robust crop. The family stayed up late at night cutting the eyes off old potatoes, which we planted first thing in the morning before they dried out. The potato crop failed too. Father always seemed to plant the wrong crop in the wrong place at the wrong time.

One night during our first winter in Antioch, I was awakened in the middle of the night by the drip-dripping of cold rainwater on my face. I moved my bed to the middle of the room to stay dry. Because we never could afford to fix the leaky roof, moving my bed became an annual ritual.

When my classmates asked if I would like to join the local Boy Scout troop, I said yes and was very excited until I found out I would have to buy my own uniform—at a cost of about a dollar and a half. I knew without asking that my folks could not afford that, so I declined.

Father required us to come home directly from school to work in the fields. Most of my classmates didn't have to work every day after school and on weekends too, but Julio and I did. Wherever we lived, Father knew exactly how long the walk from school took with no dawdling. A couple of days before I was going to graduate from grade school, we were dismissed early. I figured I had some time to kill. It turned out my father was in town getting a haircut, and he saw all the kids on the street. He came to the school and found me playing basketball on the playground. A few days earlier, he had promised to buy me some long pants for graduation. But he got so mad at me for not coming home right away that he refused to buy new pants for me, and I graduated in my old knickers.

We looked forward to one week's vacation spent every summer with relatives. I'll never forget one trip to San Francisco, where we stayed with my Aunt Tillie, my mother's older sister. She claimed to

9

be able to tell fortunes with tarot cards. I asked her to tell me mine.

She spread the cards out before her and studied them. "Your fortune says you're going to be very successful in business."

"What kind of business?"

"It's fluid," Aunt Tillie said, still searching the cards. "I'm looking . . . I'm looking . . . it's either the oil business . . . or the wine business."

Julio

Our father had more or less stumbled into farming. His family lived in Fossano, Italy—about twenty miles south of Torino. My father's parents ran a small inn located adjacent to a livestock auction yard. Once a week, when there was an auction, they would have a full house for a night or two. As their ten children grew, the family inn could not support them all. The economic conditions in Italy were so bad that they ended up leaving, just as millions of their countrymen were forced to do, looking for jobs and a better life.

The United States had not been my father's first choice. His three older brothers had gone to South America. Francesco found work in the canning business in southern Brazil, while Giorgio and Mauricio thrashed grain on the plains of Argentina. My father's two brothers wrote him about the opportunities for work. He followed them to Argentina, but disliked life on the pampas so much that he soon returned to Italy, which was still deep in a depression. He bought a one-way ticket and headed for America.

My father came by steamship from the port of Genoa, arriving at Ellis Island with only a few dollars. Ernest remembers hearing that although Father's destination was California, he had money to get only as far as Pennsylvania. He worked awhile with other Italian immigrants in the coal mines, eventually saving enough money for train fare to California.

I know from my father's own stories that he arrived in time for the

Great Earthquake of 1906, and that he watched San Francisco burn from across the bay in Oakland. Unskilled and unable to speak much English, he hired on as a ditchdigger. For fifty cents a day he shoveled trenches in streets for new sewage lines.

Italians have always enjoyed wine with their meals, and in those days the boardinghouses that put them up served wine directly from large barrels. Seeing an opportunity, my father became a small-time wine dealer. He bought wine from family wineries, stamped "Gallo" on the barrels, and supplied boarding houses in the Italian quarters.

Ernest and I remember different stories as to how our father and mother met, but in each version they met because of wine. Either he met my mother's father, Battista Bianco, at an Oakland boardinghouse while Grandpa was selling his wine (the way I thought it happened), or out in the Valley when our father came across the backyard winery in Hanford (Ernest's version). Grandpa must have liked what he saw because soon my father was meeting the three unmarried Bianco daughters. I understand it was pretty much love at first sight for my father and mother. She was the middle sister, the more subdued and quieter one. They were married in Hanford by a justice of the peace on March 18, 1908. She was twenty-one, he was twenty-five.

I was born in Oakland on March 21, 1910.

I grew up speaking both Italian and English. My father's English was limited—he spoke to Mama and she to him in the Piedmontese dialect. He had learned English later in life, while she had learned it in grade school in Hanford.

One of my earliest memories is of Mama, in her kitchen, preparing meals for our boarders. Also, for a while she fed hot lunches to highschool kids. I remember the big kids clamoring for more of her steaming spaghetti.

My mother was very much like her mother: hardworking, yet warm and compassionate. They were both great cooks. Grandma Bianco's three daughters all carried on with her recipes. My favorite was her ravioli, which is a very difficult dish to make from scratch. Growing up, if we were going to have company for Sunday dinner, Mama would start on Saturday morning, rolling out the dough by hand the way Grandma must have taught her. It took most of the weekend. You can't get anything like it in restaurants. My mother's ravioli recipe has passed down through the family—Aileen makes it, and so does Ernest's wife, Amelia.

I have many memories, good and bad, of the farm in Antioch. The only thing that grew in abundance there were the native tules. At some point, my father decided to get sheep, figuring they would eat anything. Unfortunately, they didn't like the tules, but were more than willing to eat everything else. They kept drifting over dangerously close to the vineyard. It was my job to keep them out. One day, our small flock of sheep was being especially stubborn, forcing me to run up and down the bluffs safeguarding the vineyard. Finally, I sat down to rest. My father returned from town to find me asleep under a tree and the sheep in the vineyard, stripping the vines. He ordered me into the barn, where he lashed me on the backside with his belt. I remember the strap not hurting nearly as much as the buckle.

In those days whippings from Father were frequent. His temper was like a volcano; he was very volatile and excitable. He would have something bothering him, something he wouldn't talk about, and then anything we said or did would send him into a rage. We learned to do as we were told in the hope of not setting him off. My father would get over it pretty quickly, then we'd get on with our lives.

That first fall on the farm, Ernest and I picked our first grapes, learning how to use the wooden-handled harvesting knives so that we didn't cut ourselves on the sharp blades. After picking all day, we loaded boxes of grapes onto Father's Model-T Ford flatbed truck. For two weeks he drove the load to the Oakland produce market every morning, while we stayed home to pick. On mornings when the truck wouldn't start, we would pull it with a plow horse so the truck could get going enough for Father to pop the clutch. He had limited success selling our grapes, which did not compare well to other table grapes at market.

Our family expanded on the farm. It was there that my younger brother, Joseph, was born on September 11, 1919.

Within a couple of years, farming in Antioch had defeated us—the salty swamps that defied planting, the winter flooding, the destructive spring frosts. My father decided it was time to move on and try our luck elsewhere.

In 1921, when I was eleven, we left the farm with whatever we could load onto our truck. With our parents and the baby in the cab, there was no room inside for me and Ernest, so we rode atop the load on a floppy old mattress.

WE STAYED FOR ABOUT A YEAR at a farmhouse in Livermore, California. Located about thirty miles east of San Francisco, the place had recently been vacated by my father's brother Mike, who had married my mother's sister Celia. My aunt and uncle had moved to Oakland.

In the barn Mike had left a twenty-gallon pot still, with two burners and a large pressure tank. Mike promised my father a cut of the action if he would keep the still going. Bootlegging was a real service to his thirsty countrymen, Uncle Mike often boasted.

The operation came to a sudden end on May 6, 1922. On that day, Ernest had gone into town with Father on errands. I was left to mind the still. As the distillate slowly dripped out of the still, it went directly into a gallon jug. It took about an hour to fill a jug, and then it had to be quickly replaced with an empty one so no liquor was lost. That was my job.

After slipping an empty jug into place, I went into the house for a bite to eat. Mama fixed sandwiches. I was eating and chatting with her, when suddenly there was a loud commotion outside.

We peered out the kitchen window. A large canvas-draped truck had pulled up in a cloud of dust and men were scrambling out of the back, some carrying long-handled axes. They ran into the barn.

My mother and I watched from inside. After finding no one in the barn, a group of men came out and ran around back, where they searched the tall brush and a dry creek area below, apparently for the still operator.

In a few minutes, two men approached the house.

Mama opened the door.

The men identified themselves as federal agents.

"Lady, is it your barn?" one agent asked.

"No," she said. "It's rented out."

It wasn't long before my father and Ernest pulled into the yard. My father was questioned at length by the agents. He more or less gave the same answers as Mama, but the agents were unconvinced. Though they did not arrest him, they informed him that they intended to seek a criminal complaint against him.

My father's involvement in Mike's business resulted in his being charged with violating the Volstead Act. Though the charges were eventually dropped, my mother, frightened and embarrassed by the raid, insisted that we relocate.

When I was twelve, we moved to Escalon in the San Joaquin Valley, California's great inland valley, some 250 miles long and, at average, 50 miles wide. My father had heard of the Valley's fertile soil and extended growing seasons.

The price of grapes for homemade wine had been rising since the advent of Prohibition; Father purchased, in June 1922, a twenty-acre vineyard in Escalon planted with Carignane and Alicante grapes. We moved into a run-down house on the property.

When spring came, Father decided the vines needed protection from the frost. I don't know where he got the idea, but he went to town and bought old car tires, which he brought back and directed Ernest and me to distribute throughout our vineyard. The next morning when the temperature dropped to near freezing, we were up at three A.M. setting the tires on fire. We raised the damnedest smoke, which at daybreak covered the town of Escalon with dark black clouds smelling of burned rubber. When the smoke cleared away enough for us to return to the vineyard, we found the vines completely charred.

Across the street, our neighbor had opened up the gates in his irrigation canal and flooded his vineyard. His vines were untouched by the frost, and he ended up with a full crop of grapes that year.

From then on, we always irrigated our vineyards during the frost danger—and still do. We use well water, which comes from beneath the surface at around 65 degrees, much warmer than the air during a freezing frost. The soil absorbs this water and releases enough heat close to the ground to keep the vines from freezing.

We would have many farming successes in the Valley. But we would also suffer some terrible setbacks.

The Valley became home, and still is today.

2

THE ROARING
TWENTIES:
CHICAGO, HOBOKEN

Ernest

My father's timing couldn't have been better.

In 1923 he started making a good return in farming for the first time, as the demand for wine grapes skyrocketed. Before Prohibition, the price of grapes had been between $5 and $7 a ton. For a few years after the beginning of Prohibition, grapes brought $120 or more a ton.

The 1919 Volstead Act, which made provision for enforcement of Prohibition, had stopped the production and sale of all alcoholic beverages, except for a few wineries licensed to stay in operation to produce a limited amount of wine for "medicinal and religious" purposes. However, a family was permitted to make up to two hundred gallons of wine per year for its own use. As a result, home winemaking had become an annual event for most immigrant families who had come to America to find a better future—but not to give up their heritage. Here, as in the "old country," these newest Americans still enjoyed wine of their own making with their meals.

The grapes bought by home winemakers were officially called

"juice" grapes, even though everyone knew their juice would be fermented into wine. The biggest markets for wine grapes were in big eastern cities like Chicago and New York, where the influx of immigrants was heaviest.

For two years my father sold his grapes to a shipper for a fixed price, the way most California growers sold their grapes. Each year, the vast majority of the California grape harvest ended up being shipped east.

In 1924, father sold his Escalon vineyard. With some help from the Bank of Italy, he purchased a 40-acre vineyard two miles west of Modesto on Maze Road. He paid $1,000 an acre, then spent $8,000 to have a contractor build a three-bedroom, one-bath Spanish-style home on the parcel. A few years later, he bought an adjacent 30-acre vineyard.

Modesto turned out to be a very good place to settle. Situated near the northern tip of the San Joaquin Valley, we are located 75 miles south of Sacramento, the state capital, and 90 miles southeast of San Francisco. Modesto is the county seat of Stanislaus County, which comprises nearly one million acres of fertile farmland; it is larger than the state of Rhode Island.

Most of the day-to-day work involved with our expanding vineyard operations fell to Julio and me. In the spring and summer we would be up at daybreak to sulfur the vines. Back then there was no machinery to do it as there is today. Each of us carried a small burlap sack of sulfur that we sprinkled on the vines by hand. We'd have to stop whenever the wind came up, usually late morning. But by then, we'd be covered with sulfur, and our reddened eyes would burn all day long.

In 1925 my father was approached by a Chicago grape buyer named Joe Gazzara. He proposed that we ship our grapes to him on consignment for sale in Chicago. Gazzara would negotiate the best price for them on the railroad sales tracks. After deducting his commission and the freight charges, he would pay the rest of the money to my father. My father agreed because it sounded like a way to make more money. To ensure that he wouldn't be cheated, my father traveled to Chicago to supervise the sale of his grapes. When he returned home several weeks later, he complained vehemently about the haggling and under-handed tactics of the dealers on the tracks.

"I made more money," he admitted, "but those people are the worst element. Their word is *inutile* [useless]. They make a deal with you and then they break it."

He vowed never to go back.

The following year I volunteered to go to Chicago in his place. I knew my father could be a difficult man, and I wondered how much of his trouble in Chicago came from his own stubborn inclination not to deal with people who, in his opinion, had not lived up to their word.

Although I was only seventeen and still in high school, I felt I could do the job. I had no selling experience and knew nothing about the conditions on the tracks—other than the very dark picture painted by my father.

Much to my pleasure, my father agreed to let me go to Chicago, and my high-school teachers allowed me six weeks off in order to gain "practical experience" in the family business.

In September 1926, I took the train for Chicago. As we departed the Valley, it was quite hot, and once we worked our way up the Sierra Nevada and down the eastern slope, it turned warm again. Inside the passenger compartment—this was well before air-conditioning—temperatures soared. Whenever I opened the window for ventilation, smoke and soot from the locomotive blew inside. We had no choice but to keep the window shut and swelter a good part of the way.

My father told of a train ride he had taken in the opposite direction two decades earlier. He'd made the trip west after working in the coal mines of Pennsylvania for six months to earn enough money to buy a railroad ticket to California. He didn't know enough English to order meals, but the train stopped often and he discovered that there were pie vendors at every station. He soon learned how to say "pie," and he ate pies, at a nickel each, all the way to California.

I traveled two thousand miles to Chicago in a third-class seat. Five days and four nights in a straight-back wooden seat—I could not afford sleeper-car fares.

I FOUND MYSELF on a chilly day in October 1926 standing in front of railcars loaded with my father's grapes. By then I had been in Chicago for six weeks.

As on most days, close to a hundred shippers were trying to sell two hundred or so railcars filled with wine grapes that lined the side tracks of the Santa Fe Railroad yard at Twenty-first Street and Archer Avenue.

The grape season was winding down and there would be no new shipments arriving. All of us were anxious to unload the last of our grapes so we could start home.

The buyers I sought were dealers looking to purchase grapes by the railcar load. Each boxcar held around 1,100 twenty-five-pound boxes of grapes—approximately thirteen tons in all. After purchasing a carload, the dealer would slide open the side door, prop a ladder leading to the floor of the car, and sell grapes, in lots of 20 to 200 boxes, to a mixture of Italians, Jews, and Croatians who came down to the rail yard during the day to buy grapes to make their wine. It sometimes took a dealer three or four days to empty a carload. The home winemakers would often inspect car after car before deciding which one to buy from. They bought on price, sweetness, intensity of color, and freshness.

I took my hands out of my pockets when I noticed two men moving down the line of railcars in my direction. They were serious buyers or they wouldn't be out in such cold weather. When they reached me they looked around, as if expecting someone older to step forward.

The dealers on these tracks were seasonal commodity jobbers. In the fall, when grapes were in, they handled grapes. Later in the year they might sell Christmas trees, and in the summer, melons and other fruit. In between times, they would hire themselves out by the day as carpenters or plumbers or bricklayers. They were street-savvy, out-to-make-a-buck types who loved to haggle.

Without prompting, I explained that my grapes were "direct from my father's vineyards." Every other day for more than a month, I had been receiving a carload of grapes from Modesto.

"Any Alicante?" one of the men asked.

Alicante was a thick-skinned variety that held up well in shipping. On account of its durability and ruby-red juice, which turned into a hearty, inky-dark red wine, it enjoyed great popularity in the eastern markets. Alicante, which alone had little taste, consistently brought the highest price per lug each season because it could be "cut" with cheaper muscat grapes and produce what most immigrants of the day considered a decent wine.

"No Alicante," I admitted, but I told them I had some very good Zinfandel and Carignane.

Zinfandel, the most-cultivated of any California "juice" grape variety, was well known to the trade. Carignane was also a popular grape with home winemakers.

The men wanted to look at the grapes.

I swung up the ladder leaning into the doorway of the car and scrambled to the top of the boxes stacked inside. The prospective buyers followed me up the ladder and into the dark, narrow crawl space atop the grapes. I directed the beam of a flashlight down into a box of red grapes. Reaching in, I grabbed a bunch. The dealers tasted them, not bothering to spit out the seeds.

Price was based not just on quality and variety but also weight. One of the men asked me to remove a few top boxes, so they could see down into the next tier of grapes, and I complied. It was what dealers did to check out the grapes underneath, not only to look for mold but to make sure that the boxes were well filled.

California's large, established shippers "house-packed" their grapes in packing houses to ensure consistent quality and weight in each box.

They spent money for lids and fancy labels. Many of their representatives were here in the Santa Fe yard, and I had to compete with them. Our grapes, thrown into boxes in the fields by the pickers and lacking lids and labels, could never look as good. We had the box company stencil GALLO and a red rooster (*gallo* is Italian for "rooster") on the end of each box, but of course, the name meant nothing to anyone. My father, who had made only the one trip to Chicago, was not a known grower or shipper. But price came down to supply and demand, I soon realized.

The two dealers, uninterested in our grapes, left.

Suddenly an angry man was upon me, yelling and cursing in a mix of English and Italian, that the grapes he'd bought several days earlier had been packed lightly in the boxes and didn't weigh as much as they should. The man claimed he had lost money and demanded that I refund him ten cents a box—more than a hundred dollars.

The man's claim was without merit. The grapes had been weighed when loaded into the car and the contents of each box averaged twenty-five pounds.

The dealer's real but unspoken gripe, I knew, was that with fluctuating grape prices he hadn't been able to sell the carload he bought from me for more than he had paid.

It was this sort of delayed haggling that had so frustrated my father, who would have stood his ground and lost a customer. This was the reason why he hadn't wanted to go back. He could not adjust himself to this type of negotiating.

In one important way I differed from my father. Each deal stood on its own. I was always ready to try to make sure that anyone who dealt with me was satisfied. In short, I had no intention of losing a customer.

"Okay, tell you what," I said. "I'll give you a break on the next carload."

The man didn't say anything.

"Is that fair?" I asked.

It was the least I could do, the man grumbled.

"Fine. I have a carload right here," I went on, "that I have priced at a dollar thirty a box."

The man pointed out that that was a dime a box more than he'd paid for my grapes two days ago.

Of course it was, I allowed. This load was better quality and the market was stronger today. I had several buyers who wanted it, I explained.

"You say ya gonna give me a break," the man exploded. "I didn't think ya gonna breaka my neck!"

I didn't say anything.

Besides, the man complained, they are not so fresh.

These grapes would make a fine, hearty wine, I countered. "For you," I added, "I'll take a dime off."

The man was unconvinced.

We talked a while longer. Then, with apparent reluctance, I agreed to knock an additional nickel off the per-box price.

He was happy to have knocked fifteen cents off.

It was the price I had wanted all along. We were both happy.

The buyer and I went behind the railcar to conclude the transaction. The man removed one shoe and peeled off a smelly wool sock, from which he retrieved a wad of equally fragrant hundred-dollar bills. Such precautions were not uncommon. It could be dangerous walking around the rail yard with cash. He counted out twelve bills and some smaller ones, and handed them to me.

Never wanting to linger around the yard with so much cash on me, I took a cab directly downtown to the Continental Bank. I deposited the money, then wrote a check out to my father, which I put in the mail that afternoon.

For the season, I sold seventeen carloads of grapes—approximately 220 tons. There were no sales commissions to pay because I had handled everything myself. After deducting for my room, board, and transportation, I had sent home a shade over $17,000—several thousand dollars more than we had made on our grapes the previous year.

To put this amount of money in perspective: That winter, men's all-wool suits in the Sears, Roebuck catalog cost "up to $27.50," and a one-horse plow, $5.98. A two-year-old Ford coupe was priced at $360. A four-acre poultry ranch in Santa Rosa, California, was on the market for $3,000. A prime fifty-two-acre Alicante and Zinfandel vineyard in Sonoma County was listed for $23,000.

And the United States' budget deficit stood at $408,000.

Julio

Those who did not live through the Great Depression can't understand how tough things were back then.

The misfortune began for our family, and many others, in October 1929. I was nineteen, and had graduated from Modesto High School four months earlier.

After high school I hadn't been interested in going to college. In fact, through the years I never took an agriculture or viticulture class. Everything I knew or would ever know I learned from doing. I'm not saying that's the best way, just that it's the way I did it. I was a fair student in school, and a pretty good athlete, though I never had the time to compete on a team.

On the twenty-ninth day of October, I stood with a group of grape shippers around a campfire we had built between rows of refrigerated cars at the Erie Railroad sales yard outside Hoboken, New Jersey. The flames were fed with wood splintered off bracings for the railcars. We were all chilled to the bone, and very dejected.

Jack Riorda, an experienced shipper for the very large Italian Swiss Colony vineyards, said the market was as bad as he had ever seen it. Riorda was stuck with a dozen carloads—more than 150 tons of grapes—that he couldn't sell.

It was Riorda who had convinced me to bring my father's grapes to the Erie sales yard this season. For the past two years, I had been going to the Pennsylvania Railroad's auction yard at nearby Kearny, north of Newark, New Jersey.

As our shipping business expanded and we began handling neighbors' grapes, Chicago alone was not a sufficient market. Ernest had found himself at a disadvantage with our increasing volume. Shrewd buyers in the yard would go down to the incoming tracks and count how many carloads he had coming in from Modesto. They would wait him out, knowing that our grapes weren't getting any fresher, until eventually he had to lower his prices. What was needed was another market to which Ernest could divert grapes when the Chicago prices were too low. That's why our father started sending me to New Jersey.

At the Kearny auction yard, however, shippers were stuck with whatever wholesale price the local market supported. On average, for the past two seasons I had done all right at auction, but I had come to the Erie sales yard this year in the hope of getting higher prices for our grapes.

When the market was strong, shippers did get higher prices at the Erie yard. But the market was weak, and shippers were hurting. With worsening weather on top of it, the tracks were deserted. There wasn't a grape buyer in sight.

A newsboy hurried down the tracks, calling out: "*Extra,* afternoon extra—stock-market *stampede!*"

Buying a stack of papers, we all read in silence. That day alone—October 29, 1929, known to history as Black Tuesday—prices across the board had slumped $14 billion, a staggering figure in those days. It was a complete collapse of the country's economy.

I asked Riorda what he was going to do.

He shook his head.

Like Ernest, I had still been in high school the first season I came east. I had arrived at Grand Central Station without knowing a soul in

New York City or having a clue as to where I should stay. Grabbing a cab at the train station, I asked the driver to drop me at a clean but inexpensive hotel. Let out in the heart of Times Square, I stood there with my bag in hand, looking up at the tallest buildings I had ever seen. Early the next morning, after catching a ferry across the Hudson to the Kearny auction yard, I realized just how out of the way Times Square was for my purposes. The next year and from then on, I stayed at the Cosmopolitan Hotel, located in New York City's produce area and recommended by other shippers.

"There's nothing we can do," Riorda finally answered. "Nothing at all but take a big loss."

Without buyers, the grapes would rot where they stood. It would be a disaster.

"I'll be damned if I'll do that," I said.

Riorda looked at me in amazement.

I was stuck with seven full carloads Ernest had been unable to sell in Chicago. These grapes, a hundred tons or so, had arrived at Hoboken in pretty bad shape—mold was already setting in.

"I won't sit here and lose them all," I said. "I'll divert over to Kearny. Dump them on the auction."

I was willing to gamble we could get *something* for the grapes at auction, and that would be better than standing by while they rotted on the tracks.

But there was a problem. Riorda pointed out that I would use up my diversion. He had a point:

After a shipper had paid one-way freight charges—say west to east, as from Modesto to Chicago—the railroads allowed, at no extra charge, for a carload to continue moving in the same direction. So we hadn't paid anything extra when Ernest sent our grapes from Chicago to New Jersey. In New Jersey, we had one free local diversion coming. This diversion allowed a buyer to have a railcar moved to another location at no additional expense. In other words, the buyer did not incur freight charges. While not critical in the sales yards, where the buyers most often sold the grapes directly out of the railroad cars, diversions were very important to the sale of grapes at auction. Grapes at auction were moved to sales yards or neighborhood spurs for subsequent resale. In moving our grapes from the sales yard to the auction yard, I would be using our one free local diversion. With no diversion remaining, buyers would have to pay freight charges.

"Who is going to buy your grapes at auction if they have to transport them out of the yard at their own expense?" Riorda wanted to know. He said I was crazy if I thought someone was going to buy my grapes and pay the railroad to move them or pay to have their trucks and men come over from Brooklyn to haul them away. "Not in this market," he added.

Lots of grapes could be cheaply bought this day that *did* have a local railroad diversion remaining.

I tried not to catch Riorda's gloom. "It's bad in either case, but I have to try."

"You'll be worse off sitting over there at Kearny than you are here," he warned.

But I'd made up my mind.

"I'm diverting. See you, Jack."

Ernest

That year, 1929, was my fourth consecutive season selling my father's grapes in Chicago.

In those days I stayed at a small four-story hotel that didn't have an elevator. I always made sure to get a corner room—at a rate of eight dollars per week, payable in advance. My hotel was located at Clark and Jackson streets. I would take the streetcar that stopped on the corner and ride south on Clark to Twenty-first Street, where the sales track was located at Archer Avenue.

Chicago in 1929 was not a beautiful city. All the buildings were heated with coal then, and as a result, there was heavy smoke and soot in the air. If you went out in the morning with a white shirt on, by noon you had a black ring around your collar. The Lake Shore Drive area that would later make Chicago one of the most beautiful cities in the country was back then undeveloped.

Nine years of Prohibition had turned this midwestern city into a battlefield. The "noble experiment" wasn't so noble after all—it had ignited the biggest crime wave ever in this country, surpassed only by the traffic in illicit drugs a half century later. Chicago's warring gangs, competing for control of the city's bootleg liquor and beer business, enforced their will with ruthless violence.

The Santa Fe Railroad yard was no exception. Men in pearl-gray hats with narrow black bands waited patiently at the main gate. Unchallenged by police or railroad security, they collected a four-cent-per-box "hoodlum tax" on every lug of grapes that left the yard, thereby ensuring that the load of grapes would arrive safely home with the buyer. Nobody questioned the payments or, as far as I could tell, even felt badly about having to make them.

Muggings in and around the yard were not uncommon. At times the assailant would be a stranger with a gun. But at other times, it might be an irate buyer who was determined to get his money back from the shipper who had "cheated" him. Or, sometimes a devious buyer would have a partner waiting to hold you up and relieve you of your cash, ending up with both the grapes and the money.

Being unarmed, I decided, was not advisable.

Upon my arrival that fall, I had mentioned to a Chicago policeman that I wanted a gun for protection, since I carried sizable amounts of cash. The cop said, "I've got a bargain for you," and pulled out an extra gun. I bought the .32 Smith & Wesson for ten dollars.

Whenever I found myself heading into the dark crawl space of a railcar on my hands and knees with someone who looked rough or acted suspicious, I would jerk on my coat lapel and cause my handgun to fall from a hidden pocket I'd had sewn in my jacket. Then, I'd non-chalantly pick up the revolver and put it back inside my jacket.

The cash I carried was very important to my family, and I was not going to let anyone take it away.

WHEN I FIRST READ OF THE STOCK-MARKET COLLAPSE late that Octo-ber, I had no idea at first just how terribly my family would be affected.

I knew my parents had put their life savings into buying stock in A. P. Giannini's bank—his Bank of Italy had been renamed Bank of America. At home, it was not uncommon for me to leave the field and go into the house two or three times a day to call the broker to see how our bank stock was doing. In those days, investors in Giannini's bank used to stop each other on the street and compare notes. "The stock went up a dollar and I own a thousand shares. I made a thousand dol-lars yesterday!" My parents owned a little more than two thousand shares of bank stock—by then being traded as Transamerica—but not a single share of any other stock.

The financial section of the paper soon revealed just how bad things were. On Black Tuesday, the bank's stock had bucked the trend and closed up slightly at $67 a share. But the next day, having overnight accumulated a tremendous volume of sell-short and selling orders, it opened at only $20, and it closed out the day at $42.

My father had to consider this a disaster.

Julio

Still trying to unload the grapes I'd found myself saddled with that fall of '29, the first person I sought out at the Kearny auction yard was old Louie Facito, the bald-headed, cigar-chomping head auctioneer who probably knew more about selling grapes than any man alive.

"What? You back again?" Louie asked.

"Yeah, I am."

"Don't tell me you got grapes?"

"Seven cars."

"There's no market here, kid."

When I had let Louie know, weeks earlier, that I was going to skip Kearny in favor of the Erie sales yard in Hoboken that year, the old man had graciously wished me well. But he added prophetically: "Maybe I'll see you again."

"I diverted them from Hoboken," I explained.

"You diverted? How the *hell* you expect to sell 'em if you don't got no diversion?"

"I couldn't sell them over there anyway. Just do the best you can for me, Louie."

"I'll do what I can, but it's gonna be tough. You wait," Louie said before disappearing.

I knew the setup here at Kearny. This one market served ten million residents in a thirty-five-mile-diameter circle of which New York City was the hub. New York City provided a market for about 20 percent of all California wine grapes shipped out of state. The Pennsylvania Railroad's Kearny auction yard was to the grape business what Wall Street was to the investment crowd. It was a huge field of parallel tracks on which loaded railcars were parked. Between them ran narrow platforms. Each car was open, and samples of the grapes were placed outside for inspection. The yard could hold several thousand cars at one time. As many as eight hundred cars full of grapes rolled in daily. A single "grape train" would often stretch for a mile. Fast "specials" brought grapes from California to New York in ten days. The grapes were iced on the way so that when they arrived they would not be spoiled.

Dealers, who were middlemen between the grape shippers and home winemakers, were given catalogs listing the cars to be offered on each day. They looked at the grape samples, made notes on their lists, and later bid for what they wanted in the jammed auction room. The minimum purchase was one carload—no split lots were allowed. So rapid was bidding at times that it wasn't unusual for half a million dollars' worth of grapes to be sold in an afternoon.

In good times, the average dealer would buy two or three cars and have the railroad divert them to a siding near his own neighborhood. He would spread the word to local families who were known to make their own wine. They would come down to buy enough grapes for the year's supply of wine. Grapes that dealers bought at auction for $1.00 to $2.00 a lug would retail to home winemakers for $1.25 to slightly over $2.50. A lug would make two to two and a half gallons of homemade wine.

But these were not good times.

When Louie returned, he explained that he had spoken to an *amico* who worked for the railroad. He had managed to get a second local diversion to another rail yard for my grapes—at no extra cost.

"Now we just gotta sell 'em," Louie added. At auction an hour or so later, I stood on the platform next to the auctioneer when my carloads came up for sale.

Louie, stripped to the waist and with a towel wrapped around his neck to wipe the sweat that streamed off his face, had really been flying through the lots, as usual. For my seven carloads, he jabbed a tobacco-stained forefinger again and again at the crowd, rattled off rising prices so quickly I could hardly keep up.

I was delighted to see so much action.

When the bidding seemed to lose some steam, I whispered, "Take it, Louie."

Louie mumbled something that I didn't get.

This time, I was more urgent: *"Take it."*

"I don't *have* it," Louie said out of the corner of his mouth. Veins had popped out on his neck, and sweat poured down his face.

It was the oldest trick in the auctioneer's book. Louie was trying desperately to get some action going for my grapes by pretending there were competitive bids from the floor when there were none. Since so many bidders made subtle signals known only to the auctioneer so as not to tip their hand, it was common for active bidding to be taking place among seemingly disinterested shippers.

"Sold!" Louie hollered, pointing to a big-time buyer.

From the back of the room came a loud protest. "No! You think I'm crazy? I didn't buy!"

"What you move you hand for?" Louie argued. "All right, we do it—*again!*"

Louie had gotten out of the jam.

On the second go-around, the bidding was much more low-key. I ended up selling for a nickel per lug *less* than the coast-to-coast freight charges of sixty cents a box, but better than losing the entire seven carloads of grapes.

NINETEEN TWENTY-NINE TURNED OUT TO BE a disastrous year in the grape-shipping business. On top of that loss came the collapse of my father's Transamerica stock.

Beginning in around 1927, whenever he had extra money, my father, like many Italian immigrants, had invested in A. P. Giannini's Bank of America by buying stock in its holding company, Transamerica.

It was easy to see why the old-time Italians had confidence in Giannini. He was a different type of banker in his day. He took care of the hardworking farmers. A man you could approach, he wouldn't keep you waiting in the lobby and have you escorted into some private office. For years, he sat right out where everyone could see and talk to him. He didn't just stay in the bank as most bankers did. He'd come down to the Valley, meet the farmers, get his shoes dirty.

My father's financial problems weren't limited to the stock-market crash. Just a month earlier he had purchased 160 acres of raw land directly across from our home on Maze Road. Initially, he had intended to finance the purchase by selling some of his Transamerica stock—then near its all-time high. He had been convinced, though, by the Bank of America branch manager in Modesto to hold on to his stock. The bank would lend him the money he needed to purchase the property, with his stock serving as collateral.

When the crash came and the value of his stock dropped, the bank started pressuring Father to reduce his debt to them at a time when he had no way of doing so.

I never heard Father blame the banker for his terrible advice. My father felt responsible for this error in judgment.

After the crash, not only was my father's stock worth a fraction of its cost, but we were burdened with a new mortgage on bare land that wouldn't make money until it was developed and producing a crop.

After having had some years of moderate prosperity, Father suddenly found himself in a serious financial squeeze.

Ernest

That fall of '29, Julio and I had no time to stew about things beyond our control.

Father had stopped picking our grapes because he didn't know if they would sell. Overextended at the bank and still smarting from his stock losses, my father listened when Uncle Mike came along touting a get-rich-quick scheme. Mike proposed that Father make wine from his unpicked grapes, which Mike would use as fermented mash to make distilled spirits. My father would receive a cut of what could be big profits.

While Julio and I were still back east trying desperately to get rid of the carloads of our grapes we still had on the track, my father decided to go along with Mike's plan. They set to work building four underground storage tanks right next to our house.

By the time Mama reached Julio and me by telephone, she was beside herself. Father was well along in crushing, and had started filling the tanks. She pleaded with us to return home at once to keep him from getting in trouble again.

Julio and I wrapped up our business as soon as possible, returning home in early November. Father had a crew out in the vineyards picking the rest of our grapes, now well past their prime and breaking down. Using a hand crusher, he was crushing grapes, juice, skins, and stems directly into the open manhole at the top of each tank, about six feet high and at least as wide. A couple of the tanks were already half full.

My brother and I put a stop to the activity.

"Don't even give it a second thought," I remember telling my father, reminding him that he had put the family through this once before.

Mama, never the silent type, strongly voiced her fear that Father's bootlegging activities could hurt Julio's and my future.

Realizing that the entire family opposed the idea, Father capitulated.

With no market for our grapes, we left the rest of that year's crop on the vine.

Julio

My brother and I next found ourselves faced with developing the newly acquired 160 acres across the road.

We measured off the land, deciding how we wanted to plant it. The uneven land had to be leveled off and gullies filled for proper irrigation and drainage.

My father went to town and returned with a rented Best Caterpillar tractor, a heavy-duty machine required for the job, and a ten-yard earthmover to pull behind it. "They charged me twenty dollars a day," he complained. "But they never say how long is a day."

Ernest and I took turns driving the tractor. I drove all night, warming my hands now and then over the blue flames shooting out of the tractor's vertical exhaust pipe. Ernest took over at daybreak. In that way, we kept the rented rig running twenty-four hours a day.

By then it was winter. Not knowing any better and pushed by our father, we continued to level the land in spite of the heavy rains. We were unaware of the damage we were doing to the soil by working it wet. By the time we finished, it was too late to plant grapes. We put beans and melons in that first year.

We planted grapes the following fall. After plowing long furrows, we went along and placed the cuttings in the ground. We used cuttings off other vines in those days, not nursery rootstock like today. We pushed the dirt back into the holes with a short-handled hoe, then stomped the ground pat.

By working the land wet that winter, we ended up weakening it—in places, severely. For years we had difficulty with some areas: red spider mites and other forms of disease, and poor crop set. Major portions of the vineyard had to be replanted.

But, as our neighbors who heard the rumble of the tractor night and day that winter knew, we were in a hurry.

3

END OF CHILDHOOD

Ernest

While 1929 was a struggle, the grape market in 1930 was even worse, and our finances worsened.

Our father could be very difficult to be around. Quick-tempered, he was often dictatorial and demanding. As Julio and I came of age, we were determined to be treated with respect. If not, we would leave his house.

Finally, in the summer of '30, we felt we had no choice but to go. We packed our belongings in a single suitcase and drove into the Imperial Valley just north of the U.S.-Mexico border to check out the produce business. Most large grape shippers handled melons, lettuce, and tomatoes in the summer, sending them by rail to the same eastern markets. With our farming and shipping experience, we felt that the produce business might hold some promise for us.

The hotel we stopped at in El Centro, the only one in town, wanted a dollar a day for a room for two. We couldn't afford that, we admitted. The understanding desk clerk accepted fifty cents a night.

Our stay in El Centro was cut short. Through our aunts, Mama pleaded with us to return because Father could not manage all the work alone. Things would change, he promised us upon our return.

After graduating from high school in 1927, I had attended Modesto Junior College for two years, taking only those courses I thought would help me in business—English, economics, business law, public speaking. I felt it imperative to be able to communicate effectively, as well as to be able to understand the terms of a contract. I like learning and have always had a curious mind. For a while I considered the law. After about age ten, whenever I went on vacation and stayed with my aunt and uncle in Oakland, I would spend most days in courtroom galleries, fascinated by the presentations and legal arguments of lawyers trying cases.

The most valuable course I took in high school was "bonehead" English, which I was required to take for graduation in my senior year after failing a mandatory composition test the previous year. Not all the students were motivated to do well; whenever the teacher would step out into the hallway the rowdier ones would start throwing papers and erasers, generally raising Cain. More than once I stood up and said something like "We're not going to get out of this school if we don't pass the English test!" Once, I had to defend myself in a fistfight with one fellow who took strong exception to my lecturing. Although I was smaller in stature than most of my classmates—I had been called Nino, which in Italian means small—I usually won fights using the element of surprise by striking first to the nose.

I took that English class seriously, and I'm very glad I did. I believe I learned in that class how to write concisely and with brevity. Since then it has always irritated me to try to make sense of rambling letters or reports with page-long paragraphs. When you write succinctly and effectively, it is easier to organize your thoughts and make them unmistakably clear to others.

After leaving home with Julio for that short time in 1930, I had come back to my father's house with the understanding that I would be given, or at least be able to purchase, a few acres from him so I could begin building a business for myself. It did not happen.

Having worked fourteen-hour days, seven days a week, for a number of years, I had nothing to show for it. My father paid us no regular salary. The only money we drew went for clothes and other bare necessities.

This could not continue. I was planning to get married in 1931, and I wanted to build a future for myself and my new wife.

I had met my future wife's father, Giuseppe Franzia, a wine-grape grower and shipper from Ripon, on the sales tracks in Chicago. Early one November in Chicago, Franzia had come up to me and asked when I was planning to return home.

Tomorrow, I said.

"I'm done," he said, "but I wait for you and we go back together."

We met at the train station the next morning and found seats together in a crowded coach car. He was carrying a large covered laundry basket, which he shoved under the seat. At noontime he brought out the basket. Inside were slabs of cheese and salami, bread, whole garlics, and huge red onions, which he sliced with a pocketknife. Soon, the passengers around us began moving away. Franzia pulled a bottle of homemade wine out of the basket to wash down the meal. Before the trip was over, he invited me to visit him at home sometime soon.

A month or so later, I did. When I arrived, I found him catnapping on a bench in the yard.

I woke him up, and as we chatted, I spotted a very attractive young woman peeking out from behind a screen door. While Franzia kept me outside with talk about grapes, irrigation, and fertilizers, I kept wondering how I could get inside the house. Finally invited in for a glass of wine, I met his daughter, Amelia, who became my first girlfriend.

On August 23, 1931, Amelia and I were married at her little Catholic church at Simm's Station, fourteen miles from Modesto. Julio served as best man. Not being experienced with weddings, as soon as the priest pronounced us "man and wife," I turned around and walked off with Amelia—neglecting to kiss her. It was a grievous error I have spent much time remedying. There were five hundred relatives and friends present. Our wedding dinner was held in Franzia's large cellar under the house. Afterward, Amelia and I drove directly to the Modesto railroad station, where we boarded a train to Chicago. My annual trip east to sell grapes would have to serve as a honeymoon.

We took a small apartment downtown. At night I returned from the rail yard to Amelia—and her brother John, who was also in town selling grapes. He had taken me up on my unfortunate offer for him to stay with us. "Not a good idea," Amelia had said when I first told her. She was right. Three was an awkward number for a honeymoon. A few nights into this unsatisfactory arrangement, Amelia and I decided to stage a loud argument as to whether or not the stew she had made was any good. With each of us demanding that he take a position, my brother-in-law found himself caught in the middle of what appeared to be our first marital spat. He soon left to find a peaceful hotel room, and at last we were alone.

Julio

I didn't go back east again to sell grapes after 1930. In 1931, the market was a little stronger, but we still did not do very well.

We had the help of only one regular employee. Jesse Jenkins had come to us a year earlier asking for a job one day when Ernest and I were out pruning vines. He told us that he'd been working as a foreman for "Old Man" Covell, a big rancher and the richest man in Modesto. Jesse had recently been let go.

We told Jenkins that we had a lot of work and could use his help, but we could only afford to pay him fifteen cents an hour—ten cents an hour less than he had made with Covell. With that, Jenkins picked up a pair of pruning shears and started to work. (He stayed with us for thirty-seven years, spending a good portion of that time driving a truck—something he told us he had always wanted to do—making deliveries to our Modesto winery.)

In 1932, my father bought a run-down raisin-grape ranch in Fresno, about a hundred miles south of Modesto. I couldn't understand why he would buy a ranch that was so far away, with marginal vineyards that required so much work. He had picked it up on a bank foreclosure and thought he had gotten it cheap. But what good is cheap land, I wondered even then, if it's not productive?

Ernest and I did not see the Fresno ranch before he bought it. He and my mother moved down there in the spring of 1932. My brother Joe went down there as soon as he finished the school year in Modesto.

Most of the 225 acres were hardpan clay overrun with weeds and Bermuda grass. It was some of the most godforsaken land I had ever seen. The Thompson and muscat vineyards on the ranch were old, and they were infested with weeds that quickly grew higher than the vines.

Father tried to bring the vineyards back into production, but it took a lot of effort and cost money. From time to time, he called us to ask for some equipment or because he needed some work done. I would go down there for a day or two at a time and help him.

In 1932 Ernest went to Chicago as usual, and I stayed in Modesto to oversee the shipping of our grapes. One night a buddy invited me to come along with him to a dance at the American Legion.

Aileen Lowe and I had noticed each other in high school, but had never even talked until we ran into each other at that dance. Although she had arrived with a date, we danced most of the evening. When the dance was over, I borrowed a pen from the guy to write her phone number on the cuff of my shirt because I didn't have any paper.

Aileen and I went together for a year. Unable to afford a traditional wedding, we eloped to Reno in May 1933, and were married by a Catholic priest. Aileen made her own wedding dress.

A blonde of German-Austrian descent, Aileen, twenty, was the first non-Italian in the family. My mother warmly and graciously welcomed her into the family when I took her down to Fresno shortly after our wedding. Mother also set out to show my new wife how to cook some of her favorite dishes.

Ernest

In the fall of 1932, the nation showed no signs of recovery. Crippled like the rest of the economy, the grape-shipping business was in shambles.

In Chicago, the grape market began to weaken on me at the height of the season. My father, it turned out, had promised other growers more than he should have for their grapes. When prices dipped, we decided to hold and not sell, in the hope that prices would recover later in the season. I wired him to stop sending grapes. He did, even leaving some of our own crop on the vine.

The market never did recover, and by season's end I was stuck with nearly *seventy railcars* of unsold grapes. They had cost 60 cents a box to ship east, and there was another 20 to 30 cents a box due in demurrage (a charge for extra storage time) because they had been sitting so long in the railcars in Chicago while I tried to sell them. Whether we sold the grapes or not, we owed the railroad nearly a dollar per box — approximately $70,000. The market was so bad I couldn't sell the grapes even for what I owed for demurrage. I wasn't alone. Lots of shippers went into bankruptcy before Thanksgiving.

I returned home that year to further calamity. My father had made raisins from his Fresno grape crop, but with that market very bad also, he had been unable to sell them. We were in arrears on our loans and mortgages. The bank, growers, our box company, and a long line of other creditors were hounding us. There was no money to pay them.

The coming of the new year, 1933, marked the depth of the Depression for us and many Americans. Even with the promise of a popular new president taking office in January 1933, the nation slid deeper into depression. I believe, however, that we were lucky Franklin D. Roosevelt came along when he did, as his economic plan—which included repeal of Prohibition—and social reforms ended up saving our country.

Julio and I were responsible for pruning the Modesto vineyards, now totaling 270 acres. We had no money to buy gasoline to run the tractor, or even to purchase feed for our mules. We pastured them along the highway at night for a free meal.

In past years my father had always been able to borrow for operating expenses for the upcoming season. But by the spring of '33 he was unable to raise cash—either to pay expenses for the next harvest, or to stave off unpaid creditors left over from the disastrous 1932 season. My father discussed filing bankruptcy. I did not like that idea at all and talked him out of it.

I went to Bank of America and tried to borrow for our day-to-day farm expenses to carry us through to harvest. The bank turned me down. At that time, the economy was so bad that banks had very serious problems of their own. Not only would they not lend us anything, but they wanted my father's outstanding loans repaid.

In May 1933 I negotiated a government-insured loan from the Federal Land Bank, which was trying to help farmers through the nation's fiscal emergency. I could only borrow $16,000, not nearly what we needed. It was only a short-term solution.

It didn't take much foresight on my part to recognize that the grape-shipping business catering to home winemakers would dwindle with repeal of Prohibition. Upon legalization of alcoholic beverages, commercial winemaking would certainly give birth to a brand new industry.

Prohibition had been a total failure. No law was going to stop people from drinking. It was a simple matter of supply and demand. Thirteen years of Prohibition wrecked a legitimate industry, switching the business to people who were willing to break the law to meet a need and made money doing so.

As early as December 1932, with talk of repeal in the air, I had spoken to my father about the possibility of our starting a winery. During my seven consecutive winters in Chicago (Father never went east again after his one trip in 1925), I had heard fascinating stories from old-timers who had been in the wine business before Prohibition.

Discussions with my father about the wine business continued for a time. My father opposed the idea of a new venture. He was so overwhelmed and depressed by his financial losses that he became bearish on everything.

My father occasionally seemed attentive to my ideas, but too often he had the demeanor of a man obviously in failing health. It was as if he didn't have any strength left. Despondent and distracted, he couldn't imagine starting a new business.

It became clear to me that my father wouldn't or couldn't make up his mind about the wine business. As summer neared, I announced that I intended to proceed with or without him. "I understand why you want to get moving," my father replied, "but I can't take the risk."

I decided to set out on my own.

What did I need?

I needed a winery and a supply of grapes, and I didn't have the money for either one. I had spoken to the operator of a pre-Prohibition winery in Escalon and had a commitment from him to make a little wine for me if I brought him the grapes and removed the wine from his place soon after it was made. For his fee the winemaker would take some wine—ten gallons off the top for every ton of grapes crushed.

As for the grapes, even though prices were depressed I didn't have money to buy them. I came up with a profit-sharing plan whereby I would credit growers with two thirds of the value of the wine made from their grapes—paying them after I sold the wine. The cash market for grapes was expected to be so low that I soon had growers willing to bring me their grapes.

I found a central location near a railroad spur for my "bonded warehouse" on Bluxome Street in San Francisco, and on June 14, 1933, I submitted my application to the government for a permit.

Julio

On June 20, 1933, I left Modesto in our flatbed truck to take my father some farm equipment he needed in Fresno, and also to pick up my brother Joe, who was to spend his summer vacation with us in Modesto.

Aileen, my bride of six weeks, came along for the ride.

On the outskirts of Fresno, at White's Bridge Road near Arthur Avenue, we turned up a long drive, and pulled up in front of an unpainted farmhouse.

As soon as I stepped from the truck, I spotted my mother and father in a nearby field. Father was pitching hay over the side of a wagon. Mama was on top of the wagon, leveling the load with a pitchfork.

Mama came right over, greeting us with embraces. She took Aileen into the house to start lunch.

My father had remained at the wagon, trying to finish the job. I went to help him. As usual those days, he was irritable and in no mood to talk.

Though my parents and their two hired hands had been working the place for more than a year, I couldn't see much progress.

After unloading the truck, we went inside to eat lunch. Joe, out of school for the summer, was anxious to start his vacation. Mama said his bag had been packed since dawn.

When it was time to leave, the three of us piled into the truck, with my little brother in the middle.

Mama said something through the open window about not caring

43

what happened to her as long as "my boys get along always." Her comment about "not caring what happened" to herself caught me by surprise. I would never forget it.

As we pulled away, Mama smiled and waved.

Next to her stood my father, his head down and his faded felt hat hiding his eyes, shoulders slumped forward.

The next day, when the phone rang in our Modesto home, Aileen answered it. Ernest and I were both working out in the vineyards.

It was a reporter from the local newspaper, wanting to know if he'd reached the family of Joe and Susie Gallo.

Yes.

Was she a relative?

Yes, their daughter-in-law.

"Seems Mr. and Mrs. Gallo were just found shot to death at their place in Fresno," the reporter said.

Ernest happened to come in right after she hung up, and Aileen told him about the call. He changed, and left for Fresno right away.

Ernest

I made the drive to Fresno in a daze.

When I arrived at the funeral home, the county coroner was waiting. He asked me to step into a back room with him. I did, and identified the two bodies on metal gurneys as my mother and father.

They had been found by the hired hands shortly before lunch. Mama was dead on the ground out by the barn, where she had been feeding the livestock when she was shot in the back of the head. My father was in the house, dead from a self-inflicted gunshot wound to the temple. A handgun was on the floor next to him. No notes were found.

I was interviewed that afternoon by the coroner.

Asked for a possible motive, I told of my father's financial difficulties, explaining how worried and depressed he had been for some time.

The coroner asked if I was satisfied in my own mind that it was a case of murder and suicide.

I answered yes.

Before returning to Modesto that day, I visited my parents' place. The back door was unlocked. I sat at the kitchen table for a while.

My father had been a very sick man to have decided that his life wasn't worth living. But what I could not understand—and still do not to this day—is why he took my mother with him.

I went back outside.

I would never set foot in that house again. This land was not fertile. These two hundred acres had beaten my parents. I wanted no part of this run-down raisin farm, and neither did Julio. We would sell it just as soon as we could find a buyer.

My parents had little to show for all their years of hard work.

Julio

Aileen says my parents' service was very nice, but I don't remember it or the burial. I do know that we kept their bodies in the front room of our house for a couple of days, which was common in those days, and our relatives came to pay their respects.

I recall not wanting to go into the front room. I'd never seen death before. Their bodies were here, but the people they had once been were gone forever. While I honored my father, my mother I loved deeply. Her life had not been easy. She had tried so hard to make a happy life for us. Now she was gone.

We did not dwell on our losses. Ernest and I and our wives kept busy. We all did what we could for young Joe. None of us talked much then or later about what happened. What was there to say?

4

MODESTO'S NEWEST WINERY

Ernest

I never considered for a moment the thought of giving up, letting the bankers take charge, and liquidating our parents' estates for whatever cash we could realize. I took for granted the need to fight to save the vineyards and our home. I was determined to make good on the pile of debts our parents had left behind without selling the properties, except Fresno.

By any measure, our parents' estates were insolvent and unable to pay their debts. Bank of America had been named in Mother's handwritten will as executor of her estate. She had left all her real and personal property "to my three sons . . . to be divided in equal parts as soon as each one becomes 21 years of age." Though my father had died intestate, not uncommon in those days, the same three-way split would take place if his estate had any remaining value.

I petitioned the probate court to be named executor of my father's estate. The only liquid assets in his estate were $1,100 in cash and 2,225 shares of Transamerica stock, then trading for only $7.50 a share—for a total value of $16,688. However, most of the stock, 2,000 shares, was pledged to and held by the Bank of America as security for Father's debt to the bank. At the time of his death, those debts totaled $29,718, while the available liquid assets were only $2,788. It was impossible to pay his estate's debts out of available current assets. Reaching solvency without disposing of the Modesto vineyards would not be easy.

I asked for and received court permission to continue my father's grape-growing business "for the purpose of realizing the greatest return" for the estate.

My mother's estate had nearly $5,300 in liquid assets. Of that, $2,300 went to pay estate administration costs. With Bank of America as executor of her estate, I could not use any of the remaining cash to pay the claims against my father's estate, or even the operating expenses of continuing his business.

We pleaded for patience from the creditors. At first they were resistant, fearing that the estates could never pay them. Only when they saw how determined we were did they agree not to require immediate payment.

Instead of going into the wine business alone with a San Francisco warehouse, I asked Julio if he would join me in starting a winery.

Since we didn't have the money to build a winery on the vineyard property, as other growers were doing, I proposed renting a building in Modesto and turning it into a winery. We would have to buy the equipment to outfit it on credit.

"We can get grapes on a share deal with growers," I explained, "without having to pay anything up front."

My brother was the one person I knew who was willing to work as hard and as long as I did.

Together, I figured we could make it.

Julio

I had been thinking about my future since the death of my parents. Up to then I had planned to continue working the vineyards for my father.

Now Ernest and I found ourselves each with heavy burdens. Like my brother, I was determined not to lose our Modesto home and vineyards. We were both married and shared the hope of raising families and making a decent living. Too, we had to think about our younger brother, who would soon be entering his freshman year of high school. The court would eventually appoint us his legal guardians.

Staying together in Modesto was a must. I had been thinking about trying to get into the cattle business about the time Ernest approached me with his plan to start a winery.

I recognized that my older brother was ambitious and driven. An aggressive, hardworking guy, Ernest had never been afraid to buck the tide. I don't think I was as ambitious as he was, but we were both willing to put all our effort into being the best we could be. We had always worked well side by side. Our personalities seemed to complement one another. Growing up, we had not fought as most boys do. Of course, we might have been too worn out by all our chores to have any energy for roughhousing.

I caught some of Ernest's enthusiasm for the wine business. Wine would certainly be in demand when people could legally drink again.

I asked him how much money we would need to get started.

He wasn't sure.

I told him I had saved some money.

It hadn't been easy, since Father had never paid us regular salaries. But through the years whenever Mama managed to find a few dollars now and then to sneak to us—I don't know how she did it on her tight budget most years—I had saved it.

Some of the loudest arguments I heard my father get into were with

Uncle Mike over whether it was better to know how to make money or how to save it. They were real donnybrooks, often during big holiday dinners. "If you know how to make money, you don't have to save it," Mike would crow. "Money is to enjoy! Spend it!" Uncle Mike followed his own advice, managing to live at times with fine cars and sharp big-city clothes. He always had an angle. My father, who was much more conservative, came down on the side of saving money. I now understand how losing money was more painful for my father than it would be for someone like Mike, who would just shrug it off and figure out a way to get back on his feet.

This is one of the few times that I took my father's side in an argument. I mean, what's the use of making money if you are going to go and get careless with it? If you work hard for your money, you'd better save it.

But in 1933, I was willing to invest my life's savings, every penny of it, in starting our winery. Exactly $900.23.

Ernest

I went to the local branch of the Bank of America. The bank my parents and many other Italian immigrants had trusted so much would not lend us money to start a winery. Not only did the local bank manager turn me down cold, but he reminded me that the bank was still waiting to be repaid for the loan Father had died owing.

By 1933 the Depression was so deep that many banks were failing. To most Americans the future looked bleak. In the midst of this, my brother and I were trying to start a new business.

At the time I didn't think much about all the handicaps we faced. But looking back, I can see that the odds were greatly against our surviving in the wine business. With no money or experience, we would find ourselves up against seasoned, well-financed businessmen. The competition would be brutal: men like Angelo Petri, owner of the Petri

Cigar Company, J. B. and Lorenzo Cella of the Roma Wine Company, Samuele Sebastiani, Krikor Arakelian, and the Rossi twins of Italian Swiss Colony. Fruit Industries, probably the largest winery at repeal, had the services of Walter Taylor and the legendary A. R. Morrow, both experienced pre-Prohibition wine men.

In some cases, these wineries had remained in business during Prohibition, legally producing sacramental and medicinal wines. They would start off with facilities, know-how, and even inventories of wine—all major advantages. Many of these pre-Prohibition wineries, owned and operated by experienced wine producers, were well financed. Unlike us, they were able to borrow millions of dollars from private and government sources to build and expand their facilities. They had huge wineries and inventories.

Take John B. Cella's Roma Wine Company, for example. At Repeal, Roma had a million gallons of dessert wine on hand, meaning the company was worth at least a million dollars to start with. Italian Swiss Colony (ISC), founded by Andrea Sbarboro in Asti, California, in 1881, was owned by a group of men who had a great background in wine and almost unlimited access to capital.

Then there were the large cooperatives of grape growers that were forming. Fruit Industries, for example, consisted of member wineries totaling eight million gallons in capacity. There were rumors throughout the fall of 1933 and into 1934 that Fruit Industries was trying to put together a group of wineries to form a new California Wine Association. Before Prohibition, CWA had been so powerful a monopoly that it had accounted for about 85 percent of all California wine sales.

There would be many new wineries starting up—in fact, 804 new wineries were in business in California within a few years. Though we were going up against men who had money, experience, and connections, none of which we had, I was strangely unintimidated.

• • •

IN A WAY, I BELIEVE that my father and uncle were both right about money. If you know how to make money but can't save it, you're going to lose out. And if you can only save it but can't make it, you will never have much in this life. To be successful, you have to be able to make money and also be smart enough to invest it safely.

I went to San Francisco to ask my mother's sister Aunt Celia, who had divorced Uncle Mike a few years earlier, for a loan to start a winery.

As I was explaining our plans, she abruptly changed the subject: She wanted to know when she would be repaid $4,000 she had earlier lent my father. Knowing how bad things were in Modesto, she had already filed documents with the probate court to assert her claim against my father's estate. Now Aunt Celia had no interest in loaning us start-up money.

I stopped to see my mother's other sister, Tillie, who also lived in San Francisco. "I'm sorry, I just don't have the money to lose," she told me.

I came home.

Julio would make his own personal appeals to our aunts, I found out later, but they turned him down as well.

One of the wealthiest men in Modesto was Claude Maze, a neighbor on Maze Road, which was named after him. It was Maze who had sold my father the bulk of his Modesto vineyards. Maze had his own extensive vineyards and had shipped his grapes with us for a few years. Julio and I went to speak to Claude, finding him in a field. We outlined our sketchy plans.

When the old man didn't say anything, Julio finally asked, "So, Claude, you want to come in with us?"

Maze slowly wiped his brow with a kerchief. "Tell me, just what are you boys going to do with the wine after you make it?"

Julio and I looked at each other. Mumbling our good-byes, we turned and walked home through the vineyards.

With the Depression, it was the worst of times to be asking anyone, even close relatives, for money. But I did so, convinced that we could make a go of the wine business.

My wife, Amelia, volunteered to ask her own family for help. She planned to speak to her mother, who everyone considered a softer touch than her father.

I had the highest regard for my mother-in-law. I knew her to be loving and supportive. I also knew her amazing story. Teresa and Giuseppe Franzia had not known each other in Italy. After Franzia ended up in California around the turn of the century and saved some money, he wrote to a girl he had known back home in Savona, near Genoa, sending her a hundred dollars to pay for her trip to America so she could marry him. The woman was insulted, and word spread around the local area about the rather unusual offer. A young woman from the neighboring town of Vado Ligure stepped forward and said she would be happy to go. When Teresa got off the train in California, Franzia was there to meet her. He was very disappointed when he first saw her, he would later admit, because she was small—about five feet tall. He wondered how in the world she was going to work in the fields and shoulder all the other burdens of farm life. Before long, Franzia's reservations were dispelled. Besides bearing eight children and handling the family's finances, Teresa Franzia worked the fields as hard as any man.

Amelia went to see her mother, who agreed to loan me five thousand dollars. A while later, she also co-signed a surety bond.

As it turned out, I am very glad I did not take my father-in-law's advice on one point. On Amelia's and my wedding day, her father had taken me aside. "Once a man gets married," he told me, "the farther away he takes his wife from her mother the better off he is."

Like I said, good thing I didn't listen.

. . .

JULIO AND I BEGAN LOOKING for suitable space to rent for a winery in Modesto. We were shown an empty warehouse for rent downtown on the corner of Eleventh and D streets. Owned by the local feeder railroad, the Modesto and Empire Traction Company, the building was 125 feet long and 78 feet wide. A rail spur ran directly to an outside loading dock, which would eliminate having to truck barrels of wine to the railhead.

George Beard ran the local railroad and had taken us to the warehouse. "I want to help you get started with your winery," he said. "You can have it for a hundred dollars a month."

Julio and I thought the building would work nicely, but we couldn't afford such steep rent.

"I very much appreciate your wanting to help us," I said. "You could help us even more by letting us have it for fifty dollars a month."

"I don't want to help you that much," Beard said. "Tell you what— seventy-five dollars."

"Sixty a month and we'll take it," I countered.

Beard accepted.

On August 17, 1933, we signed a lease.

IN EARLY AUGUST, Julio and I had jointly filed an application with the state for a "bonded winery premises."

Accompanying the application was a letter I dictated to Amelia, which she typed up in our cramped winery office. Our first "secretary" used a fifty-gallon barrel set on end for a desk and a ten-gallon one for a seat.

Amelia also took care of our books and swept the floors at night— doing just about everything Julio and I didn't have time to do. Later that fall, when we needed government tax stamps to put on barrels before shipping our wine, she would get up at four o'clock in the morning and drive to Stockton to buy the excise revenue stamps so we would have them when we had a shipment to get out that day. She was a great help, and never drew a dime in salary.

Our permit for Winery No. 3597 was approved on September 22, 1933.

There was much to do in a short time. We had to have a fully operable winery by the time the grapes were ready to harvest, or we would miss this year's crush and be out of business before we started.

We found a company in San Francisco that had built crushers and presses before Prohibition. In anticipation of Repeal, Rossi Machine Company had been reconditioning surplus equipment from wineries abandoned during Prohibition. Luckily the owner was venturesome, and he gave us a crusher and press on extended terms.

I learned from the Franzia brothers where they were buying their tanks. The redwood tank manufacturer, Pacific Tank and Pipe of San Francisco, required more persuasion on my part, as cooperage was in great demand, what with all the new wineries starting up. I had to admit that we couldn't afford to pay cash for the tanks. Instead, I offered to pay on trade acceptances due in six months or less. Much to my surprise, the Pacific Tank manager heard me out and, when I was finished, said, "All right, we'll do it." They initially provided us with 50,000 gallons of cooperage—every bit of it on credit.

The rest of our beginning equipment included four fermenting tanks, each with a capacity of around 3,000 gallons, an electric crusher and stemmer, a must pump, a wine pump, an ebulliometer to measure alcohol levels, a saccharometer to measure sugar levels, and an old-fashioned thermometer.

As a cooper was installing the redwood tanks and driving the hoops on the tanks, he made quite a racket. Passersby heard the noise from the street, and more than a few growers, in town for supplies, stopped to check out Modesto's newest winery. They were looking to sell their grapes, but we did not have any money. Instead I offered them the profit-sharing deal that I had come up with earlier: We would make the wine and credit a grower with two thirds of the wine, approximately 100 gallons of wine per ton of grapes he delivered to us. We would sell the wine after Repeal went into effect on December 5, 1933, and pay them when we were paid.

Though now having a license and facilities to make wine, we had a problem in that the only wine Julio and I had ever made was home-made wine. I remember as a kid stomping grapes with my bare feet. We helped our father put the crushed grapes in a small tank, ferment-ing the juice with the skins. When the sugar fermented out in a week or two, we transferred the wine into a barrel. As we drew the wine down and the family drank it, the barrel got more air inside. Our homemade wine tasted like grape juice in December and vinegar in June.

Obviously, we did not know anything about commercial winemak-ing. Though money was tight, we searched for a qualified winemaker to hire. But the wait for Repeal to come about had been too long for many experienced winemakers from the pre-Prohibition times. Those who had been relatively old in 1919 had either died or retired. Of the surviving handful of knowledgeable winemakers, those who weren't starting their own wineries had already been hired by the big wineries like Fruit Industries and Italian Swiss Colony. Unable to hire experi-enced winemaking help, Julio and I would be completely on our own.

I went to the Modesto library to look for a book on winemaking. I told the librarian what I had in mind, but she found nothing on the shelves. After all, we were just ending more than a decade of national Prohibition, during which there had been no call for winemaking liter-ature. As I turned to leave, she remembered some old pamphlets in the basement. "There might be some about winemaking from before Pro-hibition," she said. "Why don't you go down and see?"

I went downstairs and found a stack of magazines and pamphlets. I went through it, and found a pamphlet on fermentation and one on the care of wine by Professor Frederic T. Bioletti of the Department of Viticulture and Enology at the University of California at Davis, published prior to Prohibition. Bioletti had been in the forefront of research being done in enology around the turn of the century. The pamphlets were among a series published by the university, making results of various enological experiments available to early winemakers. These were exactly what we needed.

"You're welcome to them," the librarian said.

This was the beginning of our knowledge about making commercial wine, such as how to have a sound, clean fermentation, and how to clarify the wine. These old pamphlets probably saved us from going out of business our very first year—as did those new wineries that produced undrinkable wines.

IN SPITE OF FINDING THIS VALUABLE INFORMATION, had we taken a personal inventory at that time, our prospects would have looked very dismal:

Experience in producing commercial wine: none.
Experience in marketing wine: none.
Available cash: $900.23.
Borrowed funds: $5,000.

But I would have added this important intangible:

Confidence: Unbounded!

Why was I so confident? Because at the time, all of twenty-four years of age, I honestly felt that I could do anything anyone else could do—not because I was brilliant or well educated, but because I was willing to devote as much time and effort as was necessary, regardless of the sacrifice. And I knew that my brother Julio, equally dedicated to doing a good job, would make a dependable, hardworking partner.

Though others underestimated our capacities, Julio and I did not.

Julio

When our first commercial crush started in September 1933, we were up before dawn. We went into the growers' vineyards before the harvest, checking to see that the grapes were fully mature and had no mold.

When a loaded truck came in, we would dump the grapes into the crusher. After crushing the grapes into must, we pumped it into six-foot-high fermenting tanks.

The next morning, I climbed up the side of a fermenting tank, which was open at the top. The must had started to ferment overnight. At the top, the pomace—consisting of crushed stems and skins, which gives the wine color—was expanding like rising bread dough.

If the pomace cap was allowed to dry out, vinegar gnats would develop. Standing on a two-by-twelve plank that ran across the top of the tank, I used a long, blunt-ended paddle to punch down the pomace. This had to be done, I found out, twice a day during fermentation.

Several times a day I took the saccharometer and tested the sugar level. When it reached zero, in a week or so, the wine was bone-dry.

Only then did we begin pumping it out into redwood cooperage. These tanks were filled and closed. Here, the sediment, or lees, dropped out of the wine, settling to the bottom of the tank.

When we tried our first vintage, it tasted good to us. It would soften some with age. Crushing, fermenting, and clarifying filled our tanks to capacity. We realized that we would soon exceed our permit's 50,000-gallon storage capacity. But with everything running so smoothly and growers lining up to bring their grapes to us, we didn't want to stop.

In early October we took out a bond guaranteeing tax payments to support more gallonage, and notified the regulatory agency—the predecessor to the Bureau of Alcohol, Tobacco, and Firearms—that we wished to increase our capacity.

I remember sleeping at the winery and waking up to the alarm clock so as to switch tanks when necessary. We often worked around the clock—sometimes as long as thirty-six hours straight. Ernest and I went home during that first crush only to bathe, change clothes, and eat a hot meal.

That first year, crushing various grape varieties—the juice all ended up being blended together—we made exactly 177,847 gallons of red table wine.

But as December arrived, and the repeal of Prohibition with it, we hadn't sold a drop.

5

SAVING THE
VINEYARDS

Ernest

Now that we had wine, I started to think about selling it.

At the beginning of December, a form letter arrived air-mail from Chicago. Charles Barbera, a veteran grape dealer to whom I had sold grapes for several years at the Santa Fe yard, wrote that he was gearing up to start bottling wine upon Repeal. He wanted to hear from anyone who had bulk wine for sale.

Instead of calling or writing back, I hurried home and packed. Wanting to get to Barbera before other wine producers did, I boarded a DC-3 airliner to Chicago that afternoon—for my first plane ride. Air transportation was then in its infancy. In those days, planes stopped every few hundred miles for gas. We flew no higher than 5,000 feet, flying through canyons and skimming around mountains much higher than us. It turned out to be a turbulent, white-knuckle journey. Though flying was expensive and not very safe in those days, it gave me the advantage over rivals who traveled, much more slowly, by rail.

The next morning, I was waiting at Barbera's office when he arrived for work.

"I just wrote you a letter," he said.

"Is that so? What about?"

"I'm going into the bottling business. I wanted to know if you knew where I could buy some wine."

My brother and I had started our own winery, I explained. "As it happens," I said, "I have samples."

Though I didn't want to appear too anxious, the first payments on our winery equipment were due that month. To meet our obligations, we had to start selling wine.

"Let's see what you have," he said.

I took out my samples.

Immediately upon Repeal, the newly constituted wine industry was based on wineries that produced bulk wine which was sold (and shipped by rail in barrels or tank cars) to bottlers in various big-city markets. After bottling the wine in their plants, the bottlers sold it under their own labels to retailers in their area. Had marketing surveys been conducted back then, the wine consumers of the day would have been found to live mostly in large cities and to be Italian or Eastern European. The "average American" living in the Heartland had not yet developed a taste for wine. Sales by wineries to bottlers, and then by bottlers to retailers, were made principally on price alone. Though upon Repeal a few large wineries did bottle and distribute some of their products, in addition to selling in bulk, the modern-day wine industry began as a commodity business, with no national brands. No winery spent money on advertising or promotion.

Barbera liked what he tasted. He ordered 120 fifty-gallon barrels of wine that morning—6,000 gallons at 50 cents per gallon.

I had made my first wine sale.

I stayed on the move, selling wine. Often, on first calls to bottlers, I was openly stared at. I could almost hear them wondering how someone so young (twenty-four years old) could be the owner of a California winery. Invariably they would ask, "How old are you?"

"Thirty last March," I would shoot back.

I arrived in New York City that winter in the snow. I took a cab from Grand Central Station to Times Square, where I spotted the new Emerson Hotel and checked in.

What made selling wine those days extra challenging was locating potential customers. After fourteen years of Prohibition, there weren't any listings in the telephone book for wine bottlers. Along with skilled winemakers, merchants of wine had disappeared. Where to start in a place like New York?

I knew that during Prohibition wine had continued to be used sacramentally in the practice of the Jewish and Catholic faiths, so I headed for the Lower East Side, found a synagogue, and told the rabbi my problem. He gave me the name and address of another rabbi.

I tramped through the snow for blocks. The address turned out to be a subbasement under a tenement. I walked down some cement steps and pushed open the windowless door.

Stepping into a cold, dank room about twenty feet by forty feet in size, I was met by the familiar pleasant odor of wine. There were rows of tables with at least twenty women standing at them filling bottles from wine barrels, and labeling by hand.

A woman came forward, asking what I wanted.

I told her I wished to see the rabbi.

"The rabbi is not here," she said. "What do you want to see him about?"

"I want to sell him some wine."

"Wait a minute."

She went through a door at the back of the room. Soon, she returned with the rabbi, who had a flowing beard and a wide-brimmed black hat.

The rabbi asked if I had samples.

I pulled from a brown paper bag one of the two "tenth"-size bottles of wine I was carrying. The wine in both these bottles I had drawn out of the same tank in Modesto the day of my departure.

The night before in my hotel room I had checked my samples. The wine, being only six weeks old, was cloudy. I poured and repoured the wine through a paper filter over the bathroom sink until it cleared.

The rabbi poured from the bottle and tasted the wine. "What is your price?"

Fifty cents a gallon, I answered.

The rabbi put down his glass. "I have no market for wine this cheap."

"Oh. Can you afford ninety cents a gallon?"

"Yes."

I took out my second bottle of the same wine.

The rabbi tasted it. "This is the kind of wine I want. Send me a hundred barrels."

It was, as I look back on it now, a valuable lesson that I did not profit from. The correlation between price and perceived quality should have been obvious—then, and now, many people believe the more they pay for a wine, the better it is. But it went against my grain. I felt then, and feel to this day, that in the long run a business must be built upon giving the consumer the best quality at a fair price.

On New Year's Eve, I went around the corner from my hotel to the heart of Times Square. The throng increased as I inched my way forward. So many people were so tightly jammed into the area that I could have lifted my feet from the ground without falling.

When the clock struck midnight, the illuminated sphere dropped, indicating the arrival of the new year.

I was very thankful that 1933 had passed.

BACK IN MODESTO, I WENT TO SEE the local branch manager of Bank of America.

I was shocked when the banker said that he wouldn't lend us five hundred dollars to buy the barrels in which to ship Charlie Barbera his wine.

"I've already *sold* the wine," I protested. "As soon as the wine is received on the other end, I'll have payment. Your loan will be immediately repaid."

Things were tough, the banker explained, as if I didn't know the country was in the midst of the Depression.

But I refused to take no for an answer. "This wine is *sold*," I repeated. "You'll be repaid in no more than two weeks."

These barrels represented our first orders—we had to start somewhere! I kept assuring the banker that we would repay the loan as soon as the wine reached Chicago and Barbera sent me a check. There was no risk for him in advancing me the money.

It took me two hours of talking.

Finally, the banker agreed.

"Don't come back to borrow any more money this year," he said after I signed the note.

As promised, we paid the loan plus interest within two weeks.

Julio

Ernest and I were at the rear of the winery rolling the first order of barrels of wine we were shipping east onto a railcar when my old friend Jack Riorda showed up for a visit.

Riorda had also left the grape-shipping business for the wine business, having just opened a Napa winery.

"What in the world are you fellows doing?" he wanted to know.

"We've just barreled this wine and we're shipping it to Chicago," I explained.

Riorda's expression turned from confusion to disbelief. "That's ridiculous! That wine will never carry to the East. It's too new. It's still fermenting! It'll blow the ends out of those barrels!"

The wine had seemed stable enough to us and, after one final filtering, seemed to be holding its clarity just fine.

"We're not gonna ship our wine now, let me tell you," Riorda said. "We're gonna age it for a year at least and we'll get a dollar a gallon then. That's how you have to do it, boys."

"The wine is sound and our buyers want it and we need the money," Ernest said.

"You'll get it back on the next train," Riorda warned.

Ernest and I looked at each other. We went back to loading the barrels.

Jack was wrong when he said our wine was unsuitable and would be returned. In fact, we wired Barbera that if he wanted more, to let us know. He did, and soon we had a second carload of wine headed his way.

Years later, not long before Barbera died, he visited us in California. By then his wine distribution business, Pacific Wine Company, was one of the largest in Chicago. We were at Ernest's house, enjoying the dinner and conversation about the old days, when Charlie suddenly seemed to turn serious.

"You know, I never told you guys this," he began, "but remember that first carload of wine you sent me? Well—it was the best damn wine you ever made! When you started watering down your wine later, it wasn't nearly as good."

Charlie burst into laughter, and we joined him.

That first carload of wine had been heavy because it was so young, not having time to precipitate tartrates. It was a natural full-bodied wine, just like what Charlie had made at home from our grapes during Prohibition—and to his dying day he preferred that to wine made by modern winemaking methods.

ERNEST SOLD ALL OUR WINE that first year.

There was no letup at all from our busy fall and winter. No vacation or days off for either of us—just work and more work, seven days a week. And they were long days. Sometimes, after working eighteen hours, we would be called out in the middle of the night and go down to the winery because of some problem. We were going to make damn sure that we didn't fail.

Our wives recognized the pressure we were under. They put up with our long hours and supported us in every way possible. While Amelia helped out at the winery, Aileen ran the household, cooking and cleaning. They both worked very hard, and never complained.

The five of us lived together on Maze Road—Aileen and me in the back bedroom that Ernest and I had shared growing up, Ernest and Amelia in our parents' corner bedroom, and Joe in his front bedroom.

Despite the uncertainty of our new winery, Aileen and I saw no reason to delay having children. In that regard, 1934 turned out to be a good year. Our first child was born that August. We named him Robert Julio.

Come fall, Ernest and I decided to expand the winery. We had survived the first round, which I credit to the toughness of youth and our willingness to work hard.

To expand for that second season we needed more grapes, more equipment and tanks, more of everything.

A major concern was acquiring additional cooperage, which was expensive and in demand, owing to all the new wineries starting up.

When we asked Pacific Redwood Company of San Francisco for more cooperage on credit terms, the owner of the company, an old German named Schmidt, came to Modesto to check us out.

I took Schmidt through the winery—our rented warehouse was getting crowded—and pointed out where we would install the new cooperage.

Schmidt took it all in, then asked me where I lived.

"We live on a ranch out on Maze Road," I said.

"Can we go out and take a look?"

"Sure."

We drove out Maze Road and I gave him a tour of the vineyards. The 160 acres across the street that Ernest and I had worked and planted four years earlier had come into full production the previous year.

We pulled into the yard behind the house, and went in the back door. Aileen was in the kitchen trying to make lunch, and our baby, Bob, just a month old, was in his crib crying. There she was with her hands full, and there I am arriving with an unexpected guest for lunch.

Without hesitation, Schmidt reached into the crib and picked up our baby, explaining, "Oh, I know about babies." He began pacing back and forth, patting Bob gently on the back. Soon, little Bob was quiet. When Schmidt bent over and placed him back in his crib, our son was sound asleep.

"We raised four kids," he said. "They grow up so fast."

Through lunch, Schmidt didn't talk business at all. Instead, he chatted mostly about kids and family life with my wife. He was obviously a good-hearted, down-to-earth guy, which I appreciated, but while he was talking with Aileen, all I could think about was *Am I going to get the tanks?*

After lunch we drove back to town. On the ride, I started to bring up the subject of more cooperage.

Schmidt stopped me short. "I have a cooper putting in tanks at another winery. When he's finished, I'll have him come over to your place. Don't worry, you'll have your tanks. You pay me when you can."

That was that. Schmidt had found a hardworking family man, and he could see that Ernest and I were determined to succeed. He decided that E. & J. Gallo Winery was worth taking a chance on.

It was the way business was done back then. Get to know a man and trust what you see. Gain each other's confidence, and seal the deal on your word and a handshake.

I miss those days.

Ernest

We had turned a profit our first year.

Our growers were delighted. In those days, a ton of grapes produced approximately 150 gallons of wine. Under our "share" deal with them, growers had been credited with 100 gallons of wine for every ton of grapes they delivered to us. As I had sold our wine for an average of 50 cents a gallon, the growers received $50 per ton compared to the $14 per ton cash price paid by wineries that season.

We purchased our father's estate's grapes on the same basis. In fact, without the money earned from its wine grapes, the estate would not have had sufficient money to pay off its liabilities.

When we started out, Julio and I drew salaries of $60 a month. We poured every cent back into the business. Even so, we still needed to borrow to operate the winery—and would for years to come.

I went back to Bank of America for a loan in the fall of 1934. Our business was expanding and we had substantial expenses to meet in order to make it through the next harvest and crush. Also, we wanted to be in a position to buy grapes outright from growers for cash. We knew if we had cash we could buy grapes for less than what it would cost us to pay the growers in wine on a share deal.

"Look, how do I know your wine won't turn sour?" the banker wanted to know.

I pointed out that we had successfully made wine the previous year.

"But what if you end up making vinegar this year?" the banker asked. "You'll go out of business and we'll lose our money."

Not only did we have a year's experience to prove we knew how to make good, sound wine, I argued, but we had sold all our wine, paid off our growers, were current on our equipment payments, and had steady customers. Our profit was a shade over $30,000.

Bank of America made us a modest loan that second year, but I got the distinct impression that we were not at the top of the bank's list of valued customers.

A. E. Sbarboro, the son of one of the founders of Italian Swiss Colony, was a Bank of America director at the time. It did cause me to wonder about the bank's loan policy—official or unofficial—toward other wineries. I have since heard it said that Sbarboro, a member of the bank's powerful loan committee, had early on described "the Gallo boys . . . [as] newcomers who shouldn't be financed."*

We smaller operators should not have given ISC any reason to worry. Upon Repeal, ISC picked up where it had left off before Prohibition: as one of the country's biggest wineries, with a storage capacity of 4.5 million gallons. Only Fruit Industries, with 8 million gallons, and Roma Winery, with 6.7 million gallons, were larger.

Understanding the importance of developing a solid banking relationship, I began looking for a bank that would be comfortable with us.

We sold all our 1934 vintage—some 230,000 gallons, as well as wine we purchased from other wineries. Even so, there was no assurance that we were going to make it in this business. The odds were still against us. Others better equipped than we were had already failed.

A whole generation of wine drinkers had disappeared during Prohibition. For the U.S. wine industry as a whole, it was very much like having to start all over again.

In countries like France, Italy, and Spain, they had continued making and drinking wine. In so many ways they were ahead of us. There were no guarantees we would catch up or that the United States would ever become a wine-drinking country. Immediately upon Repeal, hard liquor and beer sales bounced back with a vigor that revealed a pent-up demand. Meanwhile, wine was a necessity to only a small section of our population. Not only did our revived industry have to rebuild its

---

*Burke H. Critchfield of Bank of America, in an interview conducted March 9, 1970, for the Oral History Project, University of California at Berkeley.

internal machinery (modern wineries, more cooperage, etc.) but we had to also promote a larger market for our product.

Although our company had paid off Bank of America in a timely manner that second year, the bank wasn't willing to meet our borrowing requirements in 1935. About then, we heard of a small, aggressive bank in Sacramento called Capital National Bank. I called the bank's president, George Zoller, and told him about our winery. "I'd like to borrow eighty thousand dollars," I said.

"What for?"

"To buy grapes," I answered. "And to get us through the crush and shipping our wine east."

He asked me to be in his office at eight o'clock the following morning.

This was before freeways and interstate highways, of course, so it was a two-and-a-half-hour drive from Modesto to Sacramento. I left at five A.M. to get there on time.

After talking for a few minutes in Zoller's office, he said, "Look, I'll be at your winery tomorrow morning at eight o'clock. If I like what I see, I'll lend you the money."

He was in Modesto at eight A.M. sharp, pulling up to the corner of Eleventh and D streets. Inside the winery, I let him set the pace. He didn't linger. We walked right through the building in about one minute.

Outside again, Zoller said, "I think you're going to make it, young man. You've got the loan."

I had found just the banker we needed.

For the '33 and '34 seasons, we crushed the estates' grapes, paying for them according to our profit-sharing arrangement. The return on these grapes ranged from $50 to $60 a ton, compared to an average $15 a ton they would have brought on the cash market.

This revenue from the winery helped the estates reach solvency, which in turn allowed us to keep the land. I think we surprised and impressed some creditors and bankers who in the beginning didn't give us much of a chance.

To help pay all the obligations of my father's estate, I had sold the Fresno ranch, for which the estate had to take a promissory note for most of the proceeds. Also, in September 1934 I was able to restructure the remaining estate debt with a new long-term loan from the Federal Land Bank.

After our parents' estates closed in 1935, Julio, Joe, and I inherited the estate valued at $61,800, net after obligations. The principal assets were the equity in 270 acres on Maze Road, a 20-acre vineyard in nearby Keyes, and our parents' Transamerica stock.

The bank, having been paid off, released the two thousand shares of Transamerica stock it held as security. We kept the stock until the following year, when we sold it for $12 a share.

To operate the vineyards, we formed a general partnership. Julio and I and our brother, Joe, fifteen, became equal partners in Gallo Brothers Ranch.

We had saved the family vineyards.

6

GROWING ON A
HANDSHAKE

Ernest

On August 16, 1935, my brother Julio and I were present for the first annual membership meeting of the Wine Institute at the Palace Hotel in San Francisco. Forming this trade organization, which would become increasingly effective in later years, was an important step for the wine industry.

There were some very good reasons to organize; one of them was to work to change restrictive trade barriers that interfered with orderly commerce in wine. Repeal of national Prohibition had left the states free to operate under whatever local liquor laws were in effect or were later enacted. Individual states began passing a great volume of confusing and inconsistent legislation that hampered wine distribution. Some states didn't enact any new laws at all, thereby retaining local Prohibition. Twenty-two states remained dry.

The wine industry had never up to this time been united in a successful organization. We did not even have a list of the various state regulations. We had practically a new industry, without quality stan-

71

dards. We had a Congress and more than twenty state legislatures, including California's, convening to decide meaningful issues of taxes, licenses, quality standards, and commerce. We had to reduce federal red tape. We had to resist tariff reductions on French, Spanish, and Italian wines. We had to start an educational campaign to make people more "wine-conscious" and to start publicizing California wines.

There was much work to be done. Now, as I review the minutes of that first meeting, I'm struck by how many of the same battles we're still waging six decades later.

For the next several years, Julio and I were too busy to be greatly involved in industry matters. In time that would change. But back then we were hard at work to improve the quality of our wine, expand and modernize our facilities, obtain distribution, push sales, and develop new markets for our wine.

We had a lot to do at home.

Overproduction soon plagued the industry. Gigantic grape crops came in in three of the next four years, far more than the new wineries—many of them already struggling—and the state's raisin packers and table-grape shippers could handle. Grape prices weakened.

Naturally, wine prices fell. By 1935, table-wine prices averaged 21 cents a gallon, less than half of what I had sold our wines for in 1933. Hit especially hard were those North Coast wineries that had been aging their wines for a year or two: Instead of selling it for 50 to 60 cents a gallon, they were now lucky to get half that price. In fact, some sold wine to us for as low as 8 cents a gallon.

Before Prohibition, California wines had begun winning international awards, but this reputation had faded by the time Repeal came. With our domestic wine industry shut down for fourteen years, consumers, retailers, and distributors knew little about wine. They needed to be educated about it, as did most vintners.

Opportunity seekers flooded the wine industry. Like us, many had no experience in wine production and sale, and no capital. They bought grapes on the open market as cheaply as possible—not caring whether the growers could cover their costs—produced wine as cheaply as possible, and sold it the only way they knew how: on price. No attention was given to producing a sound product. Many soon went out of business.

It was a needed shakeout.

Still, there were formidable competitors. In the marketplace, I ran into prominent vintners like John B. Cella, Walter Taylor, Louis Petri, and Samuele Sebastiani, among others.

Petri and I seemed often to end up on the same train heading east. Whenever we did, we sat together. He was a very nice guy, and always good company. When we arrived, I'd tell him the bottlers I was going to visit. If he didn't have any ideas, I'd even suggest where he might want to go so that we wouldn't run into each other. There were enough bottlers to go around.

Petri's father, Angelo, had made his money in the cigar business. I remember having lunch with Lou and his father at the Fior d'Italia in North Beach in the late 1940s or early 1950s. Angelo Petri was the kind of guy who liked to brag, and he said, "We are worth a million dollars!" That sounded like all the money in the world. Puffing on a cigar made at his own factory and waving his hands at me, he added, "A fellow like you, you are probably worth fifty thousand maybe. We could lose fifty thousand for twenty years in a row before we would go broke. If you lose it in one year, you are out of business." He was right, though I had no intention of proving him so.

With Repeal on the horizon, Petri had leased three plants in Sonoma and Napa counties and had started producing table wines. A year later, the Petri Wine Company added a winery in Escalon and started making dessert wines. They became well-financed, big-volume producers with whom my brother and I would find ourselves two decades later locked in a head-to-head battle as to who would be number one.

Even in the early days, Lou Petri and I conducted business quite differently. He would take bottlers out to dinner, I would later hear, and just shoot the breeze with them. Everyone liked Lou, of course. But often, by the time they parted, Petri had not even brought up the subject of selling his wine. That went against what I had learned on the tracks. You find your buyer, figure out a way to give him the product he needs, and close the deal. From the beginning, I was always interested in knowing about my customer's business. How much wine was he selling? How come he was buying so few tank cars of my wine? What was keeping him from selling more? What could I do to help him sell more? How much wine was his competitor selling? This approach made sense to me. I'll add this: No bottler could say I ever left town without trying to help him do better.

Meanwhile, Julio and I were working extremely hard to produce and market a sound product. We made a good sound table wine, but I don't know that our wine was much better than the wines being made by Cella, Petri, Sebastiani, and others.

Though it was our policy to sell our total output each year, we were still having to borrow from the bank to finance the tonnage of grapes needed to keep up with our increasing sales.

The borrowing cycle worked like this: At harvest time we needed cash to buy grapes and to build our inventory of wine. So we borrowed during the months of August, September, October, and November. As we sold the wine, money came in, and we paid back the bank. When it was harvest time again, we used our own money to buy grapes until it ran out. Then, we borrowed again from the bank.

What I've just described is a healthy cycle, one still practiced by wineries and their banks today.

The first sign of a winery in trouble is when it can't repay the bank everything prior to commencing the next borrowing cycle. Loans that are delinquent start being rolled over, and soon the winery is buried in debt. The bank will eventually stop making loans. When it does, the beleaguered winery is out of business.

Julio

Unlike many wineries, we never had any trouble selling what we produced—actually more than we produced. We kept costs down, even though we were always trying to improve our wines. Ernest always sold the wine. He is a great salesman and he had the product. Ernest left no stone unturned trying to find customers. He was always one step ahead of the other guy.

From the start we had to purchase bulk wine to blend with our own in order to meet our sales commitments. Actually, the wine we purchased for blending improved our wines, since nearly all of the wine we bought at that time came from the North Coast.

I began making regular buying trips into Sonoma and Napa counties, leaving home as early as three or four o'clock in the morning, often in the thick fog that blankets the Valley floor in the winter.

There were many small growers who crushed their own grapes scattered through the hills and valleys of the North Coast. I would go up the Napa Valley and then down and over to Sonoma. At each stop I'd meet the owner, climb a ladder to the top of each of his tanks, and get samples to take back home. Sometimes I wouldn't get back to Modesto until ten o'clock at night. The next morning I would taste the wines. Ernest would also, if he was home. If the wine was okay, I'd call the winery owner and make him an offer.

By the end of the 1935 crush, we were using every available foot of space at Eleventh and D. We then had about 350,000 gallons of storage capacity, but it wasn't nearly enough—we had sold over 450,000 gallons of wine the previous year. In 1935, we sold 941,000 gallons.

We needed more room.

With Ernest back east on a sales trip, I went out with our landlord, George Beard of the local railroad.

We drove around for hours, with Beard pointing to empty, dusty lots: "You could build there."

Although the lots in the industrial section of town seemed plenty big to me, I wasn't enthusiastic about any of them. Had we located in that section of town, where things were already being built up, it wouldn't have been long before we would have run out of room and been forced to relocate again. But I wasn't the one who anticipated such rapid growth and the need for more land. It was George Beard.

"I'm going to take you out of town on the other side of the creek," he finally said.

"What's out there?" I asked.

"Nothing, yet."

We crossed a creek bed and parked the car. Soon, we were walking through a grain field situated between the railroad tracks and Fairbanks Avenue.

"We've got forty acres here," Beard said. "I can sell you a piece of it. Let's say from the irrigation district canal to the power lines to the creek."

"Gee, that's pretty big," I said. "How many acres you think that is?"

"I guess about ten. Let's pace it off."

Beard took a pad and pencil from his pocket and took off, with me following him. Beard was a pretty tall guy and his paces were long, but I stayed up. When we finished, he did some figuring on his pad.

"It's more than ten acres," he announced, "but we'll just call it an even ten."

"How much is it going to cost?"

"You can have it for three hundred fifty an acre."

"That seems like a lot," I said. "Why don't you just cut it in half and give me five acres."

"Hell, no, I'm going to give you the whole ten acres. Not only that, but I'm going to reserve the other thirty acres for you. You'll need them someday, Julio."

"Never. Not that much."

I had seen my father stuck with more empty land than he could support—and I did not ever want to find myself in that position. Going through the Depression tended to make a person cautious about money and land. From the beginning, Ernest and I were very conservative in business. That never changed through the years. I can tell you we've always made every dollar count.

At the time, Beard had bigger plans for us than I did. "I'm going to keep them for you anyway," he said.

We closed the deal for the ten acres on a handshake, and Beard had a rail spur line laid directly to the site of our new winery.

It wasn't many years before Beard was proved right. Eventually we needed every bit of that extra 30 acres that Beard kept reserved for us—and then some. Today, in fact, the winery takes up 250 acres.

And today, in addition to transporting much of our volume by truck, we ship 10,000 railcars of wine each year out of town on the Modesto and Empire Traction Railroad.

I guess Beard knew a customer with potential when he saw one.

Ernest

During the first stage of construction on our new winery, I was confined to a tuberculosis ward north of San Francisco. That's where I stayed for the first six months of 1936.

When a phlegmy cough kept getting worse, I went to the doctor. "You've got TB," he informed me. "You're not going home."

With no miracle drugs in those days, treatment consisted of isolation, bed rest, and a pneumothoraxic procedure in which your infected lung was partially collapsed, inhibiting its use and promoting healing. You either recovered, or didn't.

I had no real worry that anything tragic would happen to me. I was thankful that the disease was identified early, while in only one lung. This incident made me a lifelong believer in going to the doctor at the first sign of anything wrong, and seeking the best medical care possible. At the time, there was no question in my mind that I wouldn't get well. I guess I'm a guy with perpetual optimism. On the ward, I'd see these poor guys worrying, fretting, and being very pessimistic about their chances. As they obviously feared, a lot of them did die.

That's when I came to the conclusion that mental attitude has a lot to do with health. Over the years, I've seen perfectly healthy people who worry incessantly about everything, and damned if they didn't end up dying young. Whereas people who learn how to see the best in everything tend to live longer, and are a lot happier along the way.

During my six months in the hospital, Amelia visited me regularly, bringing news about the family. When Julio came to see me, we would discuss what was going on at the winery.

I wasn't too concerned about the business, even though it wasn't the best time for me to be away. Our business was still very much touch and go, but I trusted Julio to handle things. By then, we had hired a few good men, so he had some help. Still, there was no one to take all the eastern sales trips I had been making—spending half the year on the road. Julio could not leave the winery unsupervised in order to go on the road for any length of time. He would have to make all sales over the telephone.

The previous year, I'd given some thought as to how best to expand our operation. It occurred to me that we might want to merge with the Franzia brothers. We had run out of room, while they had a winery in their vineyard. We were competing with them for bulk sales, though we were selling wine faster than they were. I spoke to Amelia's brothers. They thought a merger sounded pretty good, but when they discussed it with their father, he reportedly hollered, "Hell, no! What do we need with their junk?"

While to this day I'm not sure what Franzia meant by our "junk," his strong opposition killed any further talk of a Gallo-Franzia merger. "We don't need them," I told Julio. "We'll do it on our own."

Julio

The first stage of construction on our new creekside property was the concrete wine-storage tanks. Aboveground concrete tanks were relatively new in our industry. But with the volume we were selling, we needed bigger tanks than we could get using redwood.

Looking for a contractor who could handle the work, I was referred to the San Francisco firm Cahill Construction—one of the largest in the West. Normally I don't think they would have been interested in our tank job, but it was the middle of the Depression and jobs were scarce, so owner John Cahill himself came to Modesto.

I took him out to the Fairbanks Avenue property.

Cahill, an elderly man by then, was an expert builder who could foresee a future in the wine industry. We talked about tank sizes, and how they could be built.

"They'll have to be strong," I cautioned.

Cahill looked at me. "When I get through building them," he said, "you can roll them down a hill."

"Well, I don't care about rolling them down a hill. Just so they hold our wine."

We settled on six clusters of four 40,000-gallon tanks—twenty-four tanks totaling one million gallons of storage capacity. Cahill agreed to build them at a total cost of $50,000.

I thought we were in pretty good hands, but it turned out the Cahill firm didn't even have a transit mixer in those days. They just sent out a crew with a regular cement mixer and went to work, shoveling the gravel and sand and dumping the concrete into wooden forms by hand.

A wine tank had to be built monolithically; in other words, you had to keep pouring once you started. If you stopped, you'd end up with joints that would leak. So they started in the morning and went clear through the day and into the night, for as many days as it took to complete a tank. Once in a while, workers would climb inside and run vibrators down the wet walls to make sure there weren't any air pockets that would later spring leaks.

Since this was all so new and I didn't want to take any chances, I spent most days and nights with our construction crew, led by Audrey James, who remained with us until his retirement many years later.

Once the tanks were completed, we turned our attention to building concrete structures for our shipping department and to house our crushing and refrigeration equipment and fermenting tanks.

We consulted with wine industry experts at the University of California Berkeley and Davis campuses as to how to modernize and make more efficient the entire winemaking process from beginning to end. We visited UC Berkeley and spoke to Professor William V. Cruess of the enology department. Later, he would comment that we asked more questions in a day than anyone before or since.

Despite my comments to George Beard, we weren't exactly thinking small. At a time when only two or three wineries had a capacity as large as six million gallons, Ernest and I would end up with a one-million-gallon plant when our construction project was finished.

I never gave any thought to being the biggest. Maybe that's what Ernest had in mind all along, but it wasn't my ambition. In a nutshell, my main goal from the beginning was to do everything possible to give the consumer good wines at affordable prices. I figured that if we met that goal, we couldn't go wrong.

We met our deadline: The twenty-four new storage tanks, each one the size of an average home, were completed in May 1936, in time for the next crush. We also installed twenty-four cement fermenters having a total capacity of 140,000 gallons. Only then did work start on the other structures.

That May, Aileen met her own deadline. She presented us with our only daughter, Susann Aileen.

I REMEMBER THE DAY ERNEST came home from the hospital and we drove out to see the new concrete tanks. Though still weak, he insisted on climbing the ladder up the side of a tank. He wanted to see what we had built.

I followed behind him, planning to catch him if he slipped. We went to the catwalk on top of a massive tank. We stood side by side, looking out for many miles.

At that moment I'm sure we both appreciated what a solid foundation we'd laid for the future.

7

"SOMETHING TO CROW ABOUT"

Ernest

In the fall of '37, the owner of Napa's Beaulieu Vineyards, Georges de Latour, found himself with 400,000 gallons of dry wine he couldn't sell.

Julio and I went to Napa one Saturday. We tasted his red wine from the previous harvest and found it to be good and full-bodied. We offered him eight cents a gallon.

After some hemming and hawing, he accepted. De Latour told us we had to start hauling the wine out on Monday, as he needed the space for his current grape crop, then being harvested.

"You going to pay me first," he stated.

"No," I said. "We'll pay you in ninety days."

De Latour looked like he was going to have a heart attack. "How I know you'll pay me?"

I shrugged. "We always pay our bills."

De Latour said he wanted to come to Modesto to see our operation and financial statement.

He arrived the next morning in a limousine.

I took him into our tiny office and showed him our financial statement. To a conservative Frenchman, it was not at all good. He started perspiring.

I went on about how in the four years we had been in business, we had never missed paying a creditor on time.

"Okay," he finally said. "Take the wine on Monday and pay me in ninety days."

Even then I knew it wasn't our price, or my persuasive argument, and certainly not our financial statement that had finally convinced him. Rather, it was his pressing need to empty his tanks in time for the upcoming crush. To this day, though, I am not sure why a fellow like de Latour couldn't sell all his wine, when we could sell all of ours.

That same year we put in a still, which enabled us to enter the fortified-wine business for the first time. U.S. consumption at that time had come to favor dessert wines, such as ports and sherries with an alcohol content of 20 percent—in 1938, 42 million gallons in these categories had been sold, compared to 21 million gallons of table wine. Before Prohibition, California's wine output was 60 percent table and 40 percent dessert. Upon Repeal, those figures flip-flopped in favor of dessert wines. Many of the older wine drinkers who had preferred table wine before Prohibition were gone, and the younger wine consumers who replaced them had different tastes in wine. The public would continue to favor dessert over table wines for the next thirty years. Also catching vintners off guard was the fact that the consumption of homemade wine continued at a very high level; in 1937 it was estimated that home winemakers made 35 million gallons of wine.

To our rapidly expanding table-wine business we were able to add fortified wines such as port, sherry, muscatel, and white port, dramatically increasing our volume and sales every year. In 1937 we made 310,000 gallons of dessert wine and four times that amount of table wine.

Now with the distillery, Julio and I realized that we needed to plant grape varieties that were more suitable for fortified wines. We located three available parcels totaling some 440 acres of farmland adjacent to the 20-acre vineyard that we had inherited from our parents in Keyes, a few miles down the road from Modesto. It was very fertile land, some of the best we had ever seen, and surprisingly cheap—the asking price was only eighty dollars an acre.

We walked it, then stopped to talk to the neighbor, Charlie Mollard, an old Frenchman who had sold my father the original 20 acres back in 1922. We told him that we were thinking about buying the adjacent land, and asked him what he thought.

"Didn't you see the morning glory?" he asked.

"Yes," I said.

"How the hell can you farm that?"

Invasive morning glory weeds *were* out of control.

"Well, we thought we'd buy it," I answered, "then kill the weeds and plant grapes."

The Frenchman shook his head. "Before you kill the morning glory, it'll kill you."

Julio and I had already discussed the weed infestation. The morning glory were thick and obnoxious, it was true, and in those days such problems weren't understood and handled as effortlessly as today. Still, we had a plan.

"The land is cheap," I explained, "so we can afford to buy two mules and a weed cutter, then put a man on the rig and have him cut the weeds off below the ground surface. As soon as he's covered the property once, he'll start over, and keep doing it over and over. We'll not let the plants ever see the sun. If we continue that for a year or so, the roots will have to die."

"Cut the weeds under the surface for a year!" The Frenchman looked at us like we had lost our minds.

But that's exactly what we did. In a year, we had killed the morning

84

glory. We then planted grapes on what turned out to be some of the best farm land in California—all for the price of only eighty dollars an acre, plus the cost of a man driving a two-mule team for a year.

MANY WINERIES THAT HADN'T already gone broke in the five years since Repeal were straining under the weight of the borrowing they had done to build or modernize plants and buy equipment. With the supply of wine exceeding demand every single year, many wineries were forced to sell their wine for whatever price they could get, even if they made no profit at that price. Even so, many wineries found themselves holding large inventories of unsold wine, unable to pay their bills.

When it became apparent by summertime that the harvest of '38 was going to be another bumper crop, growers and vintners alike clamored for something to be done to keep surplus wine from hitting the market.

As a result of chaotic conditions in the marketplace, Wine Institute members pushed for a first-ever industry-supported advertising and promotional campaign to bring California wines to the attention of more consumers.

The California Marketing Act, passed in the early 1930s, provided for producers of crops to finance promotion of their products throughout the country and around the world by means of a "marketing order." To finance the wine campaign, the first marketing order for wine became effective later that year after the required 65 percent of the state's wineries voted for it. The order, which called for a mandatory assessment of one cent per gallon on dessert wine and one half cent per gallon on table wine, raised $440,000 its first year. Most of the money went for the national advertising campaign. Another important activity funded under the order was trade barrier work.

Trade barriers were becoming increasingly restrictive. In the forty-four states where wine sales were legal, there were forty-four different tax and alcoholic-beverage distribution systems written into law.

I thought the marketing order a good idea and voted for it; wine was not the first industry to benefit from such an order. But I subsequently joined others in questioning how our money was being collected and spent. We made good on our threat to withhold our payments, and the state director of agriculture filed suit. We eventually settled our disagreements and paid the assessments.

SOON AFTER REPEAL, many growers started banding together to form cooperative wineries, which crushed grower-members' grapes and produced their wine.

A co-op such as Fruit Industries, whose leadership included such powerful men as Walter Taylor, A. R. Morrow, and Antonio Perelli-Minetti, had tremendous advantages over other wineries. They were farmers' cooperatives, so the government provided them with tax advantages as well as low-interest loans.

Generally, growers went the co-op route during difficult times. Either they were dissatisfied with the grape prices paid by wineries, or they feared being unable to find buyers and hoped somehow to salvage their crop. They were winery owners, but primarily in the table-grape-shipping or raisin business. By making wine with whatever grapes they couldn't sell, co-ops could turn a perishable crop into a storageable product, which they hoped to sell later. Their wineries were largely salvage operations.

The willingness of many wineries to crush every grape not used elsewhere resulted in wine surpluses, since wine production was not tied to the public's demand for wine.

The economics of the grape industry are different than those of most industries. In few other industries does a surplus of raw materials mean a surplus of the end product. For example, one season's surplus of wheat does not mean that cracker companies will suddenly find themselves with an oversupply of crackers. The wheat surplus is the farmer's problem, and possibly the government's—but not Nabisco's. But whenever there was an oversupply of grapes, it was a certainty that the surplus would become the wine industry's problem. ("Wineries Slashing Prices," ran the headline in the *San Francisco Chronicle*. The story: "A fundamental imbalance between supply, which is abundant, and demand, which is sluggish, has prompted wineries, distributors and retailers to drop prices on virtually all varieties of California wine." The date: July 13, 1993. Some things never change.)

With the wine industry facing a disaster, the answer to the 1938 surplus problem turned out to be brandy. The Bank of America, with large loans out to wineries that were in trouble, assigned vice president Burke Critchfield to work with vintners in coming up with the so-called "grape prorate," which was financed with the help of the federal Reconstruction Finance Corporation. Under this program, growers received $15 per ton for 55 percent of the tonnage that they delivered to wineries. They received an advance of $12.50 per ton for 30 percent of the tonnage they delivered, and the winery was required to make these grapes, or to have them made, into beverage brandy, which was to be held off the market for at least two years. The remaining 15 percent of the tonnage was to be made into the kind of brandy used to make dessert wines, and for this tonnage the grower received no advance. Thus, the average grower received $12 per ton for his grapes, with the prospect of receiving more if brandy was sold for more than was needed to cover the costs of the program.

We produced our first brandy in 1938—about 10,000 barrels—and built a new warehouse in which to store it. Under the terms of this complex program, vintners were given first option to purchase the brandy they had produced. Some did, others didn't. We did, and most of it we sold to Seagram for a higher price later, during the war. At that time, there was a shortage of liquor owing to the government's requiring grain and sugar to be used for food, alcohol for synthetic rubber, and other war needs.

When the 1938 surplus crisis passed, a postmortem showed that growers had received between $13 and $15 a ton for their grapes—more than the disastrous prices anticipated before the prorate. While this program took care of 1938's surplus, it was never used again.

In 1939, an oversupply of grapes again dictated a downward pressure on prices. John B. Cella of Roma Wine Company and Louis M. Martini were offering to buy grapes for as little as $6 a ton and finding takers. At that price, growers were not even compensated for their out-of-pocket costs. Many had to accept such a price; the alternative was to leave the grapes on the vine to rot.

That year's sinking grape prices pushed wine prices to bottlers lower: down to 11 cents per gallon for table wine and 24 cents per gallon for dessert wines. Even at those depressed prices, many wineries ended up with unsold inventories.

Alarmed because so many of the wineries and growers in trouble owed his bank money, A. P. Giannini, the founder of Bank of America, swung into action.

In 1939, Bank of America set up under its control Central California Wineries (CCW). Through this umbrella group, the bank sought to refinance, direct, and control the sales and pricing policies of member wineries. The bank wanted to bolster prices so that the wineries could make enough money to meet their obligations. One look at the list of members, which included several large, well-known wineries, indicated just how bad times had become.

Petri, Roma, and Italian Swiss Colony, all having problems, welcomed the idea. Lou Petri came to Modesto to talk to me about the merits of CCW, stating that this would stabilize prices at a level all of us could live with.

I heard him out, then said I wanted no part of it. I felt then, as I do now, that I like a free hand in doing business. Nothing Petri said that day changed my mind. It just didn't make sense to me.

As it turned out, it wasn't long before federal prosecutors were investigating the parties involved in CCW because they thought the plan violated antitrust laws. One of the prosecutors was a brilliant young San Francisco lawyer of Italian descent named Joseph Alioto, who later gained his reputation by representing private plaintiffs in suits against large companies charging antitrust violations (and who eventually was elected mayor of San Francisco). However, no charges were ever filed, and CCW voluntarily disbanded in 1942.

In the meantime, Julio and I were emptying our cellars every year—selling all the wine we made as well as the extra we bought from other wineries.

Most wineries in those days had an independent broker who handled their sales. The problem was that selling a winery's production wasn't nearly as important to the broker as it was to that winery. We never used a broker. I stayed on the road myself five, six months out of the year, establishing relationships with bottlers. I got to know their businesses at least as well as they did.

These bottlers were men who had started their new business because they thought they saw a new, exciting opportunity. They seemed to value my advising them on the basis of the experience I had gained in my dealings with other bottlers. They also appreciated dealing directly with the owner of a winery.

Many wineries were owned by men who could make wine, but who seemed to assume that after doing so there would be a sure market for their wine. It didn't work that way, however. Not then, and not now.

Julio

Our banker, George Zoller of Capital National, made regular trips to Modesto to see how we were doing. On one trip he brought with him the bank's chairman of the board, Alden Anderson, a former lieutenant governor of California.

They came in and we gave them the tour—this must have been just before we put in our still. Every year our plans kept getting bigger and bolder, and this year was no different. I enthusiastically told them where we were going and how we figured we were going to get there. It all meant our needing to borrow more money, of course.

When I was finished, Anderson said, "Listen, play it close to the vest. It's tough times out there."

I had never heard such caution from Zoller. Obviously, his chairman was a lot more conservative.

My disappointment must have been obvious because as they were walking out the door, Zoller turned and whispered in my ear, "Go ahead, Julio. Go all out."

That was what I wanted to hear. Go all out we did, that year and every year. And whenever we needed it, George Zoller and his bank were there.

OUR YOUNGER BROTHER, JOE, graduated from high school in 1937 and the following year enrolled at Modesto Junior College. Ernest and I urged him to take science courses that would prepare him to transfer to the University of California at Davis, where he could major in enology.

We thought that it would be a good fit for Joe to come into the winery after college as a winemaking partner. Neither Ernest nor I had ever taken an enology class in our lives, and having our younger brother join us with such technical expertise would have been a great advantage. But Joe wasn't very motivated in school, and his grades suffered. Eventually, he dropped out of college.

Joe made it clear that he was not interested in making a career of the winery. He told me he wanted to be on his own and maybe go into cattle ranching.

I was very disappointed. Ernest and I were spread awfully thin. Being able to count on Joe joining us as a partner at some point would have been a real weight off us.

As it was, one of us always had to be at the winery. With Ernest on the road so much, the production end of the business fell my way just as naturally as sales had become his field. That was fine with me. I had learned from the trips I made east that I didn't like being on the road so much, and I found office and administrative work taxing. I always liked farming best, so staying back to handle the vineyards and winemaking suited me. We each had confidence in the other's ability to handle his own side of the business.

Though by then we had a ranch foreman, field men, and winery workers, it seemed there was always something that needed my immediate attention, whether it was checking the irrigation in the fields early in the morning or staying at the winery until late at night making sure the winemaking equipment and process were running smoothly. That work load and responsibility weighed heavily on me.

One night at home, Aileen and I were having dinner around ten o'clock. We were just about finished when I felt a stab in my abdomen and started to black out from the pain. I almost fell out of the chair.

Aileen helped me get to the couch and called our longtime family physician, Dr. Maxwell. He said it sounded like appendicitis and to bring me to the hospital right away. Dr. Maxwell didn't operate anymore because of bad eyesight, but he said he was going to call in Dr. Husband, "the best surgeon in town."

I went off to the hospital. About an hour later, Dr. Husband showed up. It seemed that Dr. Maxwell had finally located him at a cocktail party. Someone had handed Dr. Husband a cup of hot coffee before he came into the examining room to see me.

The doctor poked a finger painfully in my gut. "Your appendix has to come out right away," he announced.

When I heard that, I practically jumped off the table.

"I'm not going to let you operate!"

They had to strap me down.

"You don't understand—Ernest is back east!"

Dr. Husband went out for more coffee, and the nurses kept trying to

91

reassure me that everything would be fine—they would sober up the surgeon and he would do a good job and, anyway, Dr. Maxwell would be there. But the fact that I was going to be operated on by one doctor who had been drinking and another who couldn't see wasn't my main concern.

"We just have to wait until Ernest gets back," I explained. "Then I promise I'll come back and you can operate."

As they placed the gas mask over my face, I was thinking, *There is so much work to be done . . . With Ernest gone I need to be there . . . I have to talk them out of this . . .*

Lucky for me they didn't listen, as my appendix had burst. I was in the hospital for a week to allow the poison to drain from my system. Though the scar those two characters left behind looks like they operated with a dull knife, they saved my life.

That's the extent to which I put work before my own health. This was to catch up with me in a serious way before long. Regrettably, in those early years I also often put business before family, missing out on much at home, where Aileen had her hands more than full after the birth of our third child, Philip, in early 1939. Looking back, I wouldn't say that I'd do it again.

I'm sure that part of the obligation I felt was because my business partner was also my brother. If I hadn't held up my end, he would have had to pick up the slack, and he was already as overworked as I was.

In a partnership, you've got that responsibility. I'm convinced it's tougher to be partners than to be an individual in business. In a partnership, you are inclined to push yourself more than you would on your own.

In a good partnership, you don't work yourself until you drop because you think your partner wants you to. You do it because *you* want to.

That's the best motivation in the world.

·　　·　　·

IN LATE 1939, A REPORTER for the Modesto *Bee* called and said he wanted to write a story about our winery. He explained that he was doing a series of articles for the paper on local industries.

I invited him over.

We sat for a while in the office. As he took notes, I told him about my grandfather's winery in Hanford and my father's grape-shipping business.

"I see. They taught you how to make wine?"

"Well, not really. We made basement wine at home."

I told him how we had to study the pamphlets Ernest had found at the library because we had started with no commercial winemaking experience.

"You mean you started from scratch?"

"That's right."

"How many gallons of wine do you make a year now?"

"Three million."

"Three *million gallons?*"

He had heard me right. Since our first crush at the new facility, we had expanded our volume by some 500,000 gallons each year.

The reporter seemed shocked that one of the state's ten largest wineries—just six years after Repeal—was located right here in Modesto. If I had allowed myself to think much about it, it probably would have amazed me too. We *had* come a long way in a short time. But day in and day out, I was too busy just doing it to think much about where we had started.

We were now making a wide variety of wines, including sherry, port, angelica, muscatel, white port, Chablis, Tokay, claret, Burgundy, Sauterne, Rhine, Barbarone, and dry muscat. We still sold our products only in bulk shipped by rail or truck to wholesalers, who bottled it under their brands for the retail trade.

I took the reporter for a walk around the winery. On the south side of the plant I pointed out the area where the trucks filled with lug boxes of grapes were unloaded onto a conveyor belt, which dumped them into large rotary centrifugal crushers. The stems were separated in the same operation and came out at one end while the juice and pulp were pumped into the 20,000-gallon fermenting tanks.

I explained how dessert wine is made. During fermentation, a natural process, grape sugar converts to alcohol. Dessert wine is partially fermented; this takes only two or three days. It is then pumped to tanks, where it is fortified by the addition of grape brandy until it has an alcoholic content of 20 percent. But with a table wine (defined for purposes of taxation as under 14 percent alcohol), natural fermentation of the grape sugar is allowed to continue until it ceases—when all the sugar has been converted to alcohol.

Next, I showed where the wine was placed in storage tanks for settling and clarification. Finally, I explained how the wine was cooled in refrigeration coils to 17 degrees, which cold-stabilized it—precipitating any solid tartrates (a by-product of the fermentation process) that remained. The wine was kept at that temperature for two or three weeks and then filtered several times through filter presses. After that, it was stored in tanks for aging, and from there could be pumped directly into tank railcars or trucks for delivery.

The reporter's published story ended with this: "One is impressed by the orderly arrangement of the plant and consequent efficiency of labor. Although a close scientific control must be exercised at all times, 40 men can handle the plant at full capacity. The machinery and methods are the best that can be secured and, combined with careful supervision, insure a quality product."

A *quality product.* Important words to me.

Many of the wineries that had gone out of business since Repeal—I knew of a hundred that hadn't made it—had not paid close enough attention to producing sound products. It was no accident that we never had a batch of wine spoil. We watched what we were doing day and night.

We went a step further, too, in trying to anticipate our requirements. Ernest did that in sales and I did it with production. I spent my weekends driving all over the grape country—Fresno, Lodi, Sonoma—looking at the vines, trying to estimate the size and quality of the next crop. I took this time to go out and see what the crop situation was so that when it came time to buy grapes, we'd know which growers had the best grapes. We'd also have a pretty good idea of prices. Other vintners didn't do that. Once they were successful, they might have an office in San Francisco and take lots of vacation time. We didn't do that. We worked.

As I said, I do have some regrets as to the personal cost. Possibly we worked harder than we should have. Maybe we could have gotten where we are without having to knock ourselves out. Probably it wasn't necessary to work eighteen hours a day, seven days a week, and then come down in the middle of the night to attend to some detail.

But on the other hand . . . *we never had a batch of wine go bad.*

Ernest

Though we were expanding every year, we were not immune to pressing problems.

One serious threat was that around the country so many bottlers— our customers—were going out of business. Most of these bottlers were not brand builders. They knew little about quality, packaging, selling, or advertising. All they knew was that if their competitor was selling his wine to a retailer at $4 a case, he better sell his for $3.75. They bought bulk wine on price, not on quality, and were willing to switch suppliers to save as little as a penny a gallon, sometimes just half a cent a gallon. They did no advertising, and supported their brands with sales personnel they hired as cheaply as possible and did not train.

Whenever one of our bottlers went out of business we lost a customer. But my close contact with them kept us from losing money of any consequence. I usually knew their operations too well to be unpleasantly surprised.

At the time, most wineries sold their wine only in bulk to bottlers. In fact, before World War II, some 80 percent of all California wine was sold in bulk.

The Fruit Industries co-op, for example, sold to wholesalers who distributed its wine under forty different brand names in New York State alone. Roma had seventy regional labels in addition to its two more-or-less "national brands," Roma and La Bohème.

There had to be a better way to sell wine.

With more bottlers going out of business, I realized that in a short time our own survival would be in jeopardy. We would end up disappearing as so many other wineries had if we didn't develop and market our own successful brand. But up to then, national brand building in the wine business had not really been done. There was no blueprint for success.

We had labels printed and sent them to a few of our bottlers as an experiment. One brand was "Gallo Wine," with a rooster on the label. The other was for a "Modesto Wine" brand. Our New Jersey and New York bottlers would not even consider putting our labels on our products. A Florida distributor told me Gallo was a terrible name for wine. Our bottler in New Orleans did bottle a few hundred cases with our labels, but when the wine did not sell, the experiment ended in a few short months. Since we weren't advertising and had no image among retailers or consumers, it proved to be a futile effort, as it was for our competitors who tried to do this at the same time.

Low prices, lack of experience, fierce competition, and the Depression continued to take their toll on bottlers. In 1939, our New Orleans bottler, Franek & Co., could not pay the $30,000 they owed us for wine. I told Franek I could not continue supplying him in view of his losses, the amount of money he owed us, and his inability to pay. I asked if he was interested in giving us half his company in exchange for our canceling their debt. This would be a good deal for both of us. He would be able to remain in business as our partner, and we would have the opportunity to start selling our own brand.

Franek readily agreed to the deal. After we signed the papers, I came back to Modesto. A couple months later, I received anonymously a clipping from a New Orleans newspaper. The story was about Franek having been indicted for white slavery. I tried to reach Franek by telephone, and after several attempts finally did. He told me there was nothing to the charge and not to worry about it.

After I hung up, I started to wonder if he was telling me everything. After all, he had been indicted for a serious crime, with a trial set to start in a few days. I flew to New Orleans to see what was going on. Franek, it seemed, had brought a young lady over from Mississippi for questionable purposes. Subsequently convicted, he was sent to prison, whereupon we purchased his remaining share of the bottling company.

After our earlier experience, we didn't immediately switch to a "Gallo" label. Rather, we continued for some time to use Franek's "Cream of California" label, then the top-selling brand in the New Orleans area.

The following year, Distillers Outlet, a small bottler in Los Angeles, informed us it was also unable to meet its obligations to us. In a similar arrangement, we acquired 51 percent of that company. One of the previous owners, Sam Watt, stayed on to manage the operation.

As vintners had only recently begun to discover merchandising, the consumer was beginning to see wine displays and billboards advertising wine brands in limited markets. Trade magazines began to print information on merchandising. There was enough going on with wine to spark consumer interest. The marketplace was wide open, but I felt that would soon change. Bottlers were failing, and before long only those wineries that built successful national brands would survive.

With the future of the bulk-wine business looking so bleak, Julio and

I agreed that we needed to start developing a brand if we were to survive. Los Angeles seemed like a good place for me to learn how to build a brand. Distillers Outlet had no successful brands, so I would have to start from the ground up.

I was confident we had a sound product. Introducing a brand, however, was a completely new endeavor.

I spent many days in early 1940 in Los Angeles, visiting retail stores to see how wine was marketed and sold. It was quite evident how unimportant wine was to the liquor retailer of the day. Whiskey, gin, rum, and beer were what Americans were buying, so those products commanded by far the most and best shelf space. Wine was often kept on a lower shelf, or behind the counter, where a customer had to ask for it. Retailers had little interest in promoting wine sales.

We had to start doing things differently, not only to get consumers to purchase our wine over other brands, but as important, to attract attention to wine itself.

Working on a strategy, I spent many evenings at Sam Watt's house. Watt, about twenty years my senior, was a short, white-haired, dynamic fellow not above pounding on a tabletop to make his point. For starters, we came up with a design for a new label, and also for a completely different type of bottle. Up to that time, bottlers had been using common amber or brown bottles.

"Why do you use colored bottles?" I asked.

"It's just what we've always done," Watt shrugged. "Everyone is using them. They cost less."

"Wine is such a beautiful color," I went on. "If we used clear glass, people could see it better."

I wanted a bottle that was different from anything else on the market; something distinctive that would appeal to consumers more than the bottles currently being used by our competitors. I designed a high-shouldered tapered quart bottle of flint or clear glass, and had Owens-Illinois make them for us.

As for the label, we sketched many drawings at Watt's dining-room table until we came up with something we liked. It had the word "Gallo" and a small rooster set inside a small medallion above the name. Small lettering above the rooster proclaimed: "Something to Crow About."

The new label had something else, too—something that I thought would really appeal to consumers. Credit goes to Sam Watt's wife, Anne, an excellent cook, who made delicious dishes for us to complement various wines. One night, she suggested that recipes go on the side of the label.

"Great idea!" I said. "Do you have enough recipes to go on all our different types of wine?"

She smiled. Of course she did.

On each side of the new labels, we featured recipes such as "Eggs au Vin" and "Red Wine Sauce" and even "Burgundy Mint Julep." Right from the beginning, we wanted to market wine with food.

I kept visiting stores, trying to figure out ways to persuade the retailer to carry our product and convince the consumer to try it. I looked at the stores' physical layout, and asked questions of clerks and consumers alike, trying to develop different ideas. I reached some conclusions.

Everything being equal, a consumer bought brands he or she knew and had confidence in. I reasoned that knowledge of a brand came only from advertising or from one customer recommending the brand to another customer. Or, from the recommendation of the retailer.

We did not have the resources to establish consumer demand and confidence in our new brand by media advertising. We simply did not have money available to spend the large sums required even in those pre-television days to make an impression by newspaper, radio, or billboards. So consumer advertising was out.

As for one consumer recommending the brand to another, our product at the time did not have such superiority as to merit voluntary comment from consumers.

That left the retailer's recommendation. In those days, consumers bought wine most often on the basis of price or the retailer's recommendation. Since there was no future in selling on price alone, the retailer's recommendation was essential.

The chances of a retailer's telling his customers about our wine, or any wine, were slim to none. Undoubtedly he would just put our product in a hard-to-see place with all the other wines he carried. It wouldn't be anything unique.

Since the retailers were going to be so vital to establishing our brand, I visited more and more stores. By talking to retailers and seeing their stores with my own eyes and then thinking a lot about what I saw, I came to some conclusions, which, incidentally, have stood the test of time.

For example: Retailers are, as a rule, either too busy or too indifferent to vocally recommend a product for very long.

But: Effective retailer recommendation could be obtained without a retailer's saying a word—what I began to call a retailer's *silent recommendation.*

This silent recommendation could be accomplished by a product's obtaining dominant exposure, in other words, by becoming visually very important in the store. I reasoned that if a retailer gave this importance to a brand in the store, the consumer would accept this as indicative of the retailer's considered opinion as to which brand was the best—in effect, which one he was recommending, without his saying a word.

Having determined that for the time being we would be limited to promoting our brand only by this silent recommendation of the retailer, I set about to determine how we could obtain it.

Up to that time, wine was still being sold as a commodity. Bottlers used unattractive labels on almost any shape bottle that they could get cheaply, and sold principally on price. No effort was made by distributors to get any particular position in a store for their wines, since their principal lines were either liquor or beer. As a result, bottles of wine were found in nooks and crannies, usually on the bottom shelf, mixed in with everyone else's wine. Why would a customer come in, take a look at this hodgepodge, and buy *any* wine, let alone one brand over another?

I realized from my store visits that we needed somehow to get our product into a choice position in the store. If we had our wine on an eye-level shelf or as an attractive floor display that the customer could not fail to notice, this would have the effect of the retailer's saying, "Try Gallo Wine."

But how could we get our product in a good location in the stores? In those days, all a salesman would do—if he did anything—was to make a floor display by cutting open the cardboard case and leaving it on the floor for customers to pull bottles from. Understandably, retailers didn't appreciate having cut cases littering the floor and obstructing traffic.

I designed an attractive steel rack that could hold 120 bottles of wine. There was a recessed niche on the top headpiece for a single bottle. The bottle was lit from behind by an electric light bulb. The light behind the featured bottle accented and dramatized the color and clarity of the wine. My idea was for the retailer to showcase a different one of our wines in the lighted niche every day. To help ensure that the rack would be used only for our wines, "Gallo Wines" was imprinted on the metal headpiece above the lighted bottle, which was flanked by signs reading "See Its Clearness" and "Taste Its Goodness." The rack had three shelves, and a minimum of supports and framing so that the labels of the wines displayed were clearly visible.

Merchants thought the racks were so attractive that they usually placed them in the best spot on the floor.

I realized, too, that something basic was wrong in the way wine was being sold to the retailer. It had to do with the sales force. After the winery delivered the wine to its bottling companies, the bottlers usually sold the cased products to liquor or beer wholesalers. Their salesmen usually had several lines and many sizes of whiskeys, gins, cordials, imports, and beer, as well as other wine for sale. It was not unusual for a wholesale liquor distributor's salesman to have well over *five hundred items to sell*. This made it impossible for him to devote much, if any, of his effort to selling wine. Wine was just a very small end of his business. Almost as an afterthought, if at all, he would ask, "How's your wine supply?" These salesmen thus became known as "Howsyour Men." This was the accepted method of distribution for wines to the retail marketplace at that time. No one seemed to be thinking of finding a better way.

During my study of wine retailing, I realized that the wine industry could not hope to get its historic, enjoyable beverage—so associated with fine food and pleasurable times—before the American consumer without a different type of selling. To do the job right, we needed an intense sales effort. The only thing that made sense, I decided, was to have retailers called on by salesmen who concentrated all of their efforts on servicing the retailers' wine needs.

Such thinking was revolutionary at the time. I thought this kind of sales effort could help move the wine industry forward into the modern age of branded goods marketing. Wineries, retailers, and consumers all would benefit.

Likewise, I felt that we would not be able to build our own brand unless a salesman went into a store selling only one product: *our* wine. This would require the creation of a sales force that would sell only Gallo.

In this way, a salesman would not be inclined to accept no for an answer. If he didn't make a sale, he didn't eat. Too, the retailer would be more apt to buy wine if he hadn't already given the salesman a big order for liquor and beer products.

We put ads in the paper for salesmen. I wanted fellows with a background in retail service. I hired eight young men from the ranks of the soap, grocery, soft drink, and tobacco industries. Each one was given specific accounts and was required to make regular calls and file daily reports, which I always read.

They were trained to:

- Talk to retailers about the advantages of carrying our product
- Obtain the most visible position at eye level for Gallo wines
- Trim shelves with colorful point-of-sale materials
- Use bottle collars to attract consumer attention
- Rotate stock to ensure quality, and keep the Gallo shelves stocked
- Dust our bottles to keep them bright and clean
- Place counter displays in key traffic locations

All of these things had to be done on a regular basis, I counseled, in order to obtain and keep the retailer's confidence and silent recommendation. And it had to be done in each and every store. Knowing it would be quite a job did not trouble me. It was just plain common sense.

Our young and eager salespeople hit the streets in early 1941 with their mission well defined.

Our business was about to change dramatically.

8

WARTIME WINERY

Julio

When I found myself unable to sleep at night in early 1941, I knew something was wrong. It hadn't come on suddenly, but kept getting worse gradually.

Aileen thinks I hurried back to work too quickly after contracting peritonitis as a result of my burst appendix. She may be right. As I recall, it was fall, always my busiest time of the year. I had been anxious to get back to work—there was the crush, the winemaking, and preparing wine orders for shipment.

When sleep became nearly impossible, I went to the doctor. He said it was overwork. I didn't know what I could do about that because there was so much to do. "I'll be all right if I can just get some sleep," I told him. The doctor gave me sleeping pills but they didn't help much.

I would lie in bed worrying about all the things that hadn't gotten done that day. Finally, I would get out of bed. Back and forth I would go between lying awake in bed and pacing the floor. In the morning, I dressed for work at the regular time. Knowing how little sleep I had gotten, Aileen tried to convince me to stay in bed "just to rest" even if I couldn't sleep. There was too much work to be done, I told her. With so little sleep, I started my days bone tired. By the time I came home at night, I was completely exhausted. Then the cycle repeated itself. The body just doesn't get used to losing sleep. I began to lose weight too.

What was happening to me? I was a young man—why wasn't I well enough to do what I wanted to do? Worry and fatigue led to depression. Eventually, I had a complete nervous breakdown.

The only cure was rest, Dr. Maxwell said. In April 1941, he referred me to a sanitarium south of Livermore for evaluation. Ernest drove me, as he wanted to talk to the doctors himself. After examining me, the doctors told us that they would admit me. To get over this, they said, I needed to be away from the business and even the family.

Before Ernest left that day, he made a point of telling me not to worry about anything at the winery. He told me to take all the time I needed to rest and get well.

I stayed at the sanitarium for four months.

Aileen came to see me every Sunday. She told Bob and Susann— then ages six and four—that I was away on business. She left the baby, Philip, just a year old, with her mother every Sunday to come and see me. Later, when I was feeling better, she would make a picnic lunch for us to have under the shade of a big oak tree. As much as she wanted me home, Aileen never rushed me, saying again and again that she and the children were doing fine.

Ernest came to see me regularly. He always put me at ease by saying that everything was running smoothly at the winery and not to worry.

I knew that it was not easy for Ernest with me in the hospital. With our constantly expanding volume and now starting our own brand in Los Angeles, there was more work to be done than ever. While I was in the hospital, a major fire broke out in our sherry-baking room, destroying 300,000 gallons of dessert wine. No one was hurt, and insurance covered the loss. But when I heard such reports, it was hard not to feel as if I was letting Ernest down.

Coming back from this breakdown was the toughest thing I ever did. It was a long, slow road back—and there was no way to hurry it along. It just took time and rest. I had to learn how to relax, pace myself through the day, and at night let go of worries and annoyances so I could sleep. I especially had to learn how not to worry about things I had no control over.

I guess some people would rather not talk about something like this. There is nothing for me to gain by bringing it up. I'm doing so only because I know there are other people struggling with this kind of illness. I want to say to them that there is a way back. With plenty of time, rest, and support from loved ones, you can get well.

My recovery was not complete the day I walked out of the hospital in August 1941. I remained under a doctor's care. In fact, I suffered a relapse in early 1942 and was hospitalized a second time.

For relaxation, Aileen and I began taking short trips into the mountains. We would leave the kids with her parents and go away for several days. Having spent my entire life in the Valley, I found myself drawn to the mountains—even just taking a long drive through them relaxed me.

The doctors strongly advised me to eliminate things in my life that caused the most stress. While in the hospital, I had had lots of time to think. I came to realize that I needed to live differently. I could not let the pressures of work get to me so much. In the process of building the business, I had ignored my family. I had not had the time or energy to be the husband and father I wanted to be. I realized it just wasn't worth it. I had to learn how to set priorities and pace myself—not just to get well now, but for the rest of my life.

If it wasn't *that* important, then I shouldn't get out of bed in the middle of the night to run down to the winery and check on a piece of equipment. Now that we had capable employees, I needed to let one of the workers do it and then check their progress in the morning.

In 1943, I was able to start putting in a few hours a day at the winery, though it took a long time to get back full-time. More than ever, I concentrated on those areas of the business I most enjoyed: growing grapes and making wine. In the past, I had not had to worry about sales and marketing because that was Ernest's area, but I had from time to time been drawn into legal and financial matters, which could frustrate me. From then on, I would stay away from those concerns as much as possible. Ernest had always been better with numbers and legal matters than me anyway. I'd stick to what I liked best.

I looked forward most to those days I could be outdoors, working the land. I was a farmer at heart, and I always would be.

Ernest

Amelia gave me two sons. Our first, David Ernest, was born in June 1939. And in March 1941, six days after my thirty-second birthday, Joseph Ernest was born.

With our family growing, things were getting cramped at our small rented apartment in town. I thought I should try to scrape up the money to build a house. We decided to build on a site in the middle of the 160-acre vineyard Julio and I had leveled in the rain a decade earlier. (Julio would later build his family home on this same property.)

I sat down with an architect and we drew up a design. He estimated the house would cost $17,000.

"Who can afford that for a house?" I asked.

We cut some rooms out, and made others smaller. The architect came back with a revised estimate of $14,000.

"Maybe I can swing that."

We still live there today. I like to tell this story to our guests, then have them look around and say, "Ernest, this is a *lot* of house for fourteen thousand dollars."

We've added on a bit here and there since then, but I usually don't mention that.

WITH WINE SALES GOING SO WELL IN LOS ANGELES, I realized that we should start using these same techniques nationally.

I discussed it with Julio, and we decided to start bottling in Modesto and begin building our own national brand.

My brother and I were in a car driving to San Francisco on Sunday, December 7, 1941, to see a contractor about building a bottling plant for us when we heard on the radio about the Japanese attack on Pearl Harbor.

We knew we would soon be at war, and this raised immediate and obvious questions. Was it wise to expand our business in the face of such impending uncertainties?

I turned my car around and we came home.

Julio

After Pearl Harbor, events started to move fast in the wine industry, which felt the effects of war as did most other industries. The 1941 crush had been 1.1 million tons of grapes; in 1942, the crush was only about half that.

Government orders went out to make Thompson Seedless and muscat grapes into raisins for the war effort. At a drying ratio of 4 to 1, it took four tons of fresh grapes to make one ton of raisins. Fully three fourths of all raisin grapes were diverted to the war effort, with raisins part of the government's massive export program that sent essential foodstuffs to Europe.

We joined in the war effort. The government needed cream of tartar for the production of gunpowder and medicines. When you think of it, grapes are an amazing fruit: Their by-products not only help wage war but help cure, too. When wine is fermented it leaves a residue of argol, an unrefined form of tartar deposited on the sides of the tanks. Prior to the war, it had not made economic sense to recover argol—90 percent of the country's cream of tartar supply had been imported. The war changed that. With imports curtailed, we began recovering tartar from our wine sediment. During the war, we converted millions of pounds of argols into pure calcium tartrate for the war effort. When the war ended, there was no longer a demand for the product, so we shut down our tartrate-recovery program.

The government was also in great need of ethyl alcohol to make synthetic rubber, as all the natural rubber supplies from Indochina had been cut off by the advancing Japanese. Tires and other rubber products were under tight rationing. At the start of the war, the War Production Board ordered wineries to ship their distilling equipment to Kentucky to be used by distillers to produce industrial alcohol.

Though several vintners did dismantle and ship their stills, Ernest objected: "If our stills are going to make alcohol for the government, why should we let someone in Kentucky do it? We'll do it ourselves."

We finally worked out an arrangement for the wine industry's stills to stay in California for vintners to produce industrial alcohol the nine months of the year that the stills were not needed for high-proof brandy.

At first, we planned to make high-grade alcohol from grain. When we couldn't get priority to buy new equipment to break down the grain, we converted an old boiler into a grain cooker, and made a mash tub from used equipment. We purchased an old milk pasteurizer to use as a yeast-culture incubator, and three glass-lined steel tanks to use as yeast tanks. We bought a used grain elevator to move the grain into the cooker, and got all the plans registered and ready.

Just as we were about to start operating, we were notified by the Defense Supply Corporation that no grain would be available for industrial alcohol, as it was in short supply. It was suggested we could convert molasses into alcohol. Within a week, we were having blackstrap molasses delivered from the Hawaiian islands. We set up a seven-day-a-week, three-shift molasses-based distilling operation.

Converting molasses into alcohol created many problems. We soon learned that the waste disposal of the molasses stillage from a twenty-four-hour-a-day operation was roughly equivalent to the waste generated by a city of 500,000 people. The custom of disposing of winery wastes during the distilling season into deep lagoons would not work with the molasses waste because of its high nitrogen content. The syrupy aroma of molasses waste could turn in a day or two to the scent of a badly stinking pigpen. We built a pilot reclamation plant to neutralize the molasses waste, and determined that by running the stillage through large trickling filters, and settling and chlorinating it, we could produce a clean effluent that could be disposed of without much complaint from neighbors. Our experience in handling the sludge from this plant by land disposal gave us the expertise later to efficiently dispose of all of our grape stillage by similar methods.

Still, one neighbor in particular kept complaining of odor problems from the wartime molasses wastes. Every time we sent a man out to check on it, the air was odor-free. The neighbor lady explained each time that the odor had been bad but had cleared up just before our worker got there. I finally told our people that I would take care of it myself. I delivered a young pig for her children to raise in the backyard. They were delighted, and we never received another odor complaint from the lady.

The molasses-based alcohol produced on the West Coast was used mainly for production of badly needed synthetic rubber for the war effort. However, I heard that some of the alcohol was shipped to Russia, where it was used as antifreeze in the trucks and tanks fighting the Germans.

Ernest

Essential industrial items by 1942 were restricted to the war effort and we were unable to buy new equipment. So I made a deal with a failing New York bottler. In exchange for the ramshackle equipment of his bottling line, which he shipped out to us, I put him in business as one of our wholesalers.

Our first bottling line was rudimentary—single-file and only semi-automatic. We were plagued by constant breakdowns. But as newer and better equipment became available we bought it, ensuring that we had the latest technology available. We hired a number of people who had been laid off by the canneries (many closed during the war), and they became the nucleus of our bottling operation.

When our bottling operation was functioning in Modesto and a second line was added, we ceased bottling in Los Angeles, and some years later in New Orleans.

We discontinued sales of bulk wine and sold our wine only in bottles. Suddenly, we found ourselves scrambling with other wineries for more bottling equipment and supplies.

IN FEBRUARY 1942 I hired our first enologist.

With Julio still recovering his health and me needing to spend time in Los Angeles building a sales organization, we were shorthanded on the production side.

I placed a blind ad in the *Wine Review* in January 1942 seeking "someone of unusual capability in enology" who could help us improve our technical winemaking process, and our wines. In Charles Crawford, I found more than I had hoped for, and hired him.

Crawford, who has a Master of Science degree from Cornell University, was put in charge of our laboratory and given a budget to purchase scientific equipment.

At the time, I told Crawford that I considered research like savings. "If you wait until you need it, it's already too late."

Crawford said he had no intention of spending the rest of his career with a winery. He planned to return to academia so he could undertake research. He ended up doing a lot of research—and much more—from the front line of what would become the world's largest winery rather than from behind ivy-covered walls. In addition to serving as liaison with industry technical groups and government agencies, his career at the winery has included winemaking, chemical engineering, production management, quality assurance, and scientific research management.

Fortunately, Charlie Crawford found it all to his liking: He is still with us today, fifty-two years later.

IRONICALLY, THE WAR YEARS were a time of unprecedented demand for wine coupled with a problem wineries were unaccustomed to having: a scarcity of grapes for the crush.

The price of wine grapes skyrocketed from $15 a ton in 1941 to as high as $135 a ton in 1944. None of us had the grapes to make all the wine that we could sell. The drop in wine production was dramatic.

At the same time, national brands, the older as well as the newer ones, appeared on a greatly increased number of dealers' shelves. This sudden interest by retailers in wine was due simply to a wartime shortage of liquor.

A problem that arose for us in entering the bottled-goods field was to justify our competitive prices for our products. Wartime prices were controlled by the Office of Price Administration.

The OPA froze wine prices at March 1942 levels. The government assumed, incorrectly, that the price of grapes would be limited by the controlled wine prices, and never set a ceiling on the price of juice or table grapes. The high prices for grapes resulted in some very expensive crushes. The average vintner, making price-controlled wine from such expensive grapes, found it difficult to make a profit.

We had to make a case to the OPA that we were producing a quality wine. It was not difficult. Since we had started planning for our Gallo brand in 1938, we had been working steadily to improve the quality of our wines. We had planted our new vineyards to varieties of grapes that would improve our dessert wines. We had held out the best of the 1939–41 table-wine vintages to use for blending.

Our 1942 crush was small. We made slightly less than 900,000 gallons of dessert wine in 1942, versus 2.2 million gallons in 1941; and only 700,000 gallons of table wine versus 1.6 million gallons in 1941. Our crush consisted almost entirely of wine-variety grapes that improved the quality of the wine. Also, for the first time we used pure yeast culture for fermentation to give certain desirable flavors to the wine. Pure yeast cultures also ensure rapid and complete fermentation. We now had an accurate system of record-keeping and testing, so we were able to base our blends on chemical analysis as well as taste.

We also set up—for research purposes—independent comparative tasting of our wines against national brands of our major competitors, who at the time included Italian Swiss Colony, Roma, Beaulieu, Wente, Christian Brothers, and Cresta Blanca.

The tasting was "blind"—no labels showing. Points were given on the basis of a combination of appearance, aroma, and flavor. Our Burgundy came in second. Our claret tied for third. Our cocktail pale-dry sherry finished first. Our port tied for first, as did our muscatel. Our Sauterne was the only one that trailed the field, finishing fifth out of nine wines. These tasting results gave us a good measuring stick as to how we were doing. The results were mixed. We still had work to do.

"In order to establish a worthwhile brand that would sell high enough in price to show a reasonable profit," I wrote to the OPA, "it would be wise for us to put out a product that would compete in the higher priced market. This class seems to have the least competition and the greatest opportunity for the future since the greatest increase in consumption would be in better wines consumed by customers in the higher-income brackets."

Though we didn't get approved for the higher price bracket, we went to work in our assigned niche.

DURING THE WAR THE BIG LIQUOR distillers entered the wine industry, even before the government stopped the manufacture of spirits for use as beverages in the fall of 1942. With distillers also required to produce industrial alcohol for synthetic rubber, more than a few liquor distillers were worried enough to buy wineries in order to supplement their diminishing beverage lines and sales with an array of wine products.

Schenley bought Cresta Blanca only months before this country officially entered the war, and in 1942 followed with its purchase of Roma, giving Schenley a total of 32 million gallons of wine-storage capacity and displacing Fruit Industries, the large growers' cooperative, as California's biggest winemaker. That same year, National Distillers bought Italian Swiss Colony, becoming the state's third-largest wine company—behind Fruit Industries. Also that year Seagram bought control of Paul Masson, and the following year Hiram Walker Distillers bought three wineries in Sonoma and San Benito counties.

The distillers came up with a novel way to move wine through "tie-in" sales with liquor. I knew of situations during the war where a store owner had to accept ten cases of table wine he didn't want in order to buy a single case of liquor.

Overall, the shortage of liquor during the war both helped and hurt the wine industry. It helped in that some retailers bought wine to be able to get liquor, but it hurt because they didn't try very hard to sell it. Many of them just stacked the cases of wine in their storerooms or basements, which led to quite a lot of unsold wine building up during the war years.

After the war, when distributors and retailers could again get as much liquor as they wanted, they stopped buying the wines that had sat around unsold for so long. To get rid of their stock, some of which had deteriorated in quality, they would shoot wine out the door at almost any price, no matter how low.

We were not dealing with wholesale liquor dealers during the war, so our wines were never "packaged" to retailers with hard-to-get distilled spirits.

I've never understood why so many wineries—even to this day—consider the sale to the distributor the final transaction. I have felt, from the very first case we ever sold, that *wine is not sold until it is bought by the consumer.*

Julio

Distillers were the first group of well-financed outsiders—but not the last—to enter the wine industry with the intention of taking it over. The distillers soon found out that it was one thing to make whiskey in a controlled environment, and another to produce wine.

What these outsiders never seemed to understand is that winemaking is based upon agriculture, and any farmer will tell you that with agriculture you get lots of surprises. One year it's too wet and the next too dry. There's a surplus today, a shortfall tomorrow. No formula for success exists that you can write down and follow to the letter. You have to be flexible and stay on top of things at all times, because conditions change rapidly. There is simply no substitute for attention to detail.

As an example, in 1942 some of our growers started using gondolas on flatbed trucks to bring their grapes to the winery. They dumped their lugs of grapes right into these gondolas in their vineyards and then drove to the winery. However, when they arrived there was no easy way to get the grapes out of the gondolas at the crusher. We talked about putting manholes in the sides of the gondolas for the grapes to run out, but this did not seem practical. We then got the idea of using a steam shovel with a clamshell on it which could slip into the gondola and lift the grapes out, dropping them into the crusher.

One day, as I watched the clamshell unload grapes, the thought occurred to me to put hinges on one side of the gondola and have the clamshell lift the whole gondola up into the air and tip it directly into the crusher. When the hinged side opened up, all the grapes would come tumbling out. This seemed so simple that none of us could understand why we hadn't thought of it before. We tried it and it worked. This clean, labor-saving procedure is still used to this day—only instead of a portable steam shovel we now have permanent cranes in place that lift the gondolas and tilt them into the crushers.

Someone running a California winery from the headquarters of a distillery in Chicago or a New York boardroom would have difficulty coming up with such a solution.

Before the war, we had purchased grapes from a thousand-acre vineyard in Livingston, south of Modesto, owned by a large farming operation. We had had our eye on this big vineyard—the American Vineyard—thinking that it would be advantageous to own such a large supply of grapes only thirty miles from the winery. When we had approached the parent company, Valley Agriculture, about buying the American Vineyard, they quoted us a price that seemed steep.

Valley Ag was a publicly held company whose stock traded over the counter. Ernest and I bought up enough stock to get controlling interest. That way, we were able to sell off the other Valley Ag properties we didn't want and keep the American Vineyard.

We ended up selling off Valley Ag holdings that included peaches in Madera, vineyards near Fresno, figs south of Merced, and bare land in Raisin City and Tipton. In all, we sold off four thousand acres in various parts of the state, which brought in enough money to repay us for the purchase of Valley Ag. We ended up obtaining the big vineyard we wanted virtually free of cost.

It seemed that the Valley Ag manager liked hogs, and was raising them on the various properties. Ernest and I weren't much interested in hogs or pigs, having tried that once before. When we were growing up, lots of Italian families—even ones who lived in town—kept a pig in the backyard. All the table scraps went to the pig, and when it was fattened up, it was slaughtered. Just about every part was used by the family, for ham, bacon, salami, salt pork, even blood sausage. This had been our father's annual ritual, and it was a tradition we set out to carry on back in 1933, after his death.

When our "family pig" was ready to slaughter, we took it into the garage. Ernest tied the pig's hind legs with a rope. I swung the rope over a rafter, and pulled the oinking pig upside down. As we'd seen Father do, Ernest stuck it hard in the chest with a butcher knife, expecting to hit the heart, as Father always did.

Sure enough, the pig stopped squealing.

We had ready an old-fashioned laundry tub filled with hot water. It was not big enough for more than half the pig at a time. The idea was to soak one half for a few minutes, pull all the hair off, then do the same thing with the other half. We let the pig down, carried it to the tub, and dropped the hind end in the hot water. We then placed it on a table and started scraping off the hair from the hind quarters. Damned if the pig didn't let out a squeal, jump off the table, and take off.

We raced after it into the vineyards. I was faster than Ernest, and I finally got close enough to make a diving tackle. I held on until Ernest was able to get a rope around the pig's neck so we could lead it back to the garage. Tradition or not, we bought our ham and bacon after that.

Though, as I said, we were inclined to get rid of the hogs that had been thrown in with our purchase of Valley Ag, we were told by the chairman of the local draft board that they were part of the war effort. We should keep the hog operation going, he insisted. So we gathered up all the hogs from the properties we were selling and trucked them to Meyer Ranch, which grew mostly alfalfa. We fenced off a huge pen and raised thousands of pigs for the duration of the war. It turned out that the draft-board chairman was a veterinarian, so we were assured of good medical care for them.

Believing that Livingston would someday be an ideal place to plant new vineyards, we began buying out our neighbors as their ranch properties became available. The first piece we had bought—Meyer Ranch—was 160 acres. We paid $175 an acre. (We ended up purchasing twenty-eight parcels, bringing our Livingston holdings to 5,000 acres, of which more than 4,000 acres were planted in grapes as of 1993.)

Livingston became the nucleus for our experimental vineyards. In 1946 we planted more than four hundred different varieties of grapes—many of them never before grown in the region—to study their future potential. Paul Osteraas, our first viticulturist, oversaw the experimental operation in addition to his responsibilities with our other vineyards. We set up a small pilot plant at the winery so we could make small batches of wines from the grapes under study without having to mix them with our regular crush. Through the years, we learned a lot from these Livingston experiments—and still do today.

When we had planted the bulk of our Livingston acreage in vineyards, it gave us control of approximately thirty thousand tons of grapes a year and some flexibility of time in crushing them. If purchased grapes were slow to come in, we could bring in grapes faster from our vineyards. The reverse was also true: We could, within reasonable limits, delay the delivery of our own grapes to the winery if it was advantageous to put a higher priority on purchased grapes.

Eventually (1970), Livingston solved another problem for us. Distilling in Modesto was beginning to be troublesome because the town was

Earliest known picture of Ernest and Julio, 1911. About this time, Ernest, right, was sent off to live with his maternal grandparents in the San Joaquin Valley town of Hanford, while Julio remained with their parents, who operated a boardinghouse in Oakland. The separation of the young brothers was to last six years. *(Photo courtesy of Ernest and Julio Gallo)*

Ernest with his grandparents Virginia and Battista Bianco, on the porch of their Hanford home, 1912. Battista ran a small winery behind the house. During his years in Hanford, Ernest grew especially close to his grandmother. "She was a loving and nurturing woman," he says, "whom I will miss no matter how old I live to be." *(Photo courtesy of Ernest and Julio Gallo)*

Susie and Joe Gallo, Ernest and Julio's parents, on their wedding day, 1908. *(Photo courtesy of Ernest and Julio Gallo)*

Julio with his mother, circa 1915. "My mother was very much like her mother," Julio recalls. "Hardworking, yet warm and compassionate. And they were both great cooks." *(Photo courtesy of Ernest and Julio Gallo)*

Below: Julio atop a rented tractor, 1929, leveling and developing the newly acquired Modesto vineyard, which the family still owns today. "I drove all night, warming my hands over the blue flames shooting out of the tractor's vertical exhaust pipe," remembers Julio. "Ernest took over at daybreak. In that way, we kept the rented rig running twenty-four hours a day." *(Photo courtesy of Ernest and Julio Gallo)*

Ernest and Amelia Franzia Gallo on their wedding day, August 23, 1931. "Not being experienced with weddings," Ernest explains, "as soon as the priest pronounced us 'man and wife,' I turned around and walked off with Amelia—neglecting to kiss her. It was a grievous error I have spent much time remedying." *(Photo courtesy of Ernest and Julio Gallo)*

Ernest and Amelia leaving for their honeymoon to Chicago, 1931. *(Photo courtesy of Ernest and Julio Gallo)*

Below: Amelia Franzia, between her parents, Giuseppe and Teresa, with her sister, Anne (left), and five brothers, circa 1920. In 1933, after their own relatives turned Ernest and Julio down, Teresa Franzia loaned Ernest $5,000 to start E. & J. Gallo Winery. *(Photo courtesy of Ernest and Julio Gallo)*

Julio and Aileen on their wedding day, May 8, 1933. "We noticed each other in high school," Julio recalls, "but had never even talked until we ran into each other at a dance after graduation. Although she had arrived with a date, we danced most of the evening. I borrowed a pen from the guy to write her phone number on the cuff of my shirt because I didn't have any paper." *(Photo courtesy of Ernest and Julio Gallo)*

Julio at his desk, 1944. By then, he and Ernest had already divided up responsibilities at the winery, with Julio handling the vineyard and winemaking operations and Ernest concentrating on sales and marketing. *(Photo courtesy of Ernest and Julio Gallo)*

Ernest chairing a Wine Institute meeting, 1958. *(Photo courtesy of the Wine Institute)*

Early billboard campaign, Los Angeles, 1940s. *(Photo courtesy of Foster & Kleiser)*

Julio on horseback, checking the harvest, 1958. *(Photo courtesy of Ernest and Julio Gallo)*

Ernest's sons, David, middle, and Joe, right, "learning the ropes" from Ernest, 1959. Both boys graduated from Notre Dame University before going on to Stanford's MBA program. Today, Ernest's sons work on his side of the business; David heads Marketing, and Joe is in charge of Sales. *(Photo courtesy of Ernest and Julio Gallo)*

From the left: Jon Shastid, Albion Fenderson, Ernest and Julio, Ken Bertsch, and Howard Williams, in 1969. *(Photo courtesy of Ernest and Julio Gallo)*

Julio with his tasting panel, circa 1967. Left to right: Dawson Wright, George Thoukis, Dick Peterson, Manny Jaffee, Julio, Guido Croce, Charles Crawford, Geoge Fujii, and Jim Coleman. *(Photo courtesy of Ernest and Julio Gallo)*

Ernest (left) and Julio tasting their product, circa 1967. Years earlier, each had made a promise to the other: Julio promised to make more wine than Ernest could sell, and Ernest promised to sell more wine than Julio could make. In truth, they both succeeded. *(Photo courtesy of Ernest and Julio Gallo)*

Above left: Underground oak cellars at E. & J. Gallo Winery. "We had European wood shipped by train to Italy," Julio explains, "enough for 650 big upright casks. After the casks were constructed, the staves were numbered for refitting later. The casks were then disassembled and shipped to Modesto. To reassemble the casks in our cellars . . . we brought over from Spain an experienced cooper, José Lopez, and his apprentice son. They stayed two years." *(Photo courtesy of Ernest and Julio Gallo)*
Above right: E. & J. Gallo Winery's administration building in Modesto, completed in 1967, is modeled after the North Carolina state capitol, an impressive neoclassical structure with columns on all sides. "I keep waiting," Ernest says, "for a native North Carolinian to say how much our headquarters looks like his state capitol."
(Photo courtesy of Ernest and Julio Gallo)

Julio with his son, Bob, left, and son-in-law, Jim Coleman. "Bob and Jim have been with the winery for thirty-five years," Julio says. "They now run Production, having taken over the day-to-day operations I used to handle." *(Photo courtesy of Ernest and Julio Gallo)*

Julio, at right, with Aileen, and Modesto mayor Lee H. Davies, in front of the rooftop cupola of the McHenry Mansion, 1976. The mansion, built in 1880 and almost as old as Modesto itself, "had long been a favorite landmark of my wife and myself," Julio explains. After watching many original structures "slowly disappear in the name of progress in the more than fifty years we have both lived here, we were unwilling to see the house put to commercial use or fall under the wrecker's hammer." Julio and Aileen bought the old home and donated it to the city. The donation typifies Julio's philanthropic endeavors, which favor worthy local and youth organizations. (*Photo courtesy of Ernest and Julio Gallo*)

becoming built up around us. We ended up moving our entire Modesto winemaking and distilling operation to our acreage in Livingston, where it is located to this day.

NOT ONLY DID THE WAR EFFORT lead to the government's commandeering equipment and supplies—tank cars, glass, grapes—needed by the wine industry, but also the country's military buildup took men out of the wineries and vineyards. And it took our brother, Joe, then twenty-two.

Before he left, we sat Joe down for a talk. Ernest and I had deferments as a result of our war-related manufacturing: distilling alcohol for rubber, recovering cream of tartar for gunpowder and medicine, raising hogs and raisins for food—so we would be staying home to run things. We told Joe that we needed him more than ever, though, and that a partnership in the winery could be his upon his return.

Of course, Joe knew that I was still regaining my health. Ernest and I explained how we both had full plates, and having our other brother's help and commitment would give us peace of mind that wouldn't otherwise be possible.

Joe heard us out, but quickly declined our offer. He intended to raise cattle and farm when he came back, he said. He had already bought seventy acres of undeveloped farmland and had planted alfalfa for cattle. He also wanted to grow grapes. "I just don't want to come into the winery," he told us.

"Well," I said, "we want you to do what you are happy doing. And we'll help you in any way we can."

Joe left in August 1942 for basic training in Mississippi. After that he was assigned to Lowry Field in Denver, where he spent three years. He stayed in touch with us by letter, and Aileen and I went to Denver twice to visit him. Both times I brought up the topic of his joining the winery, but he still seemed uninterested. While Joe was gone, a 160-acre parcel named Tegner Ranch came up for sale. I wrote Joe, telling him that this undeveloped land was suitable for a vineyard. Before he left, Joe had made a point of asking me to keep an eye out for land for him to buy. He was interested in the Tegner acreage, it turned out. We bought it for him. I oversaw the planting of vines. We wanted the property to be producing by the time Joe came out of the Army. On his next time home on leave, I took Joe out to his property, where one of our crews was busy grafting new vines onto young root stock. He was very pleased.

When Joe heard about our large new vineyard holdings in Livingston—I told him that there was a nice house on the property—he expressed interest in getting an interim job managing that property for us when he got out of the Army. That way, he figured, he could develop his own farming and ranching interests in the area while getting a salary from us and learning how to grow grapes.

Late in the war, Joe was shipped to the Pacific. He saw action in Luzon. Joe returned to the United States in January 1946 and was discharged the following month.

Shortly after his return, Joe came over to the house for lunch with his new wife, Mary Ann, a local girl from a good family; they had married in Denver before he went overseas.

After lunch, I asked Joe to reconsider joining the winery. Now that he was married and ready to settle down with a family of his own, I had my hopes. Ernest and I still wanted him as a partner, I said. In fact, we needed him here at the winery more than ever.

"No, Julio," he answered. "I've told you before."

His rejection disappointed me. Before even leaving for overseas, he had asked for the Livingston vineyard job to get on his feet. Why, I wondered, wouldn't he consider staying in Modesto and becoming a partner in the winery?

Later, before he left, I asked him again. I was concerned that he hadn't given this decision much thought.

"I've told you I want *no* part of the winery," Joe said. "I'll go work in Livingston but that's it."

Our younger brother clearly had no desire to work his way into a winery partnership with Ernest and me. His mind was made up. He wanted to be on his own.

Never again would I ask him to join us.

Ernest

Shortly after Joe's return to Modesto, I had my own discussion with him about joining the winery.

I started by going over with him how Julio and I were spread very thin. I touched on Julio's ongoing efforts to regain his full health, and how he needed to be careful in the future not to get overworked again.

"The time is right for you to come into the winery as a partner," I said. "We need you."

Joe shook his head. "I'll have no part of it. I know what it is like working with you guys. Anytime I do anything right I never hear from you. Anytime I do something wrong, you holler."

It could be he was right. Julio and I always felt that a job well done was normal and expected, and we weren't inclined to give out a lot of compliments.

I was sorry Joe wouldn't join us. But that was his decision, and I respected it.

9

LIFE COMES TO OUR CRUSH

Ernest

When the war ended I was able to turn my attention back to developing our brand.

In 1946 I registered the Gallo trademark in most states, and started setting up distributors in state after state.

Having decided that only distributors truly committed to the wine business would be able and willing to merchandise wine properly, I set out to recruit and train a new breed of distributors never before seen in the wine industry. These distributors were willing to invest the effort necessary to scratch out space for wine on eye-level shelves where no wines had previously been placed, and somehow to make room in cold-boxes crowded with other products and on retail floors where wine displays were virtually unheard of.

In a few major markets, I chose as distributors men who had worked for us as salesmen. Sam Stukin in New York City was our first salesman; I had hired him in 1934 to sell our bulk wine. When we began bottling under our own label, I made Stukin the distributor of our wines in the metropolitan New York area, then dominated by seven other California brands.

Within three years, Gallo became the number one wine brand in New York City.

Arvin (Bud) Anderson became our distributor in San Francisco. His father, Edwin Anderson, a wine broker and early customer for our bulk wines in Los Angeles, had become manager of our New Orleans operation in the early 1940s. Bud started out working for us in Los Angeles, then came to Modesto in 1942 to work on our bottling line. In no time, he became cellar superintendent. Anxious to try sales, he asked me in 1944 if he could become our distributor in Stockton, a Central Valley town we were not in yet. I admired the young man's initiative, and told him to go to Los Angeles and spend a couple of weeks with our sales force. After he did, we appointed him our distributor in Stockton. About a year later, he asked me what we were doing in San Francisco.

"Nothing," I admitted.

Being fully occupied with opening other markets, I was still marking time before entering that big, very competitive market. Although the city had a reputation for being a sophisticated wine market, from a retailing standpoint it was fairly primitive. The average liquor store paid no attention to merchandising wine and offered no real selection of table wines. Few food stores carried a choice of wines.

"I'd like to have San Francisco," Anderson said.

"What makes you think you're qualified to run it?"

"Come to Stockton and see what I've done."

I had visited there numerous times, and knew he was doing a good job. As a one-man operation, he had sold 1,700 cases in his third month. Even so, I took him up on his invitation and made a thorough survey. In the stores I visited, our displays were prominent and our products had good shelf location.

I asked him how he proposed to launch our introduction in San Francisco. He outlined a plan for full distribution within sixty days. I gave him the job of implementing it.

None of Anderson's first group of salesmen for San Francisco had any previous wine experience. Anderson and I agreed: Choose them for their personality, confidence, and drive—we could always teach them the wine business. Nearly every one of these novice salesmen ended up as sales managers.

Up to now, we had not done much advertising. The problem was always the same: How to get product into a store? We needed something—our salesmen couldn't just walk in and say, "Here I am. I've got Gallo. Where do you want it?"

We gave Anderson the type of displays we had developed for Los Angeles, and our very popular wine racks. He determined which were the top one thousand accounts in the area. The racks would be used to help persuade retailers to give Gallo products the best floor position in those stores.

When Anderson and his men started out, they were often told by retailers that there was no room for wine. The salesmen would respond by dropping a piece of cardboard the size of a wine case on the floor, and then tell the retailer that a Gallo display rack would take about that much space and would return a substantial profit—specified by the salesman in dollars and cents.

By then we had already established in other markets a policy of trying aggressively to obtain more window displays, more shelf positions, and more overall consumer attention at the point-of-sale, or P-O-S, as marketers call it. P-O-S materials can help induce impulse buying: They can be both your "opening shot" and "closing volley" with many consumers.

In a short period of time we had learned some merchandising basics that are easily transferable to nearly any consumer product. All the efforts of producers, advertisers, distributors, and salesmen of any packaged product should be concentrated upon producing *action* in the retailer's store. That is the point at which the prospective purchaser comes face to face—often for the very first time—with your product and decides whether or not to buy it. No matter how fine the product, or how well designed the package, or how powerful the advertising, the actual sale depends ultimately upon the consumer's response at this "point of action" for the sale.

No matter how effective the advertising campaign may be, it will not result in meaningful sales if the merchandise is not conveniently positioned. Impulse buying represents a tremendous proportion of total wine sales, with many customers deciding to buy a bottle of wine after they are already in the store to purchase other items. Advertising in a market improperly worked by a sales force is like sowing seed on hard, unplowed ground. Neither will produce much result.

Many advertising dollars are wasted annually because of a failure to understand the relationship between advertising and personal sales effort, or because proper coordination of these factors is lacking. Advertising does not replace a sales force's efforts, nor is it a substitute for thorough, aggressive sales action.

Our working so hard for floor location, shelf space, and sales in San Francisco and elsewhere soon had other wine companies starting to do the same. Competition at the retail level intensified.

We impressed on our distributors' salesmen the importance of providing the best service to the retailer.

These practices, some of which I had developed in Los Angeles before the war, helped form the fundamental operating philosophy that was to drive our merchandising and brand-building efforts for the next six decades. All Gallo sales personnel must learn the procedures for making an effective sales call on a retailer. Much of it is basic common sense.

• • •

IN 1946, WHILE SURVEYING THE NEW YORK MARKET, I noticed a brand of brandy that was a very hot item. It was bottled by a rectifying operation in New Jersey. I crossed the Hudson and knocked on the door of Gordon O'Niell & Co.

Marty Taub, a partner in the firm, saw me into his office. The two of us hit it off immediately. I learned that he was in business with his two brothers and another partner in this rectifier and wholesale distributorship that served New Jersey and New York.

Taub told me about their phenomenal brandy business: Their label, "Lafayette," had become the number one–selling brandy in New York during the war.

While the brandy Julio and I had produced in 1938 was long gone, we had made a 1943 vintage, which was now ready to sell. (Brandy has to be barrel-aged for at least two years in order to be sold as brandy.)

"We have brandy," I said. "It's a great brandy. I can sell it to you at a good price."

"As far as I'm concerned," Taub said, "price is not the important question. I need to know if you can produce a brandy of the same type and quality I'm now using."

"I'd like to taste your brandy."

He opened a half pint of Lafayette and poured.

I sipped it. His brandy was extremely raw, exceptionally high in both fusel oil and aldehydes (rough stuff that occurs in drawing from too low and too high a level of the still column). It was just awful, and I told Taub so. "Our brandy is much smoother and has more flavor."

"I don't want better," Taub said. "This is the number one brandy in town. I want it exactly the same."

I asked Taub to give me a sample that I could take back to Modesto. I would see if my brother could make brandy exactly like that.

I took a sample back to Modesto and asked Julio if he could duplicate it.

"I can't make it that bad," he said after a taste of Taub's brandy.

"Look, Julio, I think we can get a starting order for five hundred barrels at a good price if you can just deliver the same stuff."

I suggested that Julio try drawing our brandy at varying plates on the still where more of the aldehydes and fusel oil were concentrated. That would make the brandy hotter and rougher-tasting—just like Taub's.

Soon after Taub received our brandy sample, he telephoned. Could I give him my personal assurance that the brandy we would ship him would be just like the sample?

"Certainly," I said. "What will you pay?"

"What do you want?"

We went back and forth for a while, until Taub finally claimed that he paid $1.15 per proof gallon. (A "proof gallon" is equal to one gallon of liquid containing 50 percent alcohol by volume.) Taub bought the brandy at 100 proof and rectified it down to 80 proof for bottling.

"Cheap," I said.

I told him I'd sell him brandy for $1.30 a gallon.

"A buck ten."

We ended up agreeing on $1.25 per gallon. As I had hoped, he gave me an opening order for five hundred barrels.

Taub eventually got out of the liquor and rectifying business and became sales manager for Sam Stukin, our New York City distributor. When our distributor decided to leave the business, Taub became our distributor in partnership with Oscar Feuerstadt.

Taub knew the New York market very well, from his years of experience in the liquor wholesale business. Whenever I went out in New York City to survey retail outlets, Taub would get behind the wheel to take me around.

It was typical on such surveys for some distributors to want to show me stores that they knew were in fine shape. Usually, their best salesman worked these stores. Or the distributor had his salespeople prepare certain stores in advance of my arrival. Naturally, he would try to keep me on a specific route. I came to call this the Wholesaler's Waltz. Invariably, I changed the route that the distributor had preplanned.

I wasn't nearly as interested in visiting stores where we were doing well. What was the point? I would rather see those outlets where we had problems that indicated a lack of adequate effort from the distributor, or on our part. That's the very reason I surveyed markets: to see how we could improve the effort of both our distributors and the winery. From the beginning of my days surveying, I insisted that the distributors abandon their planned route and get into territories they had not intended to take me.

On our first survey together, Taub pulled up to a big store. I told him to keep going.

"I thought you wanted to see stores," he protested.

"I do, but not that one. Turn left at the corner."

I have always been as interested in checking the small stores as I am the large ones. I feel that the bigger stores will automatically receive much more attention from our wholesalers because they move more product. It is more costly and time-consuming to handle the little mom-and-pop store. How they handled these smaller stores revealed a lot about the distributor's overall effort.

By the end of a long day, Taub and I had covered nearly thirty stores—a busy but normal day for me when I'm surveying stores—even now.

IN EARLY 1945 I RECEIVED A CALL from Los Angeles. A young man going door to door looking for advertising business had showed up at our offices. Sam Watt, who headed our operations there, thought the fellow was worth my talking to. It was good timing, as I had been thinking we needed to do some advertising.

I went to Los Angeles the following week and met John Freiburg, a smart young man with a photographic memory and an infectious smile. He had previously been a junior account executive in a large

New York agency, and was now trying to start his own one-man agency.

Since late 1941 we had been using on our point-of-sale material a slogan that Watt had come up with: "By golly, buy Gallo." In place of a rooster on our label, we had a seal picturing toga-clad Bacchus, the Greek god of wine, whom we dubbed "Jolly Old Gallo." From time to time, for local promotions, we hired a guy to walk in front of stores wearing a toga and a sandwich board that delivered this message on both sides: "By Golly, Be Jolly, Buy Gallo." We thought this was just great.

When Watt enthusiastically recited our slogan to Freiburg, the young man flinched.

"We need to find some inexpensive way to get *everybody* saying, 'By golly, buy Gallo,' " Watt emphasized.

"I don't know," Freiburg said hesitantly. "People might start thinking of the brand as 'Golly Wine.' "

I chuckled, but Watt didn't. The slogan was his baby and he was convinced it would take us to the top.

"It does nothing for your image," Freiburg went on. "Image is important if you are going to compete with other brands of wine."

The young man made sense to me, but Watt started arguing with him. I let them go at it for a while, then interceded. "Look, let's have John try to come up with something he likes better. If it doesn't work, we can go back to your slogan, Sam."

We decided to launch a billboard campaign in southern California. At the time, billboard space was the best medium for advertising. For our first major campaign, we started with a teaser that gave no indication as to the advertiser or product. It pictured a great number of women's lips painted with red lipstick, and the words "On Everybody's Lips." Then, two weeks later, after we had everyone's attention, we turned the line into "On Everybody's Lips: Gallo Wine."

Another campaign showed an important-looking matronly woman with big diamonds on each hand and wearing a diamond tiara, and the line: "Mrs. Primrose Quaver 3rd was dropped from the social register for not serving Gallo wines." Another had a nice-looking chef with a tall chef's hat: "Chef Ordurve Soufflay lost his job at the Waldorf for not serving Gallo wines." For still another, we pictured two giraffes crossing their necks and the line: "Necks Time Drink Gallo Wine."

I wasn't satisfied with just any billboard location. Billboard companies had A, B, C, and D types of locations, where A was the best and D the worst, and the companies expected their advertisers to accept a certain portion from each category. Whenever Freiburg contracted for a billboard campaign, I insisted on "riding" the boards—starting at five-thirty A.M., seeing and approving each one for myself.

After my tour of our billboards, I rejected a number of them. Freiburg argued that we had to accept some poorly placed ones in order to get the good ones, but I insisted that the billboard people replace the bad ones, which they did. It was imperative that I get the most out of my limited advertising budget.

I soon had Freiburg accompanying me as I traveled around the country in an effort to get established distributors to handle our wine. It wasn't always easy.

"Listen, Ernest, we've got a problem," Freiburg said our first day back from a long trip through the Midwest. "Without any national advertising, we are just another brand in all these markets. Why should a distributor take our wine? We've got to have Gallo known *nationally.* We've got to make our brand *important.*"

"I agree, John. How do you suggest we do it with our limited advertising budget?"

"I've got an idea."

Somehow, I thought he did.

"We throw a 'vintage party' during this year's crush at your house. We'll have a pretty girl take a bath in a barrel of wine and call her 'Queen of the Crush.' We'll invite everyone in town and get *Life* magazine to photograph it. We'll have fantastic national exposure at no cost."

"How are you going to get *Life* to come out?"

"I'll call them and tell them all about it."

I was skeptical about getting coverage from *Life*, then the most popular magazine in America and also the most expensive advertising medium. Putting that aside for a moment, I asked, "Who are you going to get to take a bath in wine? I'd hate to hire an actress. That would make it kind of phony, wouldn't it?"

"We won't hire anyone," Freiburg said. "I can go downtown and get a pretty girl in twenty minutes."

"Here in Modesto?" I asked.

"Yeah."

"I don't think so."

"Give me twenty minutes. If I don't have anyone, we'll call the whole thing off."

"Okay," I said, checking my watch.

Freiburg came back inside of half an hour. "I've found just the gal," he said happily. "Her name is Doreen. She's twenty-one years old and very attractive."

"Where did you find her?"

"Working at the soda fountain. She is looking forward to climbing into our barrel of wine."

"Why in the world would she want to do that?"

"Well, I told her there was going to be a party at your house and there would be many important people there and she'd be photographed by *Life* and her picture would be seen by all the Hollywood talent scouts and they'd probably all be after her for the movies."

Now all Freiburg had to do was get *Life*. Unbelievably, he did.

For our part, we put on an enthusiastic "crush festival," complete with a number of pretty young maidens lifting their skirts and trampling the grapes with bare feet as in the old days—"an important symbolic gesture of something or other," Freiburg had told *Life*.

There, on page 130 of the October 8, 1945, issue of *Life* was a full-page picture of Doreen, attired modestly in a two-piece bathing suit, climbing into "a barrel of sauterne for her coronation." The caption read, "Queen of the crush, Doreen Ronne, a 21-year-old Modesto girl who works as a secretary at the Gallo winery, crawls dutifully into a barrel for her coronation. For her royal bath 95 gallons of wine were poured into the barrel, in which foaming setting she received her crown. Later, she filled five bottles with wine from her bath, to be poured on the vineyards."

The article, "Life Goes to a Grape Crush," ran for three more pages. From a promotional point of view, it was a huge success. We could not have bought that kind of national exposure for any amount of money.

We convinced *Life* to release the picture spread to us two weeks in advance of publication so that we could have thirty thousand *Life*-sized folders with the full story ready to be merchandised to retail outlets. Brochures, store signs, and window displays about the *Life* magazine story on Gallo were ready and promotional material was rushed out to all sales staffs. This quick action on our part allowed us to take full advantage of the *Life* story.

Often, Freiburg and I would be on the road together for weeks at a time. Times were tough. Whenever we checked into a hotel, we rented one room with two beds.

I decided that with distribution now in several states, and plans to expand to others, I needed to have winery representatives living in close proximity to our distributors. They would help to train the distributors' sales forces, see that our point-of-sale material was used effectively, and so on. To hire them, Freiburg and I put want ads in local papers before our arrival, then conducted interviews. Once, in New York, the hotel management got mad at us because we filled up the lobby with job seekers waiting to be summoned to our room for interviews.

When we were making a presentation to a distributor who we wanted to handle our wine, Freiburg would open a big leather-bound book filled with our *Life* spread and trade advertisements. On the first page was a picture of a bottle of Coca-Cola. "Thirty years ago, eight people in this town turned down this franchise," Freiburg would say. "You have the same opportunity today in the wine business with Gallo."

Both Freiburg and I really believed that.

I know I never would have guessed that Coca-Cola, one of the most successful marketers in the world, would one day enter the wine business and try to take us on—but wait; I'm getting ahead of myself.

10

POSTWAR
SHAKEOUT

Ernest

There had been relatively small crushes during World War II, but that pattern changed with the record crush of 1946. Some 1.6 million tons of grapes were crushed—40 percent more than any crush in history.

That season proved to be an aberration, though. With the war over and all varieties of grapes now available to wineries, it meant that the distribution pipeline for wine could be filled immediately. In fact, the amount of wine entering distribution that year would increase dramatically—up 48 percent, from 38 million cases in 1945 to 56 million cases in 1946. Wine consumption rose some 50 percent, perhaps partly attributable to the millions of G.I.s returning home from Europe, where many had tried table wine for the first time. Personally, I believe the high prices for grapes and the tremendous volatility in wine prices in 1946 could be laid directly at the doorstep of a New Yorker named Lewis Rosenstiel.

Rosenstiel, as head of Schenley, had bought California's largest winery, Roma, from the Cella family just as the war started, retaining

John B. Cella as winery president. With wartime price controls suddenly lifted, the price of wine was free to respond to supply and demand. Because wine supplies had been so short during the war, Rosenstiel felt the demand would be great for a few years after the war.

From New York, Rosenstiel issued orders to Cella to make a great quantity of wine from the 1946 crush, far more than the Schenley-owned wineries—Roma and Cresta Blanca—could handle in their own plants. His intent was to put Schenley in the driver's seat by controlling the lion's share of California wine that autumn. As it was, Schenley (by 1944) had more than 35 million gallons of wine storage capacity in California, making it by far the state's largest wine company.

With at least one third of all California grapes off the "open market"—because they were raised by growers who belonged to cooperative wineries—Schenley was attempting to corner the market on what was left: the grapes that all the rest of us counted on to supply our production needs.

Cella went up and down the state contracting with wineries for them to make bulk wine for Schenley, agreeing to pay them whatever it cost them for grapes to fill their wineries, plus a generous per ton fee for processing. With no restraints on grape prices and the emphasis on volume with these cost-plus deals, wineries immediately started bidding against each other for grapes—using Schenley's money, of course. To the delight of growers, grape prices soon went from between $50 and $60 dollars the previous year to over $100 a ton in 1946.

Bulk wine prices followed grape prices, at which point—in the fall of '46 bulk dessert-wine prices hit an all-time high of $1.50 a gallon—Julio and I had a serious talk. This was twice the price of bulk wine during the war, and five times the price before the war. Though we were in the middle of our crush, we didn't think it was smart to compete with Schenley in buying grapes at ridiculously high prices.

Schenley had caused the price of grapes and wine to increase dramatically—but, inexplicably, it was *buying* grapes at prices artificially inflated by its own actions. Jumping on the bandwagon was yet another major distiller, National Distillers, which had purchased Italian Swiss Colony during the war.

In our judgment, Rosenstiel had made a major miscalculation here. Worse yet, other vintners were bound to suffer as a result of Schenley's actions.

We felt that grape prices were far too high. Given the size of the crop, the price of wine was too high as well, and would soon tumble.

An industry catastrophe was in the making.

Julio

We were still crushing late in the fall of '46 when I received a call from Ted Cribari of Cribari Winery in Fresno. "I hear you're picking your Missions," he said.

"That's right, we're picking."

"I have commitments for wine I can't fill," Cribari said. "Can I buy your Missions?"

That year, the Cribari family had decided to take their winery in the opposite direction we were headed: It had stopped bottling and would sell only in bulk. They had a cost-plus contract with Roma that year, meaning that they didn't mind at all paying exorbitant prices for grapes.

"Well, you know what the market is," I said.

"A hundred and twenty a ton?"

That was the highest price I'd heard this crazy year. I wanted to be sure about this. "You'll pay a hundred and twenty a ton for our Missions?"

"Yes," he said.

In the thirteen years since Repeal, California growers had received an average $34 a ton for their wine grapes. Things had gone haywire this year, all right.

"Let me get back to you," I said.

I called Ernest, who was back east. That year, as usual, we had bought grapes while they were in the range of $50 to $60 a ton. As prices began going up, we had stopped buying.

"The market doesn't make any sense," I told Ernest.

"I agree," he said. "Sell."

I called Cribari back and told him we had a deal.

"I appreciate that, Julio."

"There's just one thing. You have to pay now."

That was how Ernest and I felt about the market overall. Some people were going to end up losing their shirts, and before they did, we wanted to be paid.

Cribari sent me a check, and we trucked him three hundred tons of Missions.

It was the first and last time we ever sold grapes to another winery.

THE SITUATION IN 1946 could not have come at a worse time for us. At the end of the war, many vintners had gone back to selling in bulk. We had decided to sell our wines only in bottles. In early 1946, we invested heavily in a new state-of-the-art bottling room. With the help of Owens-Illinois, who was our supplier of bottles at that time, we designed a room that ensured that our wines would be bottled under the most sterile conditions possible. Air inside the room was filtered and under high pressure, so when the door was opened, air went out instead of in. To avoid any carton dust getting into the wines, we took the bottles out of the carton and sent them into the bottling room on a conveyor that passed through an opening in the wall. After the bottles were filled, labeled, and capped, they returned through another opening to be placed in the carton. We installed four bottling lines, though we had room for six. (We now have fourteen lines.) Our bottling room became a model for the industry.

Ernest

Within a day or two of my conversation with Julio, I ran into Bob Gibson, a Cincinnati bottler, in the lobby of a New York hotel. Gibson had recently built his own winery near Sacramento.

"Ernest, what are you doing here?" Gibson asked.

I shrugged. "Selling wine."

"Why didn't you call me first?" Gibson asked.

"You need wine?"

"Sherry. Can you give me any?"

"Yes. How much you want?" I asked.

"How much do you have?"

"Five hundred thousand gallons."

"I'll take it all."

"What will you pay?"

"A dollar fifty a gallon."

At that price, I didn't have to think twice. Julio and I had already agreed we would sell not only grapes but bulk wine as well if the price was right.

Gibson found us seats in the hotel lobby, pulled out his checkbook, and on the spot wrote out a check for $750,000 for a half million gallons of sherry.

"That wine is mine," he said.

"You've got it."

I stayed in the East until past Thanksgiving selling bulk wine. I was uneasy about where the industry was heading, and Julio was equally uneasy.

It was obvious that a large surplus of wine was being produced as a result of the distillers' misjudging consumer demand for wine —

particularly for their own brands. In light of the surplus that was bound to develop, prices were artificially high. The bottom was likely to drop out of the wine market, and soon.

When I came home, I asked our employees to assemble one noontime in our new bottling room. Our four new bottling lines were in place. With our recent push on bottled goods, we had just gone to two shifts a day.

I took off my suit jacket, turned over a wooden box, and stood atop it. "My brother and I started this business in 1933. We've had some rough times and gotten through them. We have all of you to thank for that."

This was my first speech to our employees. I wasn't the type to give inspirational addresses, and the employees who had been around for a while knew it.

"Right now, we're facing our biggest challenge ever. We need to roll up our sleeves and get in and fight. These are rough times for our industry. Some wineries aren't going to survive. Grape prices have gone crazy for no reason other than some outsiders are trying to control our industry and put as many of us as they can out of business.

"Julio and I need for each and every one of you to help us get through this. We ask you to do everything you can to help improve our efficiency. We want you to think of this as your winery, too."

I explained that we thought too much wine was being made this year and that bulk prices would surely drop. Therefore, we were going to quickly sell as much bulk wine as we could to other wineries. This meant we would end up with less wine to bottle and market under our own brand. Our bottling lines would soon be idled. But I preferred to unload our wine at today's prices, and not wait for disaster to hit.

When I was finished, a shocked Charlie Crawford came up to me. "Ernest, if you sell most of our wine to other wineries, what are we going to do come March when our distributors start running out of wine?"

"Don't worry about it," I said. "I believe that come spring, we'll be able to buy back our wine for half what we are selling it for now."

In no time, bulk wine prices peaked at $1.75 a gallon, a postwar high for dessert wines. Then the roller coaster headed down with a jolt. By the summer of 1947, retailers and distributors were overloaded with wine, and prices crashed to 38 cents a gallon. At those bargain prices, we bought back most of the same wine we had sold at $1.50 a gallon a few months earlier.

Prices stayed so low that buyers who had contracted with wineries for the 1947 vintage willingly forfeited their down payments so they wouldn't have to take delivery and make payment in full.

The Napa Valley Cooperative had sold its wine in 1946 to Schenley's Roma for 85 cents to $1.05 a gallon. Hoping that prices would go even higher, the co-op kept part of its wine off the market to sell on speculation the following year. Caught in the spiraling downturn, they ended up selling the remainder for 25 cents a gallon to us.

Unfortunately, Cribari Winery had agreed to take its fee from Roma in wine. Cribari was paid off in $1.50-a-gallon wine that they soon couldn't sell for much more than 30 cents a gallon. Al Cribari would later explain that his family's winery lost all their working capital that year. They never recovered. (Eventually, they went bankrupt, and we ended up buying their winery.)

By late 1947 the marketplace was in chaos.

Most wineries experienced large losses for 1946–47 and a sizable number went out of business—or soon would. Schenley reportedly lost $16 million. National Distillers finished $9 million in the red. Louis Petri later boasted that he had "broken even."

As near as I could determine, E. & J. Gallo was the only winery to make a profit that crazy year.

WE WERE STEADILY PUSHING OUR WAY to the top in various markets. In New York, for example, our competitors were all selling at $1.10 a bottle when we entered the market. We went along with them at first, but had a difficult time breaking in. I decided to lower our price to the natural price point of $1.00 a bottle.

I understand that the head of Roma got in touch with the heads of Petri, Italian Swiss Colony, and the Guild to beseech them to hold their prices in New York and elsewhere. "Let Gallo sell at those prices. At the rate they're selling, they have to run out of wine soon. When they do, we'll get our customers back at our prices and they will lose their standing with retailers since they will be out of stock."

It was true that we were selling a lot of wine, but what our competitors didn't fully appreciate was that just as fast as we shipped case goods from Modesto, we were buying bulk wine—for one third the price that our competitors had paid for their higher-priced inventories. As a result, there was no danger of us running out of wine. We held our prices and soon became the leading wine brand, not only in New York but elsewhere.

In the key California market—a state with the nation's highest per capita wine consumption—we became the best-selling wine brand in 1947.

OUR BATTLE WITH THE distillers was not over.

By late 1947, the distillers had fired and replaced many of their winery managers, as a result of what has been called "the circus of '46 and the debacle of '47." With much ballyhoo, Rosenstiel came to California to meet with a dozen or so "leaders of the industry." The president of Schenley was a very important man in those days. We were flattered that such a prominent industry leader was interested in talking to us.

"None of us are making money," Rosenstiel complained. The problem, he said, was an overproduction of wine. "I've got a plan and I want your support. I want it proposed to the state legislature that it pass a bill requiring the seal of California on every bottle of wine produced in this state. To qualify for the seal, wine must be four years old. That will short the amount of wine available in the country and drive prices up immediately. We'll all make money instead of losing it as we are now."

It was true that many wineries were overloaded in inventories of wine—high-cost wine produced from high-priced grapes. Of course, Rosenstiel himself had helped cause this surplus. When you have purchased grapes for $120 a ton, you need to sell your wine for more than a dollar a gallon just to pay for the grapes.

Julio and I did not have a big inventory—not that year.

Rosenstiel wanted the Wine Institute to propose the legislation to the California legislature. The chairman of the Wine Institute's board was Walter Taylor, head of the large growers' cooperative, Fruit Industries, which also had a great excess of wine on hand—some of it more than four years old. Naturally, Taylor favored the plan.

After Rosenstiel returned to New York, a lot of behind-the-scenes lobbying and vote counting went on. If the Wine Institute proposed the ageing plan to the state legislature, it had a good chance of passing. Without the industry's support, it would certainly fail.

The new head of Roma, Rosenstiel's handpicked man to run Schenley's wine business, was the recently retired Army general James Herbert. A bright and capable guy who had previously commanded the Port of Los Angeles, he possessed impressive logistical skills. In the future, I would work well with him on other matters, but on this scheme to short the California wine market, the general and I were on opposite sides of the battlefield. As far as Rosenstiel's plan was concerned, I would not even consider it. This was another fight for survival. If we lost, our winery might as well shut its doors. It would prove just as fatal to other small and medium-sized wineries who didn't have the financial wherewithal to hold their wine from the market for four years.

I had been elected to the Wine Institute's board of directors in 1943. I now called my fellow directors and lobbied hard against Rosenstiel's proposal. Among other things, I pointed out that the ageing plan would not necessarily improve wine quality. Unquestionably, improving wine quality was not Rosenstiel's intent. At the same time the president of his California wine operation was calling vintners, promising those who didn't have aged wine that he would sell them some cheap. Or if a winery needed to sell wine, he vowed to buy it for top dollar. He was making promises and throwing Schenley's money around in an effort to get votes.

Most of the smaller vintners agreed with me that the plan didn't make a bit of sense. The larger wineries with excess inventories sided with Rosenstiel. Counting heads, I realized it was going to be very close.

A Wine Institute meeting in those days was often a gloves-off fight to the finish. Old-timers like John B. Cella, A. R. Morrow, Walter Taylor, "Padre" Jimmy Vai, and Harry Baccigaluppi were rough characters who weren't afraid of confrontation. They knew what they wanted and they went after it with all their might. If you were in their way, they would just as soon run you down as not.

When it was time for the Wine Institute to take a stand on Rosenstiel's proposal, I continued my lobbying right up until the last minute. My own count showed that we could defeat the plan by a single vote.

Taylor, the chairman, put the issue up for a voice vote.

Knowing that Taylor strongly favored the measure, I demanded a roll call. Doing so was my prerogative under parliamentary rules.

Taylor agreed, and called each director's name one by one. As they cast their votes, I checked them against my list. When they came to Bruno Bisceglia, whom I had down as a solid "no" vote, he said, "Yes." As the plan would be greatly to Bisceglia's disadvantage, I doubted anything General Herbert could have promised would have convinced him to change his mind.

I jumped up. "There's been an error, Mr. Chairman."

"What error?" asked Taylor.

"I'm not sure everyone understands what a yes or no vote means. Please restate the issue and call for another vote."

143

Taylor, with a confident smile, did so. His head count before the meeting must have been different than mine—he no doubt thought there were enough votes to pass the proposal.

When the voting resumed, Bisceglia, who by then realized his mistake, voted no loud and clear.

We defeated the proposal by one vote.

At this point Taylor became enraged. "Wait a minute, Gallo! You had no right to demand another vote!"

As it was a proper vote, Taylor was hamstrung.

Noticeably embarrassed, Herbert excused himself and left the room.

A few minutes later, I walked by as Herbert came out of a phone booth in the hallway. He looked shaken.

"I was just talking to Rosenstiel," Herbert said. "He's in Europe. I started to tell him about what happened but he was yelling so loud that I told him we had a bad connection."

The general had hung up on his boss.

The defeat of the arbitrary ageing plan was the beginning of the end for Schenley and National Distillers in the wine industry. The distillers had miscalculated the nature of the wine business. During the war years the big distillers had pushed lots of wine off on retailers and so they assumed that their wine had moved out to the consumers, that they had built up brand loyalty. In reality, the retailers had resented having to take their wines in order to get their hands on hard liquor. Much of that wine pushed on retailers was still, years later, sitting in retailers' storerooms gathering dust. When the war ended and liquor flowed freely again, retailers stopped ordering the distillers' wines.

ABOUT 1949, I STARTED TAKING AN ACTIVE ROLE in trying to deal with the varied problems faced by the wine industry at large. My efforts were mostly low-key, conducted within industry committees and other such forums.

In an effort to ensure the "orderly marketing" of wine and grapes—

to everyone's benefit, we all agreed—a state marketing order designed to regulate the sale of table and dessert wines was approved in 1949, but it was not effective in keeping prices up. A stabilization order was also passed in 1949, but no funds were ever collected under this order. Neither of these interventions was the long-term solution the state's wine industry needed.

Unfortunately, not everyone saw the need for improving wine quality. For these individuals, the wine industry's sole purpose was to serve as the salvage operation of the grape industry. As one economist of the day said, "Why increase wine quality? That would just increase sales, which would raise prices, which would encourage growers to plant more grapes, which would lead to more grape surpluses."

It was fortunate for the future of the California wine industry that a majority of us refused to be persuaded by this dangerously "logical" reasoning.

If any winery in the country made a bottle of bad wine and sold it, it could hurt all of us. The consumer who bought it might never try wine again.

How could we expect to place wine into the mainstream of American life if we didn't keep trying to improve the quality of existing wines and striving to produce wines that would appeal to consumers who didn't buy our present types of wine?

Julio

Growers' cooperatives were a big part of the California wine industry by the early 1950s. The largest co-op winery of all, Allied Grape Growers, formed by Louis Petri in 1951, had 275 grower-members and 19 million gallons of wine-storage capacity. In all, there were 20 co-op wineries with a combined capacity of more than 70 million gallons—about one third of the state's total wine storage at that time.

The birthplace of co-ops was in the Lodi area, where growers got fed up with John B. Cella, who had started Roma Winery there upon repeal. Cella was always trying to drive the grape market down.

I remember one year when we were paying close to $50 a ton for grapes, Cella stopped by to complain. "You finding grapes hard to buy this year?" he asked.

"Not at all," I answered.

"So why are you paying so much?"

"We think it's the right price," I answered.

"Hell, I'll sell you my Hopper Ranch grapes for that," said Cella, trying to bluff me.

"You will? How many tons do you have?"

"Seven thousand tons on seven hundred acres."

I pulled a contract book out of my drawer and started writing in it.

"Wait a minute," Cella said. He had gone from sounding cocky to worried. "You know, I have to deliver a thousand tons a day."

"We can take a thousand tons a day." I kept writing. "I'll stop picking our own to crush yours first."

When I was finished filling out the contract for Cella to sell us 7,000 tons, I swung the book around in front of him.

"You know where to sign," I said.

He didn't like it, but he signed and delivered to us that year.

In the early days, growers in Lodi had found themselves pretty much at Cella's mercy. He would put his per-ton price up on the crusher for everyone to see, but then as the farmers brought their grapes in, if he saw a long line he'd go out and drop the price. With the long lines, it could sometimes take a grower's truck twelve hours to reach Roma's crusher—with countless price changes during the wait. Growers would sling hammocks under their trucks so they could rest without losing their place in line. Even a grower who had choice grapes when he first pulled into line never knew what price he would receive until he pulled up to the crusher. If the price was less than the cost of raising his grapes, the grower lost money that year. Two or three years like this in a row, and he could be bankrupt.

The Lodi growers finally became so dissatisfied that they started their own wineries: Seven or eight co-ops sprang up in the mid-1930s. Eventually, the co-ops so completely cut off Cella's supply of grapes that he moved his operation to Fresno.

Cella had another winery in Manteca, and over there he would seldom pay cash for grapes. Instead, he promised to pay the growers after he sold the wine. When spring came, growers would go in to see if he had sold the wine. They could never find Cella around and would end up talking to his bookkeeper. Looking up their account, the bookkeeper would say, "Yes, we sold the wine, but the crushing fee is so much and the storage fee is so much and we didn't get such a good price, so . . . you owe *us* money."

As I said, that's why some of those co-ops started up. I can't blame the growers one bit. After having been treated so badly by a winery, it took them years to gain confidence in other wineries.

The co-ops were an honest attempt by growers to bring some stability to the grape industry, and stability was badly needed. But co-ops were not the solution.

Ernest

For a while, co-ops were formidable competition.

Not only did they have access to long-term government loans to build modern plants—favorable financing that the rest of us could not get—but they also received considerable tax benefits. Their main tax advantages over regular corporations were the right to set up tax-free reserves for any purpose, and the fact that earnings were taxed only once, as personal income of the individual grower-members. Owners (or stockholders) of regular corporations have their profits taxed twice: once as corporate earnings, and again as personal income.

Another enormous advantage for co-ops, of course, was that they did not have to pay cash for their grapes.

For about thirty years the cooperative wineries gave us very tough competition. In the early 1950s, two of the five biggest wineries in the U.S. were co-ops. They wielded great influence on the wine industry. Early on, co-ops controlled annually upwards of one third of the California grape harvest.

One thing that worked against co-ops was the fact that their members had no sales or merchandising experience. By its nature, a co-op was primarily a producer, not a marketer. When the wine industry stepped up its efforts in marketing, advertising, and improved salesmanship, the co-op brands began to fade rapidly.

The decline of co-ops coincided with the increase in table wine sales—the co-ops made primarily dessert wines, which can be produced from lower-quality grapes. However, the major failure of co-ops was their lack of qualified management. Despite their numerous advantages, co-ops were unwilling to spend the money to hire or keep competent people. Even when a co-op obtained a qualified person, it was difficult for him to get a decision by the board of directors on a plan of action. The directors did not understand or appreciate sales and marketing issues, or know what to do about them.

In time, we were able to overcome the co-ops' built-in advantages. Several did remain in business through the years—mainly as suppliers of bulk wine, however, not as brand builders.

In 1950, I visited my parents' homeland for the first time.

After packing our bags, Amelia and I filled a couple of boxes with groceries. We had heard how the war and inflation had made a shambles of Italy's economy, and that poverty and hunger were widespread.

We packed tuna and sardines, threw in salamis—food we thought we could carry that would keep.

When we docked in Naples, the Italian customs agents came aboard ship. Asked what we were bringing into the country, I mentioned the groceries.

"Why are you bringing groceries?" the agent asked suspiciously.

"Well, we understand that in some of the smaller towns"—I didn't want to offend his national pride—"people may not be able to get all the food they want."

He went through the boxes, making a list of each item. Then he started totaling a long column of numbers.

"What are you doing?" I asked.

"Figuring the duty."

"The duty? We're going to give this food to people who are hungry and you want to charge us *duty*?"

"*Signore*, that is the law."

He rattled off an amount of money that was a lot more than what we had paid for the food.

I was furious. Turning to Amelia, I said, "We're not going to pay their duty. Not a damn cent!"

The agent called for his supervisor.

Not only would I not pay, but I wasn't about to walk away and leave our groceries. I wouldn't have put it past these characters to sell our offerings on the black market for four times what they had cost.

Without a word, I picked up the loaded boxes and threw them overboard.

Ashore, we rented a small car and filled the back seat with luggage, then tied the rest on the roof rack. Not having traveled abroad before, we learned a valuable lesson about overpacking. After this trip, Amelia and I traveled the world with only one suitcase apiece.

We headed north.

In Fossano, my father's hometown in the pasturelands of the Piedmont region, I located the small inn where my father had been born and raised. At this time, the downstairs was a little shop instead of the kitchen and dining room it must have been in earlier years. The upstairs appeared to have a number of small bedrooms. The place seemed so small for such a large family.

I found my father's brother Bernardo running a tiny café. I figured he must have been not quite seventy years old, but he looked ninety. Business was not good, and he seemed beaten down by dire circumstances. Yet, Bernardo struck us as a real urbane gentleman, which was surprising because he had spent his entire life in this isolated little village.

Before we left I slipped Bernardo a few hundred dollars, which he didn't want to take at first — but I insisted. I remember sending him a few checks when I returned home — then word reached me that he had died.

In Agliano di Asti, my mother's birthplace, in the heart of the picturesque Piedmont wine region, we ran into quite a scene as word spread that a Gallo from America was visiting. Droves of townsfolk poured into the streets, all of them apparently expecting me to invite them to a big dinner just like my Uncle Mike had some twenty years earlier. Out to impress my Aunt Celia's family and everyone else in town, Uncle Mike had acted like the typical rich American. On top of the world with big earnings from his bootlegging, Mike made sure he and his wife traveled in style, even shipping over his new Chrysler convertible to drive on the narrow roads through backwater villages.

I disappointed a lot of people that night because I didn't throw a big extravaganza. Instead, we had a quiet visit with a group of my uncles, aunts, and cousins on the Bianco side whom, of course, I had never before met.

One cousin took me down into his wine cellar and uncorked a bottle of his homemade Barbera. No sooner had he opened it than the whole cellar filled with the wonderful aroma of the wine. His wine was great—the family still knew how to make wine. Since then, I've had Barbera many times, but I've never found any as good as my cousin's.

Amelia wanted to see Lourdes, located at the foot of the Pyrenees in southwest France. She told me this was where "the miracle"—visions of the Virgin Mary—were said to have taken place in the last century.

Driving nearly a hundred miles out of our way to get there, we arrived at five o'clock one afternoon. We drove around on the narrow cobblestone streets until we saw a small hotel that looked comfortable. Amelia waited in the car while I went in to inquire about a room.

A young Frenchman was behind the desk. I asked him if they had a room and he said yes. He opened up the book for me to register and I wrote my name.

When he saw my name, he said, "Wait a minute." He disappeared in the back.

A woman about my age came out.

"Is your name Ernest Gallo?" she asked.

"Yes."

"Are you from California?"

"Yes."

"You are in the wine business?"

"Yes, I am."

"You are my cousin," she said.

She turned out to be the daughter of my father's sister, who had married a Frenchman and moved here long ago. The coincidence of it was amazing.

We spent the night at my cousin's small, very neat hotel. The next day we visited my elderly aunt in Toulouse. She made a splendid meal of roast veal for us, and told stories about the family and the old days.

Growing up, things were so tough for the Gallos of Fossano that before my father and the other children would leave for school they would line up and rub a piece of polenta (baked cornmeal) on a big salami that hung by the door. This gave their sparse lunch of polenta some extra flavor, while conserving the family's food supply.

Seeing the towns from which my parents had come, and learning more about the circumstances prevailing at the time, made me thankful that they had sought a better life in America.

11

THE FIFTIES:
STEADY GROWTH

Ernest

As we entered the 1950s, our wines were distributed in only a few more states than they had been at the end of the war. As a matter of fact, we had full distribution in only six states: New York, New Jersey, Kansas, Louisiana, Utah, and Connecticut.

Up to this time I had personally handled all the sales, with the help of only four or five winery representatives. It became obvious that actions and decisions were delayed because I was simply covering too many of the details. I needed to find someone whose aptitude was in sales, and who would be willing to work hard and travel extensively to help broaden our distribution network throughout the country.

I envisioned forming a talented team that could go into an area, develop a workable plan for distribution and sales, and find the right people to implement it. Setting out to build this Modesto-based team from the top down, I interviewed several individuals for the sales manager post, including Albion (Al) Fenderson, who had previously worked for distillers and the government's war production board. In our interview,

Fenderson stated unequivocally that he didn't think a sales manager should have a desk in the office, but rather, should spend his days in the field. I liked that.

I also told him I needed someone to help with the advertising. Did he think he would be able to help? I liked his response. "Yes, I can also do the advertising with one hand tied behind my back."

After I finished questioning him, Fenderson asked me to assess the future of the wine business. "There are now about ten different wineries attempting to become national brands," I remember telling him. "They can't all succeed. In my opinion, within five years' time there will only be two or three of us left."

I hired Fenderson in June 1952. When he showed up for his first day of work, he found no desk or office awaiting his arrival. I had taken him at his word. Anyway, Fenderson was not going to spend a lot of time in Modesto. He asked for ninety days to acquaint himself with the wine business, which he knew was much different than the distilling business. I gave him thirty days.

For a month Fenderson traveled around California, exploring markets and meeting our principal distributors. Then I handed him his first assignment: improving our position in Los Angeles, even though we were the leading brand in that market. From reading the daily reports and route sheets that our salesmen turned in, I believed we could do better than we were doing.

At the time, there were twenty-two salesmen in our L.A. distributorship trying to cover upwards of 5,000 accounts. Our best salesman there was handling 386 accounts himself. The problem was obvious. The salesmen could not possibly be doing justice to all their accounts. Fenderson soon developed a plan for expanding the sales force and increasing our sales pressure in the area. He sold the idea of the expansion to the sales force—salesmen universally fear that new hires will cut into their business and reduce their commissions. Each salesman could do a better job servicing his remaining accounts and actually sell more product with a smaller number of accounts, Fenderson argued. He was proved right.

Next came a similar campaign in San Francisco. Then I sent Fenderson to Bakersfield and San Diego for market surveys. When he came back to Modesto, I cross-examined him in detail about the state of the markets. I asked him how many retailers there were in San Diego who didn't carry our products.

"I don't know," Fenderson admitted.

"What about Bakersfield?"

He shook his head.

I told him in no uncertain terms that he had not done his job properly, and he should return to both locations and find out how many unsold accounts there were.

"Identify them by name and address," I explained, "and set up a program to see that they are opened up as quickly as possible."

Fenderson rushed home to get his bag, which he hadn't yet unpacked. He had been right: There was no reason to give him a desk in Modesto.

For nearly the past half century, Al Fenderson has been—and still is—a dominant influence in our sales and marketing efforts. He has been personally responsible for much of our progress.

And he has long since had a desk at the winery.

Fenderson has more than earned it.

Julio

Ernest and his sales force had been watching the success of a new kind of red wine produced by the Guild Winery of Lodi. A product called Vino da Tavola was selling well with no advertising at all. Though the majority of wine drinkers still preferred dessert wines, this new red table wine was suddenly very popular.

We set up a tasting in Production. As they always did, our winemaking staff joined me—and so did some people from Sales and Marketing. Seeing Vino da Tavola's success, our distributors were anxious for us to bring out a similar table wine.

I sipped this popular new wine, swirled it around in my mouth, and, in a nearby sink spit it out, as tasters usually do. I didn't like it.

To make sure we didn't have a bad bottle, we opened up another. It wasn't any better. Part table wine and part dessert wine, Vino da Tavola was a common Valley red wine sweetened with port.

"You really want a wine like this?" I asked.

Al Fenderson talked about how this product had found a niche in the marketplace. "But, Julio," he smiled, "if you want to make it better that would be fine."

"What we're looking for here," Fenderson said, "is a red blend that is light and mellow."

Without making a commitment one way or the other, I said we would see what we could do.

This would happen a lot over the decades: the Sales and Marketing departments would ask Production to try to develop a particular new product that had commercial potential. Though we didn't always see eye to eye in these matters, we usually agreed to see what we could come up with.

In this case, I was interested in seeing if we could develop a product that would appeal not only to Vino da Tavola's customers, but also to the many Americans who were still drinking little, if any, wine.

The typical California table wines of the day were described by a majority of consumers in surveys as "too sour." Instead of trying to change the country's tastes overnight, the wine industry needed to come up with new products that would attract those potential customers. I could see how they might like a product that was softer, smoother, and a bit sweeter than the robust Burgundies I preferred at my own table. Of course, I had been raised having wine with dinner while most Americans hadn't.

We ended up making a very soft red wine—using some quality North Coast grapes in the blend—that I liked better than Vino da Tavola. Fruitier and not so harsh, our wine did well in comparative tastings.

Fenderson came up with the name "Paisano," which I didn't like at first. In Italian, *paisano* means somebody from your village, and its connotation for me was of poor immigrants coming off the boat from Italy. But naming a product wasn't my department.

A nice compliment was passed on to me by Fenderson from an Italian opera singer friend of his. She said our new wine reminded her of the original, dry Lambruscos that she had enjoyed in Rome. She even took a case of Paisano along on her honeymoon.

The best compliment came from the consumers: Paisano became the top-selling red wine in the United States and remained so for many years.

WE WERE BUYING MORE WINE all the time from North Coast wineries. The market turmoil of the late 1940s left many of the surviving Napa and Sonoma wineries looking for financial security. At the same time, our skyrocketing volume and sales meant we needed more wine than we were producing, even though we were expanding our capacity every year. We made long-term commitments in the early fifties with the Napa Valley Cooperative, Frei Brothers (near Healdsburg, in Sonoma County), St. Helena Grape Growers Co-op, and a number of other wineries. By 1954, the wineries under contract to us had a total annual production of more than five million gallons. These wineries made the wine for us under our supervision. We then transported the wine to Modesto for blending and bottling.

We continued to purchase wine for blending purposes on the open or bulk market from such wineries as Fountain Grove, Beaulieu Vineyards, Wente Brothers, Seghesio, and Mirassou, among others.

I was convinced that people who enjoyed popular-priced wines in this country did not like the variations that occurred from year to year in European wines, but preferred a good product with assured consistency. Such wine products could only be produced by blending. This blending process became the core of our production operation.

The table wines of the early 1950s were generally technically sound, and the dessert wines, reasonably good. But most vintners understood that the wines then being produced were not enough. We needed more variety, and different tastes.

Though increased research was being conducted in viticulture and enology at the University of California at Davis, Ernest and I agreed on the need to expand our own research programs. It would be expensive, but we considered such long-range efforts to be the only way to improve the quality of our grapes and wine, as well as to develop new products. We agreed that unless more wines that people liked were produced, the wine industry would fail to attract new customers.

Our research enologists went to work on a range of projects: cold fermentation, selected yeast strains, new and improved clarifying agents, tank coatings, sterile filtration, automated blending of wines to ensure product consistency, and a complex ion-exchange technique for the cold stabilization of wine as a way to remove potassium, which causes precipitates and cloudiness.

I encouraged individual ingenuity. For example, one of our enologists, Ralph (Brad) Webb, younger brother of UC Davis enology professor A. Dinsmoor Webb, started doing some experiments on his own with something called a Millipore filter. This membrane-type filter had been developed in Germany during the war to filter airplane fuel. Since then it had been used in this country to filter water. Webb kept working with the filter until he was sure it could be used for the sterile filtration of wine. This would eliminate the need for pasteurization, which could damage wine. Webb convinced us that "membrane filtration" was the sign of the future, and he suggested that our purchasing department ask the Millipore manufacturers to make larger-sized filters for our use. We were the first winery to adopt Millipore filtration and "cold bottling," which we found improved flavor and increased the shelf life of wines. We are still using this process today.

When Webb left us in 1954 to take over operation of a new Napa winery, he gave us a list of four hundred research projects he suggested we undertake in our lab. We got around to doing most of them.

By 1958, our research department had moved into its new lab, complete with state-of-the-art equipment never before used in the wine industry. There is no doubt that the research we began four decades ago is the main reason why today's wines are much more drinkable than the wines of the fifties. These advances contributed to better wines, not only for us but for the entire wine industry, as our scientists publish their most important findings.

By the mid-1950s, and thanks to the determined efforts of Charlie Crawford, we had the largest and best staff of researchers in the industry—a distinction I'm proud to say we've maintained ever since.

Of course, winemaking is art as well as science. The human palate remains the ultimate standard by which wines are judged—and so wine quality is a very subjective thing. Our wines were constantly being tasted not only by Ernest and me and our staffs, but also by consumers we would bring in from the community for tastings.

WITH A FEW EXCEPTIONS, the nature and schedule of vineyard work hasn't changed much over the years. We start right after the crush. From late October until mid-December, unless there are heavy late fall rains, we irrigate to make sure that the vines will not suffer root injury from being too dry in the winter. Moist ground does not become as cold as dry ground.

As soon as the leaves have fallen—which means the sap has stopped running and the vines are dormant—pruning begins. This usually happens around Thanksgiving and continues until March.

In our experimental vineyards in Livingston, we had tried various methods of pruning—head pruning, cane pruning, cordon pruning—for each grape variety. The only grapes a vine will produce well grow out of the wood, or cane, that grew the previous year. Grapes will come from shoots or spurs growing off this "fruit wood." In pruning, you are planning just how much sunshine and aeration the grapes will get, decisions based largely on grape variety and local climate.

Pruning must be finished before the sap runs freely and the buds begin to swell and open. At that point, the leaves start unfolding and clusters appear. "Bloom" usually takes place between early and late May, depending on the weather.

Back before we started to introduce organic farming methods, from March on—when the buds began to swell and open—we began fighting pests like cutworm and, in the summer, leafhoppers. This required careful inspection of each vine. If the invasion was serious, the vines were dusted or sprayed. I never liked doing this, but back then we didn't have a choice. Sulfur is applied weekly—more often if it rains—between mid-April and July to prevent and control powdery mildew.

In June we go through the vineyards and thin those vines that look overcropped (that is, they support too many clusters of grapes, which affects quality), cutting off the excess grapes and letting them fall to the ground. We also thin the grapes on any vines that look weak.

What we are working for with all these trips into a vineyard during the year is full grape maturity and the best quality possible. There are no shortcuts. There are approximately seven hundred vines per acre, and we go from vine to vine several times a year—and still do today.

Once picked, grapes that went into our wines were inspected repeatedly before crushing. At that time, I can say that no grapes were crushed that I hadn't seen. No matter how large we became, this hands-on approach guided me in everything I did. I'm sure some people found me to be tough and uncompromising—when it came to maintaining quality control, I certainly was.

During the harvest in the mid-1950s, we crushed from six o'clock in the morning until ten at night. I showed up at the crusher hourly to inspect the grapes as trucks lined up waiting to be weighed and unloaded. I put a chalk mark on each truck after I inspected it. Our men knew better than to dump a truckload of grapes into the crusher that didn't have my mark on it.

CRIBARI WINERY WAS UNABLE TO RECOVER from the disastrous years 1946–47—when they had the cost-plus contract from Schenley—and ended up defaulting on their bank debt and filing for bankruptcy.

Though Ernest wasn't interested in acquiring the Cribari labels, we decided we could use a plant in Fresno, as we were crushing so many grapes from that area of the Valley for dessert wine. After purchasing Cribari in 1954, we started remodeling its Las Palmas plant, practically rebuilding the place from the ground up. Eventually there wasn't anything left from the original Cribari Winery. Today it is a modern, well-equipped winery of 94-million-gallon capacity.

Though we had been building new storage tanks at both wineries all along, in the 1950s we found ourselves without the capacity needed for an operation our size that was still growing. Since storage capacity was then the criterion of a winery's size (today the criterion is usually total sales), we didn't make *Time's* list of the five largest wineries in 1953, even though we sold more wine than all but one or two of them.

In the summer of 1955, we hurriedly began building more glass-lined storage tanks. As the summer progressed, it was obvious that there was going to be a large grape crop. I was afraid that even with the new tanks on-line we wouldn't have enough storage. At the last minute I asked the steel-tank company if they could deliver an additional tank—one million gallon capacity—by mid-September. I explained how we needed it for the crush. They weren't sure they could manufacture it in time. I put our men to work anyway, building the foundation. The day they finished, the prefabricated walls and roof for California's largest wine storage tank arrived.

By 1958 we had replaced all the wooden cooperage at Modesto and Fresno with glass-lined steel tanks. We ended up replacing all our concrete storage too. The advantages of glass-lined steel tanks—and later, stainless steel—were obvious to all wineries that shifted over. Stainless steel tanks proved to be ideal for holding wine prior to bottling. You could better control the temperature and atmosphere inside. Being able to store wine in insulated, easy-to-clean tanks contributed to the industry's ability to make fresh, fruitier wines available in quantity at a reasonable price.

Without stainless steel as the industry's standard type of large-scale wine storage, the white wine boom of the 1980s might not have been possible.

Ernest

In 1952, I began negotiating to buy Italian Swiss Colony, located in Asti in Sonoma County. With nearly 27 million gallons of wine storage, ISC was, at the time, the nation's third-largest producer of domestic wines after Roma (40 million gallons) and California Wine Association (30 million gallons).

ISC's owner, National Distillers, who had bought the firm in 1942 as a hedge against wartime restrictions on liquor, had lost interest in wine after the sudden downturn in the market following the war.

The president of National Distillers called me to ask if we would be interested in buying ISC—the winery, its labels, everything. I flew to New York and worked on coming up with an acceptable deal. When we had reached a tentative agreement—including the sales price and payment terms—I returned to Modesto.

Going the acquisition route, a common way for an organization to expand quickly, was tempting. Italian Swiss was more than twice our size. Buying ISC and its labels and adding its 27 million gallons of storage capacity to our 12 million gallons would make us the country's largest winery.

I had negotiated an option to buy ISC. The structure of the deal I had worked out in New York meant we would be buying ISC for the value of the inventory and buildings. The ISC brand, which had better sales at the time than our own label, would essentially be thrown in gratis.

Julio and I agreed that he should go up to Asti and take a look at ISC's inventory and main plant before we went any further with the deal.

Next, I went to see Fred Ferroggiaro, then chairman of the Bank of America loan committee. We would need bank financing to make this acquisition.

When I presented my plan to Ferroggiaro, his jaw dropped. He was surprised that I had been talking to National Distillers about buying ISC.

It became evident that it would take some real persuasion on my part to get the bank to make us a loan to finance the acquisition.

We probably would not have ended up back at Bank of America had George Zoller, of Capital National Bank, not gone to his club for a handball game one afternoon in 1947 and, tragically, dropped dead on the court. Capital National was subsequently bought out by Wells Fargo. When I told the new president what our borrowing needs were for the following season, he said, "I'm not sure we want to lend on wine." Stunned, I pointed out that the bank had taken care of us for years. "Look at the record," I said. "We borrowed two million dollars last year and paid it back early." He finally offered to lend us half of what we needed. "How can I operate on half?" I had asked. At the same time, the new Modesto branch manager of Bank of America—a guy named Puccinelli—had been trying to get our business back. "You belong here," he had told me more than once. "You're from Modesto and I'm Italian." When the new head of Capital National appeared so hesitant about continuing to meet our loan requirements, I switched our business to Bank of America, which has been great to us ever since. I lived to see the day they never say no.

I began to reconsider the whole ISC deal. In addition to depending on Bank of America to finance our current borrowing needs, I would be asking them to finance the acquisition, plus the operations of a larger winery—Italian Swiss Colony was more than twice our size.

I started to think about where my emphasis would be in marketing and selling. How could we be as effective in selling two brands in the same price category as we were in selling one?

When Julio returned from his trip to Asti, he described the ISC winery as a "real mess."

"What about the plant?" I asked.

"Obsolete and inefficient. We'd have to spend a lot of money to bring it up to what we are used to."

"Sounds like the only asset is the label," I said. "But I'm not sure now that I want it."

"That's a marketing decision," Julio said. "All I can say is, from a production standpoint I want no part of that place. I can't operate a winery that's in that shape."

I thought more about what we would do with the Italian Swiss Colony label. It would be an asset to someone, but would it be to us? We already had our own national label. Could we support two labels, Gallo and Italian Swiss Colony, effectively? From every point of view—advertising, marketing, production, meeting capital and borrowing needs, buying grapes, carrying inventories, building two sales organizations—we would be required to ride two horses at once. Just how could we put maximum effort on two brands? And if, with a big push from our sales force, the ISC label took sales away from Gallo, how would that help us in the long run? And if we favored the Gallo label, as I would be inclined to do, then why buy ISC in the first place?

Equally important, we would be stretched financially—assuming we could find a bank to lend us the money we needed—as well as in marketing and sales, which would make us vulnerable to our competitors.

Julio was like me. We both wanted to build things. To us, the real fun of being in business was building from the ground up. Then when you start succeeding, you can feel you have really accomplished something. To go out and purchase an existing winery and label—I finally had to ask myself: Where is the fun?

Julio and I were clear on this: Our biggest satisfaction in life comes from building and producing something that is our own.

Something with our name on it.

After notifying National Distillers that we were no longer interested in the acquisition, I called Louis Petri and told him I had baked a very good cake and he could have it if he wanted. His family friend, banker Fred Ferroggiaro, would no doubt tell him anyway.

Petri jumped at the deal, buying ISC for the figure I had hammered out in my negotiations. ISC's storage capacity added to Petri's 20 million gallons totaled 46 million gallons. Overnight, Petri became the largest wine producer in the country.

One might well ask: Why did I tip off Petri, a formidable competitor, to the deal for ISC?

Well, I knew *someone* was going to end up buying ISC from National Distillers, who were anxious to exit the wine business. From where I sat, Petri was a good choice. I never considered him much of a brand builder. The antithesis of us, Petri expanded distribution for the sake of sticking colored pins in a wall map, I think. It never made any sense to me. It was like spreading a very thin layer of manure out in a big field—you've got coverage, sure, but it isn't concentrated enough to do any good. He went into all markets as quickly as he could get there, regardless of the effectiveness of available distributors, and of what kind of support he could give his line of products. His forte, rather, was buying and selling businesses.

Also, like us, Petri had his own viable family-name national Petri wine brand that was selling well. Frankly, I suspected that Petri would spread his efforts by trying to support two competing national brands. It would divide his efforts on two fronts.

The following year, in California, the nation's single largest wine market, Italian Swiss Colony's sales dropped 20 percent and Petri's sales fell 30 percent.

Our sales increased significantly.

12

TEXAS,
THUNDERBIRD,
AND TELEVISION

Ernest

My method for opening new markets has changed little through the years. *Carefully study and take on only one major new market at a time, doing everything necessary to achieve a leading share of that market before tackling another one.*

Throughout the 1940s and 1950s we entered only a limited number of new markets every year, but when we did, we made the required effort to attain sales leadership.

We were not satisfied with our move into any market until we were the best-selling brand of wine.

From 1948 to 1955, our annual sales soared from 4 million to 16 million gallons, a 400 percent increase in seven years. U.S. wine consumption increased 18 percent over the same period. By the mid-1950s, we were selling 10 percent of all the wine sold in the U.S., even though we were distributed in only twenty states.

In 1955 we were approached about a merger by a gold-mining company that owned extensive properties and was listed on a major stock exchange. The main advantage for us would be the availability of increased financing for our future growth, and for diversification.

Julio and I talked it over. Our living requirements were modest, and did not require the sale of part of our company for us to live in our accustomed life-style. After all, each of us could eat only three meals a day and wear one suit of clothes and drive one car at a time.

Under the proposed merger, we would have been in operational control of the new company but answerable to a board of directors. By nature, we did not like having to answer to anyone. Now, if I wanted to expand advertising or distribution, I could do so. And if Julio wanted to modernize our production facilities, he could do so. The system worked well and had gotten us this far.

That ended that.

Never again did we consider a merger.

IN THE EARLY TO MID-1950S, Italian Swiss Colony had 60 percent of the Texas wine market. ISC's distributor, Lone Star, was the strongest in the state, with warehouses in all the major cities. No other national brand had been able to penetrate the market to any extent, except in Houston, where Roma was running a distant second.

Conventional wisdom has it that a consumer-products marketer with as huge a share of the market as ISC's in Texas is virtually invulnerable. But I didn't know that. In fact, at the time I viewed the situation as a golden opportunity.

Local bottlers with their own labels—none supported by advertising—provided the only real competition for ISC, and they were steadily losing ground. ISC's strategy against the local bottlers in Texas was to deeply discount in one area, while maintaining full prices elsewhere. ISC's discounted prices, meant to drive the local bottler out of business, were below the out-of-pocket cost of production for the average bottler. When the bottlers couldn't match those prices, they were slowly squeezed out of business. Then, once alone on the shelves in that market, ISC would raise its prices. In one Texas market after another, ISC repeated this practice.

The first indication that Texas might be ripe for our entry came when John Saragusa, an established Houston bottler and distributor, called us about the possibility of handling Gallo. Without a national wine brand, he was having difficulty competing with ISC.

Texas was on our "future" schedule along with other major markets we had not yet entered. I had gone to Texas annually for the past five years to survey the market and see if the time was right for our move into the state.

In those days, "consumer research" was done the hard way. Often, it consisted of Fenderson and me visiting stores and asking questions of retailers and consumers. It wasn't scientific, but it worked. We learned that the table-wine business in Texas at the time was virtually nonexistent. Dessert wines accounted for 90 percent of all wine sales.

When Saragusa telephoned, I told him that we were not then prepared to enter the Texas market—but we were keeping our eye on it.

Refusing to take no for an answer—I *liked* that about him— Saragusa said he would arrive in Modesto the next day and that he did not intend to leave until he got the Gallo franchise for his area.

Saragusa proved to be just as persuasive in person. I finally agreed to let him test the waters for us. Rather than just trying to get someone to switch from ISC's sherry to ours, I was more interested in seeing if we could develop new table-wine consumers.

I liked the idea of forging an alliance with Saragusa for the future, as he fit the mold of what I was looking for in every market: a smaller distributor to whom we could become important quickly.

We started Saragusa off with Paisano. "I know Texans aren't drinking table wine," I told him. "If they won't buy it, I'll give it away to them." I dropped the price on Paisano to the point where it was such a bargain that I hoped we would get people to at least try it. The market so heavily favored fortified wines that the real challenge here was seeing whether or not we could develop *any* table-wine business at all.

As Paisano's sales began building slowly, primarily as a result of price and word of mouth—we did no advertising whatsoever—we continued to survey the state periodically. On one trip Fenderson and I went to Houston, Dallas, Fort Worth, San Antonio, and Odessa in six days.

When I thought it was time to make a move, I called a meeting of the largest bottler in each of the five biggest markets and sat them down in a Dallas hotel suite.

"One by one you guys are being knocked out of business by Italian Swiss Colony," I began. "Let me ask you a question. Which is more important to you: to see your name on a label or to make a profit?"

When I received a unanimous response favoring turning a profit, I went on: "Then I've got a plan. I'll give you Gallo. Our full line. My brother and I will ship from California a far better quality of wine bottled at the winery. You close down your bottling plants. I'll do some advertising and we'll go after them. What do you say?"

"I'm not going to shut down my bottling plant for Christ's sake to go with you," said one bottler. "Who the hell are you?"

"Your brand just isn't known here," another bottler pointed out.

There had been a serious outbreak of skepticism.

"We're going to have a big advertising campaign," I went on. "We're going to put in lots of colorful point-of-sale materials. Each of you will have a sales force only for our wine. We're going to train your people. They're going to walk in and tell the retailer, 'We have wine bottled in California. Gallo is coming. We are their distributor and it is to your advantage to take us on and help give us a push.' "

"Why would it be to a retailer's advantage?" someone wanted to know.

"Your salesman asks the retailers, 'When did Italian Swiss Colony give you a deal? None that you can recall, right? We'll give you one on occasion. Before you know it, Italian Swiss will have to give you one too.' "

The distributors were looking at each other.

"The retailers will buy it," I said.

"What do we have to lose?" one of them asked.

They had nothing to lose.

Once these early Texas distributors closed down their plants and began working with us, they became attentive students. They followed what our people told them very carefully. We helped them to screen and hire additions to their sales forces and trained their new sales managers. When they finally hit the streets in October 1956 with our product, they were ready.

We also had gone to work on our end. We developed special advertisements to introduce Gallo to all of Texas. We launched a true "Texas-size" advertising campaign, including the most powerful statewide television, radio, and newspaper advertising the Lone Star State had ever seen for wine. We designed a sales presentation to the retailers, pointing out how little wine they were really selling and what small profits Lone Star, ISC's distributor, was allowing them to make. We promised that with our products, advertising, and merchandising we would significantly increase wine consumption. Not only would they sell a great deal more wine, but as a result of the competition between us and Italian Swiss Colony they could expect more advertising and promotion from both of us and better profits for themselves.

We prepared a total program for our distributors, down to the items and volume to be sold to each retail account, the proper shelf positioning, necessary point-of-sale material, and so on. In addition, Fenderson spent several weeks in Texas preceding the introduction of our brand, planning and preparing the detailed selling and advertising campaign for each individual market. He also handled the introductory sales meetings in each market to introduce the brand properly to the sales force.

The result was that the retailers greeted us with open arms. They gave us the shelf positioning and promotion that we wanted. Despite drastic countermeasures taken by Italian Swiss Colony, we obtained virtually 100 percent distribution and our sales grew rapidly.

Several months after introduction, Fenderson and I returned to Texas and resurveyed the state and our distribution program in every market. Everywhere we went, we were exceeding expectations. From El Paso in the west to Longview in the east, Brownsville to the south and Wichita Falls to the north, we hopped from one market to another, sometimes visiting three a day.

Prior to our entry into Texas, Italian Swiss Colony had been selling around fifty thousand cases of wine a month, representing about 80 percent of the popular-priced wine business in Texas. Our first year, we managed to sell fifty thousand cases a month too. There was little drop-off in ISC's sales volume, which proved my point that with the right products, the proper advertising and merchandising, and solid sales-manship, the total wine business could be substantially increased in Texas.

We learned from our market surveys that these new wine consumers had been induced by our advertising, products, and pricing to try wine for the very first time. Apparently they liked what they tasted, because sales continued to grow with repeat customers, a sizable portion of them buying table wines. Also, retailers found the increased margins to their liking. Not only were they selling more wine than ever before, but they were also making bigger profits per bottle.

At the beginning of the Texas campaign we had given each of our distributors there a quota for the first year, which was to equal the sales of Italian Swiss. At the end of our first year, I visited them—John

Saragusa, Mickey Goldman, Julius Scheppes, Ed Block, Phil Terk—not only to celebrate our first year's success, but to lay out our program for the second year.

At dinner with Scheppes, our Dallas distributor, I suggested matter-of-factly that I thought we could sell twice as much wine next year. He about choked.

"Ernest, you came down here last year and gave us a quota that represented practically the total wine business then being done in the state of Texas," Scheppes said. "We met it. Now, you're asking us to do *twice as much* this year! I'd like to know how you expect us to do that?"

"I guess we'll just have to double the wine market here, Julius."

I could tell that he wasn't sure if I was being serious. I was.

One of the reasons we were able to build the wine business in Texas was because we virtually introduced table wine to the general public in the state. The Texas wine market then and for some years after was not very sophisticated—though it is now. Soon after we opened in the state, a retailer mentioned how a customer had recently asked for a nice white wine to serve with chicken. The retailer had recommended a muscatel—a sweet dessert wine!

When we entered Texas, the majority of the middle- and higher-income classes were not drinking much wine of any kind. The market growth that we generated among those consumers was due to effective advertising, promotion, and the interest and cooperation of Texas retailers.

On that same trip, I stopped in Odessa to see our distributor Phil Terk and his son, Dave, who was just starting out in his father's business. At a celebration dinner, young Dave stood up with a glass of wine in hand to make a toast.

"Here's to you, Ernest Gallo. You're not only the first winery, distillery, or brewery president to ever come to Odessa, you're also the only one who ever came back!"

From there, I flew 150 miles to a place called Four Corners, aptly named because a four-way stop served as the entire downtown. This was just the kind of out-of-the-way place I liked to check on.

There was a liquor store on each corner. I went in, looked around, and talked to the retailers. None of them could believe that an owner of a large California winery would drop into such a small, isolated place to visit.

I've never been back to the Four Corners since, but I'm told that as a result of my trip, all four stores there are almost exclusive Gallo accounts.

Julio

One Saturday in late '55 or early '56, Sales and Marketing asked for a special tasting in Production. They said they would bring the wine.

Fenderson arrived with Harry Bleiweiss, one of our San Francisco salesmen, who had volunteered to study the Los Angeles market for us. In a paper bag they had a bottle of white port and a bottle of concentrated lemon juice.

With clean glasses lined up in front of us, Bleiweiss went to work. First, he opened the white port and poured some into the sink. Uncapping the lemon juice, he poured some directly into the bottle of wine — refilling it.

My winemakers and I watched with great interest.

Fenderson explained that they had just returned from a marketing survey in Los Angeles. Along with Bleiweiss, he had been trying to figure out why our white port was not selling well.

"White port is popular," Fenderson explained, "but not our white port. Not in Los Angeles or anywhere. The consumers in L.A. have become loyal to a local brand called Santa Fe. No other white port will do. But, Julio, there's something else going on."

This was turning out to be a pretty good story.

174

"Some guys are taking their white port," Fenderson went on enthusiastically, "drinking four or five ounces out of the bottle, then filling the bottle to the top with lemon juice."

Bleiweiss poured the white port–lemon juice concoction into glasses for us. I reached for mine and sipped it. I tasted it a second time to be sure.

"You know," I offered, "the trouble with white port is that it's too sweet. When they add lemon juice, it cuts that sweetness and improves the sugar-acid balance."

I took another taste. "They make a better wine out of it. They're pretty good winemakers."

"Our idea," Fenderson said, "is to mix it for them in the bottle."

I asked for comments from our winemakers. They thought we could come up with a product that had the ideal sugar-acid balance along with the lemony flavor.

"Tell Ernest we'll give it a try," I said.

We experimented and conducted many in-house tastings of our potential new product. One thing we learned over the years with new products was to be careful with our own enthusiasm. When you sip a pleasantly sweet wine at a tasting for the production team, you can easily get fooled into thinking that everyone will surely like it. But when it goes out on the market the consumers find it too sweet to drink by the glass, let alone have a second glass. We learned to proceed cautiously.

We experimented and came up with a clear, grape-based, fortified wine product that when served chilled in comparative testings was described by consumers as tasting like champagne, or like a tall, cool highball, or even like a cordial. It was not a white-port product at all, but something entirely different: wine with citrus flavoring added. The taste was very similar to the mixture Harry Bleiweiss had made for us.

Our new product led the way under a change in federal law—effective January 1955—that for the first time allowed wine other than vermouth to be made with natural flavors added. Through the Wine

Institute we had lobbied the government for the change in the law, whereby the addition of pure natural flavors to wine was permitted without payment of a special tax. We took the long-term approach: The change would open up opportunities for wineries to make products desired by a greater number of consumers.

We ended up making a stream of new products in the area of special natural flavors.

New products, of course, meant new customers.

Ernest

After Julio and his staff developed our new lemon-flavored product, Fenderson and I personally tested it in several markets.

We soon became convinced that we had something worth pursuing: a flavorful drink that would be enjoyed by a broad spectrum of consumers — including the retired and elderly on fixed incomes — as a less-expensive, lower-alcohol alternative to the popular evening cocktail.

Several months later, though, we still had no name for our new product. In fact, for the first time ever we held up product release because we couldn't find the right name. But then, we had never had a product quite like this one before.

Flying back from a market survey in Texas one morning, Fenderson and I began brainstorming names for our new product. This was nothing new: Every spare moment we tossed names out, hoping one would stick.

Though we had considered hundreds of names, none of them had clicked for me. I wanted a proprietary name that was different and totally American. This was a brand-new American wine and I felt strongly that it should stand on its own without borrowing from other brands or winemaking regions. But I was beginning to wonder if I would recognize the right name when I heard it.

"Ernest, I think I have it," Fenderson said at fifteen thousand feet somewhere between Dallas and Modesto. "It's a radically different kind of name for a wine befitting the radically different kind of wine it is. It's all-American and has an image of quality, prestige, and contemporary styling."

"So what's the name?" I asked.

"Thunderbird!" Fenderson exclaimed.

I knew instantly. "That's it."

It was an upscale, all-American name.

In May 1957 we test-marketed Thunderbird in four cities: Los Angeles, New York, Houston, and Shreveport. The brand was an overnight success, almost without any help from us. There was no advertising or point-of-sale material to speak of.

Thunderbird was such a resounding success that there was no question about making it national as fast as we could, which we did in the next few months.

In Los Angeles we sold 19,000 cases of Thunderbird the first month—about the level it maintained from then on. The same thing happened elsewhere. In Houston it did 9,000 cases its first month. I had never seen a product that went from nothing to almost full growth in thirty days.

Results were the same everywhere, as we expanded our distribution market by market. Repeat orders from retailers, sparked by consumer demand, reached a point where it became a problem to keep our distributors supplied.

In no time we began hearing about the lyrics that were sweeping the country coast to coast, apparently having started in New York. "What's the word? Thunderbird. How's it sold? Good and cold . . . "

Fenderson and I were driving through Atlanta not long after. As we waited for a light at an intersection, I rolled down the window and shouted to a man on the street, "What's the word?"

"Thunderbird!" he yelled back.

Thunderbird was not yet on sale in Atlanta.

While Thunderbird had immediately appealed to the white-port-and-lemon crowd, when served as an over-the-rocks aperitif it also appealed to Middle America and to the younger, upscale suburbanite.

We developed upbeat television commercials, including one set in Las Vegas around the Thunderbird casino. "A wine so refreshingly new . . . Thunderbird will captivate you," was the lyrical message. We also advertised extensively in the print media.

Our success with Thunderbird gave rise to dozens of me-too products, none of which ever dented Thunderbird's success.

THE SUCCESS OF THUNDERBIRD WAS RESPONSIBLE for an important internal change in the Sales and Marketing departments. I had sensed something on one of my field trips that I came to understand was inevitable: When members of our sales force became excited about a new product, as we certainly wanted them to be, they could neglect existing products.

When Paisano first came out it was greeted with a great deal of enthusiasm by our winery reps and distributors' salespeople. The results were terrific. They worked hard at getting distribution, setting up displays, all the important things to help a product move. But when Thunderbird came out, they quickly switched horses.

I decided we needed to put somebody in charge of Paisano or it would go out of business.

Procter & Gamble, probably the best consumer-products marketer in the history of American business, had developed the concept of brand management in the late 1920s. It enabled a multiple-brand organization to deal with all of its products without losing track of them.

We applied the concept to the wine business.

We assigned a brand manager to each of our brands. A brand manager has a single responsibility: to support his or her product in all ways possible. With solid brand management, no brand gets lost in the shuffle.

. . .

A BREAKTHROUGH IN COMMUNICATION HAD BURST on the scene in the late 1940s that would change forever the way American industry sold its products.

Television antennas popped up on rooftops everywhere. With early television shows like *The Ed Sullivan Show* and *I Love Lucy* came the first TV commercials, and the beginning of mass marketing as we know it today. It didn't take a genius to recognize the selling power of television.

By 1950, there were 5 million television homes; three years later, 20 million; two years after that, 31 million.

With an effective commercial on television, a product could become well known nationally in a very short period of time. Prior to TV, we had no way of mounting such a quick-hitting campaign. Radio, billboards, and newspapers had less impact—for reaching the consumer, no other medium was as effective as television. As soon as we could afford it, we began advertising on TV.

In the beginning we used only one station, in Los Angeles. As our business grew, we extended our TV coverage to other markets.

Television dramatically changed the way consumers bought wine and other products in America. For the first time people were going into a store in great numbers and asking for a particular brand. There is no doubt that television helped us, and other advertised brands, get into stores. This said, the "silent recommendation" of the retailer (communicated via positioning and point-of-sale materials) was and is still vital.

We had hired a major advertising agency, BBD&O, in 1950 and had worked with them for five years. They launched our early TV ads. One was called the "Song of the Vineman" (1952), which utilized cartoon characters, "the little vinemen," who had grapes for faces and grape leaves for garments and wandered through vineyards singing songs. Now that I think of it, this commercial was similar in style and format to the more recent and quite popular California Raisins, who sang "I Heard It Through the Grapevine" for the California Raisin Advisory Board. Our singing vinemen, unfortunately, were not nearly as effective as the singing raisins.

We ended our relationship with BBD&O in 1955. (They were to come back and handle our account for another five years in the 1960s.) After trying for a short time to develop our own advertising, Fenderson set up a dinner for us to meet the principals of a new but highly regarded New York agency named Doyle Dane Bernbach. After dinner, but before Ned Doyle could get up to make a pitch for our account, I turned to Fenderson.

"Al, what do you think of this outfit?"

"They're the best in the business," he replied.

"Fine. Let's put them to work."

Doyle seemed disappointed that he didn't get to present his ideas. "Is that all?" he asked. "Is that it?"

"Yes," I said. "You fellows ready to get to work?"

After a tour of the winery, the agency's creative team latched on to the fact that we used only the first squeezing of the grapes to make wine, with the second squeezing used for distillation into fortifying brandies. Thinking this could be an effective product-superiority claim that would appeal to consumers, they built a whole campaign around it—for television, radio, newspaper, and outdoor ads. Thus, the TV ad copy for a new product, Gallo Grenache Rosé, went like this:

Under the California sun there are special vineyards that grow the celebrated Grenache grape. A grape that has been prized for seven hundred years for its unique flavor and its unmatched bouquet. From the precious Grenache grapes in these vineyards, Gallo uses only the finest juices, only the best-tasting juice, the juice from the first squeezings of the grapes. The first luscious juice that bursts forth goes into making Gallo Grenache Rosé. Gallo Grenache Rosé, a tangy dry pink wine. So light, so bright, so right, everybody's talking about it. Gallo Grenache Rosé is so new, so deliciously different, everybody likes it. Even people who don't normally like wine. Try it chilled, over ice, or tall, cool, pink, with your favorite mixer. Any way you drink it, it's wonderful. Gallo Grenache Rosé. The Grenache Rosé made from the first squeezing of the Grenache grape.

Grenache, a French variety first planted in California around 1850, is a sweet red grape with a flowery fragrance and distinctive spicy bouquet. We fermented the white juices along with the red skins for up to seventy-two hours in order to give the wine its pink hue. Grenache rosé required little aging. Bottled when young to preserve its fresh, fruity flavors and character, it was ready to drink, usually chilled, right away.

In the early days of television, I involved myself very intensively in buying time. After we had an approved commercial, I asked for the exact time the spot would air, on what program, which program immediately preceded the spot, which program followed it, and what the other commercials would be in the same "advertisement pod." We wanted to be the first commercial in the pod. We wanted to know the ratings of the shows immediately before and after our spot. We also took into account the subject matter of the shows. And since I believed in always knowing who my competition was, we looked to see which shows appeared opposite this time on the other stations in the market. Weighing all these factors, we would make a final decision as to whether or not to buy the spot.

We used a number of celebrities in the early days—sometimes finding a talent even before they became recognized by others. For instance, we ran a series of commercials for Paisano and other products using young up-and-coming opera stars—one of them a relatively unknown soprano named Beverly Sills.

Some other celebrities who appeared in our spots over the years included Jack Haley, Tab Hunter, James Mason, Alexis Smith, Lauren

Hutton, Pearl Bailey, Nancy Wilson, Sebastian Cabot, Cesar Romero, Peter Ustinov, José Ferrer, Linda Gray, Tom Selleck, Farrah Fawcett, Sally Struthers, James Brolin, Robert Vaughn, Rich Little, Dick Cavett, Robert Morse, and Zsa Zsa Gabor. Of course, they were not all well known at the time.

In 1962, BBD&O came up with the idea of a mythical singing "vineyard giant." We did not buy the concept as originally presented, but brought it down to earth, suggesting that we cast a real person who would sing while riding a horse through wine-country settings. This led to our first major casting problem: finding somebody who could satisfactorily represent our image to the rest of the world, and who could also sing and ride a horse.

It proved impossible to find anyone with all three qualifications, so we went with an actor named Don Kent, who could sing a bit and made a good impression as a rugged westerner. The former Los Angeles motorcycle policeman could not ride a horse, however. In fact, it was Julio who taught Kent how to properly mount a horse. Whenever the singing vintner was seen at a distance on a white charger in the vineyards, a young account manager from the ad agency rode the horse.

The spots featuring Don Kent, with his baritone voice singing "Come along with me to the wine country . . . Gallo makes wine with loving care . . ." to the tune of "Jimmy Crack Corn," turned out to be our most successful television commercials up to then. It was a turning point in terms of our TV advertising. Kent soon became the wine industry's best-known and best-liked spokesman. We bought time on *Maverick* and other popular shows. The campaign ran for several years and did more than any other previous national advertising to establish the name Gallo with the public.

I am told that Kent received lots of fan mail. Some of it was addressed to me or Julio from viewers who assumed that the handsome man on horseback had to be one of us.

13

SHIPS AND GLASS

Julio

Wine can be only as good as, never better than, the grapes used to make it. Cultivating better grapes was essential for our industry to keep advancing.

The winemakers who worked for co-op wineries had it especially rough: Often they didn't get their grapes, mostly Thompson Seedless, in until the grower-members were certain they couldn't be sold for anything else. Growers liked Thompsons because they could be sold to any one of the three markets for grapes: table grapes, wine, or raisins. The grapes sometimes had been picked a week or two earlier and were already starting to get moldy before being delivered to the winery. "How can anyone make good wine out of that?" the co-op winemakers would complain. They couldn't. I would never have allowed grapes in such poor condition to go through our crusher.

Though we believed in shopping for value as much as anyone, we let growers know that to us quality was more important than price.

Wines are not made, they are grown. Better grapes are costly, but they make better wines. Since it had become well known that we would pay more in order to get good wine grapes, we were usually able to get the best on the market.

In tough times there were wineries that paid a farmer less than it cost him to grow his grapes. I have always had a deep feeling for farmers who are trying to earn a living. I know from experience how hard they work and how many difficulties they face.

In 1957 it rained on the North Coast the entire growing season. It was the worst harvest anyone in Napa and Sonoma counties could remember. At first no one could get into the vineyards to pick the crop. Finally it stopped raining in time to try to save some grapes, but most of them were in bad shape. After inspecting every fermenting tank, the state condemned most of that year's vintage. Very little wine went to market that year. The rest could be used only as distilling material for fortified wines.

When it was raining so hard and everyone knew the grape prices were bound to drop, some winery owners were rubbing their hands together, saying, "Boy, we're gonna get to make wine cheap this year!" There were always those shortsighted vintners who were happy to see the bottom fall out of the grape market. I never felt that way. In fact, market instabilities worried me.

That rainy year, we paid full price for grapes as if they had all gone into table wine without a hitch. Several North Coast wineries were very unhappy with us. But if we hadn't paid our growers a fair return on their crops, a lot of them would have gone out of business right then and there—maybe even ripped out their vineyards to plant prune trees or something else.

I felt a responsibility to our growers. We had to help them every way we could.

·   ·   ·

Transcontinental trucking is a difficult way to ship a product as heavy as wine. Some states had, and still have, weight limitations for trucks on the road.

With no economical way to move wine long-distance other than by rail, the railroads had a real monopoly. By 1957, the railroads were making life miserable for us and other wineries shipping bulk wine and case goods east. The railroads kept raising their rates and we had no choice but to pay up if we wanted our products in those markets.

We protested, for all the good it did. Although the Interstate Commerce Commission had the final authority over freight rates, the railroads were generally able to set rates as they saw fit. They tried to squeeze as much as they could out of every industry that shipped by rail.

The next thing we knew, ISC's Lou Petri bought himself a ship. Well, half a ship. Petri purchased what was left of a tanker that during the war had split in half on a voyage. The front end had sunk, but the Navy had towed the back end up to Alaska. It had been brought down to Seattle to be junked and salvaged, when Petri bought it. He'd had it towed to San Francisco's Bethlehem yard to be rebuilt at a cost of $7.5 million—fitted with a new bow, and steel tanks to hold 4 million gallons of wine.

Petri's 23,000-ton tanker started making trips through the Panama Canal and into the Gulf of Mexico to the port in Galveston Bay. The wine was then loaded onto barges with glass-lined tanks, and barged to Chicago, where Italian Swiss had a bottling plant.

Ernest and I were worried. We would be paying higher freight charges than Petri, putting us at a real disadvantage with our top competitor.

Ernest was interested in buying a ship right away. He found three smaller ones that were being auctioned off in southern California. We flew down to take a look.

On the way, I told him that I was opposed to shipping bulk wine to different locations for bottling. That might be okay for Petri—in fact, ISC had for some time been bottling in the Midwest and the East—but I wanted no part of it. I'd have to spend much of my time on the road overseeing such operations, and even then I knew there would be problems with quality control.

Some years earlier, we had decided to do all our bottling in Modesto for these same reasons. Since then, I'd become even more of a believer. We were one of the few large wineries bottling and sealing our entire output at the winery in a sterile environment—a process that I personally supervised. Many other wineries still shipped bulk wine to local bottling operations, which could not provide the same standards of quality control and hygienic bottling.

If we shipped bulk, I was also concerned about finding the right "back-hauls," as it wouldn't pay to have a ship return home empty. It turned out that Petri was already having those kinds of problems. There were chemical companies interested in shipping back to California on the S.S. *Angelo Petri*, but Petri knew better than to put chemicals in tanks that held wine.

As it was, I found out later, when we hired winemaker George Thoukis, who had worked for a short time for Italian Swiss, that there had been trouble with some red wine that had gone east by ship for bottling. When bubbles showed up inside the bottles, they investigated and found soap mixed in with the wine. Someone had forgotten the rinse cycle.

"I'm against bottling outside Modesto," I told Ernest.

"Maybe what we should do is move case goods by ship," Ernest said.

The longshoremen, not yet mechanized, were still unloading ships by hand. I pointed out that our wine would be loaded and unloaded one case at a time. The longer a ship stayed at a loading dock, the more it cost.

When we arrived in San Pedro, we went aboard the three ships that were due to be auctioned the next day. They were rusty and not in good shape at all. They were also a little small—only about two hundred feet long.

"Maybe we should buy them," Ernest said.

"What?"

"If we buy them now, we can probably get all three for under a million. If we don't buy them today, we could lose them at auction tomorrow."

"I'm not ready to buy ships," I said. "What are we going to do with them, for Christ's sake?"

"We could always go fishing," Ernest said.

Ernest

The greatest remedy for disagreement is delay.

Through the years, whenever Julio and I didn't agree on something, we dropped it and then a few days or a week later discussed the subject again. By that time, we both had been able to think about it some. As a result, the best course often dictated itself. We never made a major decision about the winery that wasn't unanimous. It wasn't a matter of his way or my way being right. As a result of our exploring an idea thoroughly, we often came up with a third alternative that neither of us had originally seen as the best way to proceed.

For all I know, this is a kind of management style taught at Harvard Business School. I do know it works, and luckily for us, Julio and I took to it naturally. We always respected each other's point of view, even when we didn't agree, or maybe, *especially* when we didn't agree. This contributed greatly to the success of our partnership.

Returning to Modesto after checking out the three ships in San Pedro, we immediately looked into the economics of building and operating a suitable dry cargo ship for transporting case goods east. Like Julio, I wasn't willing to give serious consideration to bottling anywhere but Modesto, where we could supervise the operation.

When a study we had done on wine transportation pointed out the many difficulties and costs involved with moving case goods by ship, we looked into the possibility of barges, a far smaller investment. But after checking it out further, we learned that certain times of the year the weather on the stretch between Florida and New York could be very rough. In a storm at sea, I didn't want a load of our wine on a barge three hundred feet behind a tugboat tethered only by a cable as wide as my wrist.

I contacted the president of the Santa Fe Railroad.

I explained that as a result of Petri's ship, our principal competitor was able to ship his wines to the East Coast much cheaper than we could send ours by rail. Petri was therefore able to undersell us, and any other competition, by a considerable amount. I told the president of the railroad that we had been looking into the possibility of buying our own ship, and might do so unless the railroad could meet the reduced costs that Petri had gained.

The railroad agreed immediately to seek ICC approval to lower its rates 13 percent on case goods—a significant savings for a producer shipping by rail.

IT WAS DURING OUR DISCUSSION about buying a ship that Julio first brought up the idea of building a glass plant so we could make our own bottles, thereby reducing our costs.

At the time we were purchasing bottles from United Can and Glass Company, owned by the entrepreneur Norton Simon. When we had left Owens-Illinois—because they wouldn't make our bottles out of thin-walled, lightweight glass that would lower freight costs—we had gone with United Can.

United Can had given us a good price in the beginning. But then, from time to time, the firm's plant manager, Russ Meidel, would come in and deliver news like "The union just raised the rates we have to pay by three percent. We'll have to raise your prices five percent."

Before long, Meidel would be back. The cost of sand had gone up 2 percent, it seemed, and our prices were being raised 4 percent.

One day he came in with a big smile to say that we had taken up so much capacity of their plant that they would have to build a new furnace. "That's a big investment," Meidel said. "We'll have to raise your prices."

I told him I had had enough of his constant price increases. "You must be making an inordinate amount of money off us," I said. "I want a cost-plus contract. I'm willing to pay you ten percent over your costs."

"It'll cost you more that way than it does now," Meidel said. "We're not making that much on you now."

"Who are you trying to kid?"

Meidel said anytime I wanted to see the figures, he would show me their actual costs.

I think the offer came out of his mouth without any thought. Meidel did not expect me to take him up on his offer to see the records.

The next morning, I walked into his office at nine o'clock. Meidel was surprised to see me, but when I asked to see his costs, he reluctantly pulled out a spreadsheet.

Looking at the figures, I could see that their cost was very much lower than they were charging us.

I folded up the spreadsheet and put it in my pocket.

"Wait a minute," Meidel protested. "You can't take that."

"Why not? I have to show this to my brother."

I promised to return it the next day.

Instead of going back to Modesto, I drove across the bridge to San Francisco.

At Bank of America headquarters, I sat down with Fred Ferroggiaro, chairman of the loan committee. Ferroggiaro had been the industrialist Henry J. Kaiser's banker through the years, and had helped Kaiser get into the shipbuilding business during the war, even though Kaiser had never built ships before.

"Fred, I want to borrow four million dollars."

That was an awful lot of money for a company of our size at that time.

"What for?" Ferroggiaro asked.

"Julio and I want to build a glass plant."

"A glass plant!" Ferroggiaro shouted.

I thought Ferroggiaro would go through the roof. I might as well have been asking for a loan to build a rocketship.

I took the spreadsheet from my pocket. "This is a breakdown of the costs of making glass," I explained. "It is not an estimate. This is actual costs."

When Ferroggiaro asked where I got it, I told him.

I took him over some of the figures, showing how much less it cost to make glass than what we were paying to have it manufactured.

"But you guys are in the wine business. What the *hell* do you know about making *glass*?" Ferroggiaro was yelling.

"Fred, you're shouting."

"Oh, don't pay any attention," he said. "This is the way I talk when I get real excited."

I wasn't sure whether his excitement was a good sign or a bad sign.

"I'm telling you, Fred, the more I look at these figures, the more sense it makes."

"Let me see those figures again," Ferroggiaro said.

His voice was back to normal.

A few minutes later the banker looked up. "Okay, I'll give you the money."

When I returned Meidel's spreadsheet the next day, I told him that we wanted to be relieved of our existing contract unless they could supply glass for us at substantially lower rates.

"Impossible," he said.

"Then we want out."

"You'll have to talk to Mr. Simon about that."

Norton Simon, the owner of both United Can and Glass and Hunt-Wesson, its parent corporation, had a reputation for being a very astute businessman.

A serious collector of fine art, he pointed out a large painting on the wall as he showed me into his office. It was by one of the masters, and I wouldn't have been surprised if it was worth a million dollars.

Getting down to business, I told him what we wanted to pay for glass, and if he couldn't give it to us at that price then we would build our own glass plant.

"I've got a contract with you," he said.

"Yes, to make all our clear bottles."

I explained to him about our researchers having developed a formula for a green glass but that his people had said they couldn't make the type of green bottles we needed.

"We intend to make only this type of green bottle at our plant," I explained.

Simon knew a contractual loophole when he saw one. "So you've talked to the bank and they'll loan you money to build a glass plant?"

"Yes."

"What about a warehouse?"

"What warehouse?"

"You'll need a big warehouse for storing all your bottles after you make them. Before you fill them up."

"Then we'll build a warehouse," I said.

"I'll tell you what, Ernest." Simon was a very personable guy and he had stayed on an even keel. "If you can get financing to build the plant and a big warehouse to store your glass, I'll let you out of our contract."

Though Simon was not arrogant in the slightest, I knew he was counting on my not being able to borrow the money we would need.

"Sounds fair," I said.

We ended up building our glass plant and the warehouse—250,000 square feet with a storage capacity of two million cases. Our new green bottle, called "Flavor-Guard," quickly turned into a major product advantage as it blocked harmful ultraviolet light that damages wine.

True to his word, Simon canceled our contract.

Julio

Even after we got bank financing, there had been obstacles to building a glass plant. Only one company made the kind of specialized equipment we needed, and skilled glassmakers were not easy to find.

When it came to finding the right guy to run the plant, we got lucky. I had become friendly with Nick Franzen, a United Can plant superintendent. Franzen knew the glass business inside and out, and was about ready to retire. I approached him, saying how much we needed him to teach us the process. I asked if he would be willing to come to work for us to get our new plant going and train our people.

"Five years, Julio," he said. "No more."

That was better than I'd hoped for.

"That's fine, Nick," I said. "By then, we better know what we're doing."

I didn't tell Franzen, yet, who I planned for his chief apprentice to be.

The previous spring, in '56, Aileen and I had driven to Oregon to see our oldest son, Bob, who would graduate that June from Oregon State with a degree in business technology.

Bob owed the Navy a year of active duty after graduation. When I asked what he might want to do when he came to work for the winery after his military service, Bob dropped a bombshell.

"Dad, I'm not coming to the winery," he said.

Bob went on to explain that he had been recruited on campus by a national company and how they had given him an offer to join them after the Navy—an offer he couldn't refuse.

I was floored.

I'd always assumed that Bob, our eldest of three, would join the family business. It wasn't as if we would be doing him a favor by giving him a job. I had known for some time that he had good instincts for business.

Since childhood, Bob had shown real ingenuity. When he wanted to earn money for a car at a faster rate than he could make it doing odd jobs at the winery, he started collecting scrap metal, one of the first products to be recycled in this country for profit. I had given him permission to gather scrap metal at the winery, left-over pieces from old copper stills that had been torn out, that kind of stuff. I never pried into what his plans were for reselling the metal or even if he had a market for it.

One day Bob said, "Dad, I sold my scrap metal." He showed me a check from a recycler made out to him.

I was impressed.

"You made all that from scrap metal?" I asked.

Bob smiled proudly.

"Good work, Bob. Now, after you go to the bank to cash it, remember to give your cousins David and Joe half of it."

Bob's face fell. "Why? They didn't help me."

"Ernest and I always split whatever we make at the winery. You made this off winery property so the same split applies to you. You'll be in the business someday with your cousins and they'll do the same for you."

After he paid his cousins, Bob had enough left over to buy an old Chevy convertible.

Growing up, the boys had vineyard rows to hoe in the summer. I assigned them a few rows each day, and when I came home from work I would drive by and count the rows they had done. One evening, Bob had not touched his hoeing.

When we sat down to dinner, I said, "By the way, Bob, you didn't get your rows hoed."

He came up with some excuse.

"Wait a minute," I said. "You know you have that responsibility. You have to do it."

"I'll do it tomorrow."

"No. You better go do it now."

After that, Bob made sure to get his rows done while there was still plenty of daylight.

Through the years, I had taken for granted that Bob wanted a career at the winery. Now, as he was about to graduate from college, I asked why he didn't want to join the family business.

"I want to do something on my own," he explained. "The winery is already organized and I don't want to come in as your son and step on anyone's toes."

I tried to assure him that he wouldn't, but his mind seemed made up.

On the ride home that spring, Aileen could tell I was upset. I hardly spoke a word.

What could I challenge Bob with? I'd kept thinking. *Something that would cause him to want to join us.* I needed to come up with something new that he could sink his teeth into—even become our expert in.

Bob had gone off into the Navy, and then, shortly before he was due to get out, Ernest and I began talking about building the glass plant.

I realized: *That's it.*

When I proposed to Bob that he learn the glassmaking business from the ground floor up, with Nick Franzen as his teacher, he went for it.

Within a few years, Bob was our in-house glass expert. He eventually became president of Gallo Glass as well as part owner. Ernest and I set up the plant as a separate entity not connected to the winery. We allotted our children equal shares of ownership. We gave our brother, Joe, the opportunity to invest on behalf of his three children. We saw it as a good investment for the next generation.

Not only were we saving money on our bottles, but unlike Petri, we could claim that all our wines were bottled in California.

In my mind, we now had the advantage.

MY JOY IN HAVING BOB AT MY SIDE was offset terribly the following year when our younger son, Philip, took his own life in October 1958. Phil had been in psychiatric therapy for years as a result of severe emotional problems.

Our youngest child was a sensitive and intelligent boy—the high-school vice principal had told us that Phil had tested with one of the highest I.Q.s they had ever seen in an incoming freshman. A strong and husky boy, he had enjoyed art and seemed quite talented. After graduating from high school, he had been working in our production lab. The previous summer, Phil had been Bob's best man.

Philip's loss was devastating to Aileen and me, and of course to Bob and Sue.

We buried him at St. Stanislaus Cemetery, not far from the grandparents he never met. Phil was nineteen.

14

TO THE TOP—AND
BEYOND

Julio

Our daughter, Susann, two years younger than Bob, followed him to Oregon State, where she majored in Home Economics.

When she was about sixteen, Sue had announced plans to become a nun. Naturally, we suggested she finish school before making such a decision. At college she met Jim Coleman, of Corvallis, Oregon. Sue and Jim (the son of Vera and Alfred Coleman) were married in September 1957. Aileen and I became grandparents for the first time in June 1958, when Sue gave birth to a girl, Christine. My daughter, instead of becoming a nun, ended up giving us eight grandchildren.

My first grandson was born nine months after Philip's death. I remember the first time Sue brought the new baby over for a visit. I had always been a little uncomfortable holding a small baby, but I took Gregory in my arms right away and stepped outside with him. He was asleep, and didn't let out a peep as I walked with him alone through our backyard garden, alongside the vineyard that Ernest and I had leveled in the winter of '29. Though I've always had high hopes for all the grandchildren, I couldn't have dreamed what a determined young man Greg would grow into and how he would, in a real sense, lead us into the future.

After his discharge from the U.S. Navy, Bob married Marie Damrell, a Notre Dame (Belmont, California) graduate and daughter of Judge Frank and Mae Damrell of Modesto. Bob and Marie, who had taught elementary school in San Francisco, also gave us eight grandchildren, starting in 1959 with their first, Julie. They ended up with four boys and four girls, as did Sue and Jim. We always try to equalize things in this family.

By the way, Bob assigned his sons hoeing duties too, with each boy given a differently colored ribbon to tie on a vine at the front of his row. That way Bob could tell, as he drove by on his way home, who had done his chores.

Sue's husband, Jim, who had a degree in business administration, went to work for a publishing company in Portland for a year, then came to work for the winery. After he worked in Sales for a short time, I asked him to come to work in Production, where he got involved in managing, bottling, and shipping. When we started having problems with the liners of pilfer-proof caps we were buying from Alcoa, we decided to begin making our own closures. Jim started that department for us, and we eventually spun it off into Mid-Cal Aluminum, a separate business of which he became president. His responsibilities expanded through the years, as did Bob's. Like Bob, I made sure Jim worked his way up, and in time he became responsible for production at the Modesto winery. I believe that in order for a person to be able to manage a department, he has to start at the bottom.

IN 1959 I TOOK A TWO-MONTH TRIP to Europe to survey vineyards, wineries, and winemaking equipment.

The greatest technical progress had been made in West Germany. Germany led everyone else—including France and Italy—in modern winemaking techniques and equipment. I understood they had had a similar technological lead before World War II.

As for the rest of Europe, it was still stuck in the past, with old-fashioned equipment and methods.

I was disappointed in the quality of most of the wines generally available to consumers in Europe. The exceptional wines, produced in occasional favorable vintage seasons from exclusive vineyards, received all the publicity. But they were only a fraction of the continent's total production. And they were very expensive, beyond the means of most citizens. The lower quality of everyday table wines that most of the people drank surprised me. It was the reverse of what we were trying to do in this country.

In our effort to draw greater numbers of people to the moderate use of wine, we were concentrating on producing quality wines at affordable prices. In much of Europe, where the consumption rate was up to ten times greater than in the United States, they already had their customers.

I came home and told Ernest that based on what I had seen, our vineyards and winery were among the most efficient in the world in every phase of production. We spared no expense in acquiring the best grapes. We had the most modern facilities. We had the best-equipped research laboratory and the largest staff of qualified researchers. And we had the best quality control in the industry.

As I looked ahead to the new decade, our company seemed to be in a good position to succeed in giving quality wine to consumers at reasonable prices.

Ernest

During my first term as chairman of the Wine Institute (1957–58), I summarized at our annual membership meeting some of the recent progress the industry had made. The list was long, with credit due many. Among the accomplishments I cited:

- Credit for first developing the light red-wine type we call "Vino" belonged to Guild Winery.
- Credit for developing rosé wines belonged to several people — especially to Almadén.
- For introducing cold fermentation, which had improved our white wines, credit went to the wineries of the Napa Valley: Louis Martini, the Mondavis, Beaulieu.
- For improving our white wines by bottling them young, we owed much to the wineries of both the Napa and Santa Clara valleys — as well as UC Davis, which had helped significantly in all of these developments.
- For pioneering ion-exchange resins to make wines cold-stable without oxygen pickup, credit goes to Wente Brothers.
- For improved methods of pressing white wines, Martini and Christian Brothers.
- White vermouth was pioneered by Cresta Blanca.

I also gave credit to Lou Petri, whose tanker ship saved the industry millions of dollars in transportation costs because it had provided the leverage for us to force the railroads to lower their rates.

We had done a few things ourselves. Our continuous improvement of vineyard and winery practices had contributed to the advancement of the state's grape and wine industry. We had introduced modern merchandising techniques and advertising budgets comparable to those supporting sales of other leading consumer products. We had also built the most modern glass plant on the West Coast, which resulted in keeping glass costs down, not only for ourselves but for the rest of the industry. (Due to the competition, glass prices were no longer subject to unwarranted increases.)

In the process, we had become the leading winery in the United States. In 1959, we sold 24 million gallons of wine—making us number two, behind United Vintners. The following year, we pushed over the 30-million-gallon mark to attain first place. However, it was not until 1966 that we moved into first place to stay.

In my farewell address as chairman of the Wine Institute in 1959, I stated that I did not agree with those who felt that our industry's increase in sales over the last five years—a gain of only 9 percent over the previous five years—was adequate progress. Not in the face of a 10 percent increase in population, and not in the face of a 30 percent increase in purchasing power during the same period. "And," I added, "emphatically not when we consider the superior value our product, wine, has to offer the American public in comparison to other alcoholic beverages.

When I note that this country is now consuming annually over 2.6 *billion* gallons of beer, 212 million gallons of distilled spirits, and only 149 million gallons of wine, I must ask myself: Why? *Why* is there so much more beer and liquor sold in this country than wine?

Let us look into why people choose to serve and drink each of the three kinds of alcoholic beverages—beer, liquor, and wine. There seem to be four principal reasons:

•For the taste
•For the relaxing effect
•As a social beverage, the choice being influenced by social prestige
•Reasons of health

Let us examine each of the three kinds of beverages from these four standpoints.

As for beer: Some people may drink it for the taste. As for its effect, I would say that beer is refreshing. But few, if any, drink beer for social prestige. You seldom hear of anyone drinking beer for his health.

As for distilled spirits: Few drink liquors for their taste. This is shown by the increasing use of vodka, and by the preference for lighter-bodied whiskey blends. There can be no doubt that their principal use is for effect. Liquors do have social prestige. As for health, relatively few people drink liquor for that reason.

Now, what does wine offer? In taste, wines are the most delicious of all alcoholic beverages. The dozens of wine types offer many separate and distinct pleasing flavors.

We all know that wine's effect is relaxing.

In social prestige, wine ranks the highest of all beverages, but unfortunately the particular segment of society that serves wine is, if anything, *too* high socially to influence or set a pattern for the average American family. The social appeal of wine is not getting over to most people in this country.

As for wine's health benefits, I summarized the findings of a number of early medical research projects, including:

- Dr. Eric Ogden, UC Berkeley, 1940—Found that wine stimulates digestion.
- Dr. Franz Goetzl, Permanente Foundation, 1953—After six years of experiments with hospital patients who suffered from lack of appetite, found that table wines taken with meals caused these patients to increase their food intake by more than 50 percent.
- Dr. Theodore Althausen, UC Berkeley, 1956—Found that a substance in table wines markedly helps absorb hard-to-digest fatty foods, thereby helping people who suffer from "nervous indigestion."
- Drs. Leon Greenberg and John Carpenter, Yale, 1957—Discovered

that wine materially diminishes the basic level of emotional tension, and has the properties of a natural tranquilizer.

Just a few weeks prior to my speech, Dr. Agnes Fay Morgan, UC Berkeley, had released findings suggesting that wine may prevent hardening of the arteries, the principal cause of heart disease. Experimenting with animals, she found that those given wine had significantly less cholesterol in their blood than those given an equivalent solution of alcohol.

That most Americans had not heard of these findings was, I said, "not the fault of our advertising, because under federal advertising regulations it is not permissible to advertise any medical or health claims for any alcoholic beverage. Anybody who has ever seen the kind of liquor ads that used to appear before Prohibition understands why the regulations prevent it."

I had looked up some of those old-time ads, and I told my fellow vintners about them: "In one, Rainier beer advertised itself with a picture of a woman holding a glass high like a crown of jewels and the words 'Rainier Bottled Beer—To it I owe my health—More strength and vigor in a single bottle than in a barrel of ordinary beer.' "

Ads for Canadian Club whiskey claimed it was "particularly adapted for medicinal use." Those for Duffy's Pure Malt Whiskey called it "Medicine for all mankind—The only absolutely pure malt whiskey which contains medicinal, health-giving qualities." Ads for Rock & Rye read: "For all bronchitis, consumption and all diseases of the throat and lungs—Put up in quart size bottles for family use."

Wine ads weren't free of such hyperbole. Good Samaritan California port wine and brandy ads read: "Recommended by physicians—Strengthening after illness—Possess tissue-building qualities not found in ordinary wines and brandies."

"No wonder that federal regulations were written to prevent that kind of advertising," I continued. "It is a good thing for our industry and for the public that government regulators in Washington have done such a good enforcement job in preventing that kind of advertising since repeal. Such advertising would only mislead the public, promote intemperate drinking, and provide the 'drys' with ammunition. Moreover, the health claims made before Prohibition were without scientific proof."

Personally, I believe in the health values of a moderate use of wine. At the time I made those remarks (in 1959), modern science had only begun to find evidence of wine's health benefits. Today, of course, we know much more, with leading scientific researchers at Harvard, UC Davis, and elsewhere providing indisputable proof of the health benefits of the moderate consumption of wine. As I look back now, maybe we have been very negligent these past forty years in not working to get word of these healthful benefits of wine out before the American public.

In closing my farewell remarks, I pointed out that the American public generally didn't know or appreciate the many virtues of wine. "It is not any lack of desirability in our product that causes ours to be only a baby industry in comparison to the beer and liquor industries.

"On the basis of product desirability, we should have an industry many times its present size."

We now had a steady stream of distributors from different areas coming to us and inviting us to enter their markets. Our first responsibility, as always, was to those we were already working with to build our business in their areas.

Our wholesalers were—and are—vital to our business. Each one is a link in the chain. Without them, we are dead in the water.

Through the years, I sensed that some of our competitors felt differently. They seemed to think: We sell our wine to the distributor and it's his job to sell to the retail trade. They would occasionally send someone around to tell him when he wasn't doing a good job, but they would leave it up to the distributor to correct the problem. If he didn't, they shrugged and either stayed with the distributor or went elsewhere. I have always believed that so much of selling is building relationships. When a distributor has a problem, it becomes our problem. And when they are successful, so are we.

By mid-1959, our distribution extended to slightly more than half the nation—thirty-one states.

I had long been anxious to enter the large Pennsylvania market. It was a very competitive situation, however: It would be difficult to obtain a fair market share for a new brand in a reasonable time and at an acceptable cost.

I finally decided the best way to get into Pennsylvania was to buy an existing brand. Bartolomeo Pio, Inc., which owned the popular "Pio" brand and Pio Winery in southern California, was for sale. As soon as we purchased Pio, we put "Gallo" on the label in small print and kept the "Pio" name its regular size. Gradually, over a period of several years, we made "Pio" smaller and "Gallo" larger. Eventually, we were able to eliminate "Pio" from the label altogether, successfully completing the "transition" of an existing brand to our own while maintaining all of Pio's customers.

We did the same thing in Indiana. We bought a top-selling local brand called Melody Hill and transitioned it successfully to Gallo over a period of a couple of years.

Illinois came next. With Italian Swiss Colony again dominating the market, we decided to use the same strategy we had used in Texas. The "dual supplier" concept, which we attribute to a professor of marketing at Memphis State and refined to suit our needs, worked especially well in markets with one large competitor. Our entry gave the retailer two suppliers he could play against each other for higher margins, increased advertising, and better promotions.

Fenderson liked to call this tactic "marketing jujitsu." It allows you to take on an entrenched competitor directly at his strength while at the same time giving you leverage in the market almost overnight.

It usually worked.

For lack of any real competition, Italian Swiss had 90 percent of the wine business in Chicago when we entered the market. Looking at Chicago, I realized that we probably couldn't sell more wine than was already being sold in that market. The best we could hope to do was to take business away from Italian Swiss. But in the outlying areas and the rest of the state, we again set out to expand the general wine market through aggressive advertising and merchandising.

Canvassing Chicago for a potential distributor, we talked to wholesalers who were either too big and not excited about working with us, or were unwilling to make the investment necessary to handle our full line. I decided that we should open our own distributorship for our entry into Chicago.

We set up Edgebrook Distributing; the owners were Al Fenderson; our advertising manager, Howard Williams; our national sales manager, Ken Bertsch; and Jon Shastid, an extremely bright financial expert who had joined us several years earlier. (While working for us full-time, Shastid went to night school to study law. He didn't tell me until he passed the bar exam. We expanded his duties then to include legal work as well as finances.) It hadn't been difficult to come up with the name of the new company: Three of the four lived on Edgebrook Drive in Modesto.

Fenderson brought in recruiters and hired a sales force, then put together a team of top sales managers to train the new people. He and Bertsch selected the top eighty liquor retailers in Chicago, and hit the streets for the first time in January during a bitter cold snap. They formed into two-man teams, with at least one member an experienced salesman. All of our sales executives from Modesto were involved— even Bertsch and Fenderson were on the street, helping to convince retailers that we had the "hottest brand of wine" in the country and it was really going to sell.

Chicago is a "deal" town.

"Okay, what's the deal?" retailers would ask.

We'd say: "We are going to sell you our wine at the list price."

They'd say: "At the *list* price? Are you crazy? We don't pay list price. I want a *deal*."

Alcoholic-beverage retailers in Chicago were among the toughest customers we ever faced. Most of them had been in business since the repeal of Prohibition. We had to convince them that by helping us they would be creating healthy competition that would eventually enlarge their margins and double their wine sales.

For openers, we wanted each of the top retailers to take thirty cases of wine and give our wines the best shelf space in the wine department—at least adjacent to but if possible, above ISC's position. The only incentive we offered the retailer was the profits he could expect when Swiss finally found itself facing a strong challenge in the marketplace. These dealers had never heard of being asked to take on a new item without some kind of introductory deal. And our other requirements seemed equally brazen to them.

That first day, one of the salesmen got the idea to chip in a few dollars each into a pool and the first person to sell 100 cases would win $100. Fenderson and his teammate hurried back in a few hours with orders for 100 cases, certain they had won. But they had been beaten to the finish line by supersalesman Pat Rondinella. We didn't find out until later that Rondinella had gone out to Cicero and sold 100 cases to his cousin who owned a liquor store. At that point, everyone was interested in knowing exactly how many cousins Rondinella had.

That first day, they sold fifty to sixty of the top Chicago retailers at least the minimum 30 cases and obtained everything we asked for. We seemed to be on our way.

But a year later, I was disappointed in the distribution of our products in the thousands of smaller stores and on-sale locations (restaurants with wine lists) in Chicago. In order to get the kind of intensive distribution we wanted, we closed Edgebrook Distributing and went with one of the big distributors. This was not our usual pattern. Our distributor, Joe Fusco, one of the giants in the business, had many large liquor lines and several national wine brands.

Fusco had graduated from driving bootleg beer for Al Capone to managing his own large, legitimate wholesale liquor business.* I knew that the fewer questions you asked someone with such a background, the better. But when one of them decided to tell a colorful tale about "the old days," you listened.

One night in Chicago, Fenderson and I were having dinner with Fusco at a place he had recommended that specialized in wild-boar meat. Also at the table was my youngest son, Joe, then not quite twenty and still an undergraduate at Notre Dame.

At the time, one of the most popular shows on television was *The Untouchables.* Joe had just watched a recent episode about Eliot Ness breaking up an illicit beer operation. In the end, the agents drove through the wooden doors of a warehouse in a truck with a battering ram.

"Mr. Fusco, was that a true story," Joe asked enthusiastically, "the way the G-men put the Mob out of the beer business?"

Apparently, Fusco had seen the show too. "That was a lot of bunk," he said, shaking his head. "Not true."

Fusco then commenced to tell how Ness would find out where Fusco's camouflaged beer-delivery trucks were headed and "knock 'em off" en route.

"So what did you do then?" Joe asked.

---

*Though Fusco was indicted along with Al Capone in 1931 on violations of the federal prohibition laws, he was never convicted. In 1950, Fusco gave testimony before the Senate committee investigating organized crime, chaired by Estes Kefauver. Ten days later, one of Fusco's liquor warehouses was bombed.

"We started using cars. We'd put two barrels at a time in the trunk. It was a slow way to haul merchandise, but we got the job done for a while. Until they started stopping our cars too . . ."

Though a few details varied, the ending of Fusco's story was pretty much the same as the TV show Joe had watched—with Ness and his "Untouchables" forcing Fusco and his boss, Capone, out of the illicit beer business.

Fusco's sales force gave us good saturation in the Chicago market. But I soon became discouraged by having to wait in line with other suppliers—big liquor concerns as well as numerous wine companies—to address his huge sales force. Usually, by the time I came to the podium the salesmen were tired of pep talks and anxious to leave.

I decided to try to find the "hungriest" distributor in Chicago. One we visited was Morand Distributors, a pre-Prohibition liquor house that still had a pre-Prohibition warehouse. Everything about this operation, owned by the Romano family, was antiquated. They had limited resources and no sales force of any consequence. They carried odds and ends of whiskeys and wines but weren't doing much business. The owner was getting along in years but he had two sons working for him. The Romanos struck me as honest and hardworking. But they didn't have any money and were stuck in those old facilities. Their warehouse was a small, three-story building in a residential neighborhood. They moved their case goods up and down in a tiny, slow-moving elevator.

Realizing that if we helped them modernize their business, we would become very important to their operation, I made them our Chicago distributor.

Before long, Michael and Buddy Romano demonstrated their unique abilities and were so successful in developing our brands that they rapidly outgrew their small facilities. I telephoned a Santa Fe Railroad official I knew and asked if they had a piece of property along their tracks that the Romanos could buy to build a warehouse. Once we had several possibilities, we sent our engineering people to select the best site and design a large ground-floor warehouse. We then helped the Romanos negotiate a construction loan.

When the Romanos moved in, we sent them experienced office help to bring them into the modern age of accounting and billing, and a sales manager to hire and train their sales force.

We soon became the leading wine brand in Chicago.

The Romanos grew rapidly and became so efficient and effective that other suppliers of liquor and wine rushed to them seeking them as their distributor. We had no problem with the Romanos' handling other brands so long as they maintained a separate sales force and manager for our line, which they did.

The "dual supplier" concept, so successful in both Texas and Chicago, now became our principal strategy in the next ten or fifteen states that we entered.

But some of our ways of introducing ourselves into new markets were less sophisticated. Pat Rondinella's primary area of responsibility included the state of Kansas. Just after that state finally legalized wine sales, he won Kansas over for us with his own individual style.

Rondinella was a great personality with a lot of Italian charm, and a good salesman with a gimmick and slogan: "Have spaghetti pot, will travel." When he went into Kansas, he brought his pots and pans with him. His spaghetti and Sicilian-style homemade sausage were a real hit with the Kansas distributors.

Thanks to Pat and his spaghetti—his sauce was made with our Burgundy—we soon had a higher share of market in Kansas than we did in any other state we were in at the time.

WE CONTINUED TO SURVEY all of our markets.

Fenderson and I were flying one afternoon from San Antonio to Houston, where we were to start a survey the following morning. Inasmuch as it appeared we would be landing in Houston at about five P.M., and not wanting to waste the evening I had the pilot continue on to Beaumont, a half hour away, so we could make an impromptu survey.

We hired a driver at the airport and climbed into his taxi. I instructed our driver to park in front of each store as we hurried inside, walked through the store checking the shelves. Other stores were closed. We peered through the plate-glass window to look at the wines. We had some difficulty seeing brands in the dark, and we spent a few minutes at each stop with our hands up against the windows trying to see in.

Having seen what we considered a cross-section of the stores in Beaumont, we asked the driver to hurry us to Port Arthur. Just as we were leaving the city limits, we were pulled over by two police cars with flashing lights. One screeched to a stop in front of us and the other stopped right behind us.

A tall, lanky Texas Ranger type appeared. While watching us carefully in the backseat, he asked the driver for his current taxi license. The driver didn't have one.

The officer, apologizing to us, explained that he was going to have to drive the car to the station and get things straightened out. The officer had the driver move over to the passenger side. He slipped in and drove us to the police station, with the other squad car following.

When we got to the station, Fenderson and I were placed in separate interrogation rooms.

A sergeant came in to question me.

"Look," I said, "I'm Ernest Gallo of the Gallo Winery and we're here on business."

The sergeant looked at me, smirking. "Sure you are," he said. "And I'm John Wayne."

"I've got identification."

I pulled from my pocket several letters addressed to me in Modesto.

The sergeant looked at them. "What are you doing with these letters?" he asked suspiciously.

"I tell you I'm Ernest Gallo."

I found my driver's license.

The sergeant looked at it like it was a forgery. "When and how did you arrive here in Beaumont?" he asked.

"We flew into the airport about an hour ago."

The sergeant left the room. When he came back a few minutes later, he said there had been no recent incoming flights that afternoon.

"We didn't come on a commercial flight," I explained. "We came on my private plane."

"Oh, you flew in on your own plane."

"Yes," I said, glad to be making progress.

"What's the plane's tail number?" he asked suspiciously.

"The plane's tail number?"

When I had to admit I didn't know, the sergeant looked quite satisfied with himself.

I didn't even know my car license number, I explained, let alone the number on the company plane.

I told him the name of our pilot. "Please call the airport and check out my story."

Twenty minutes later, the sergeant came in full of apologies. The reason we had been picked up, he explained, was because there had been a liquor-store holdup a few nights before, and the police officers had thought we might be the robbers "casing" other stores.

That was the last time we peered through a liquor-store window at night after closing—at least in Texas.

But it wasn't the only time we had to deal with police. One time in Denver on a market survey, I reproved the driver, Dave Gasca, our winery representative in the state, for driving too slowly. He picked it up, but at the next light he started to brake when the light changed from green to yellow.

"Go right through," I ordered.

Gasca did.

We were immediately stopped by a policeman.

"You ran a red light," the officer said. "You'll have to follow me downtown."

"Officer, please just give us a ticket," I said.

"You must be from out of town," the officer answered. "Around here, you have to go right to the station house and appear before the judge."

"I'm in a great hurry," I said. "I'm here on business for only a few hours. Why don't you take the driver with you and leave me with the car? When I'm finished, I'll go to the courthouse and pick him up."

The officer shrugged. "Sure."

Off my employee went in the squad car.

I got behind the wheel and finished the survey on my own and at my own pace. Then I went to my hotel, washed up, and changed. I had dinner reservations that night in the hotel restaurant with some of our local people.

When I sat down, someone asked, "Where's Dave?"

I had completely forgotten about him!

Very embarrassed, I said, "I guess the police still have him."

THE CALIFORNIA TABLE-WINE BUSINESS as we know it today started in the 1960s.

We introduced our "Gourmet Trio": Chablis Blanc, Pink Chablis, and Hearty Burgundy, a smooth, full-bodied wine that attracted seasoned wine consumers.

That's not to say it was easy. Take Pink Chablis for example.

Our brand manager for table wines had suggested a rosé product for the line. I took the idea to Julio, and his production team developed a slightly sweet pink wine that tasted very good.

Using Los Angeles as a test market, we released Pink Chablis with a full-page ad in the *Los Angeles Times* and lots of point-of-sale support. It was a total dud.

On the verge of failure in 1965, Pink Chablis was not only saved but "made" by what was probably the most effective commercial we have ever run on TV.

Leo Burnett creative director Cleo Hovell, who had come up with the Hamm's bear for the "Land of Sky Blue Water" commercials, presented an idea that was different than anything we had ever tried. It was a "fantasy" commercial involving a handsome prince and a beautiful princess in a surreal royal-court setting. Hovell enthusiastically acted out all the parts off a storyboard.

ANNOUNCER: Once upon a time, a handsome prince poured a goblet of wine for a beautiful princess. It was a white wine. White as the waters of the crystal fountain. White as the diamonds in her crown. It was called Chablis.

PRINCESS: It's the finest wine in all the realm.

ANNOUNCER: And so great was her praise that the wine blushed pink. Now this legendary wine is re-created for you by Ernest and Julio Gallo. Pink like rosé, drinks like Chablis. Gallo Pink Chablis. The first really new table wine in years. The smart wine for young, modern tastes. Pink like rosé, drinks like Chablis. Pink Chablis.

Everyone on my marketing team liked it, offering comments like "wonderful fantasy," "romantic," and "high class." One proposed visual trick we couldn't see but which Hovell described in detail was how the white wine would turn pink right before the viewer's eyes.

I said, "That's it—let's make it as soon as possible," and left the room.

We sent a young assistant brand manager named Skip McLaughlin back to New York to be on the set while the commercial was being shot, to help with casting and set design. Though the process of making a commercial usually influences how well it turns out, this was one of those unusual cases where it was shot without a single change from the storyboard presentation.

We first ran the commercial in Los Angeles on a Friday night. Saturday afternoon, McLaughlin called me from Los Angeles to say that Pink Chablis was flying out of the stores. For months, the retailers had had stacks of unsold Pink Chablis sitting around. By Monday morning we were shipping more product. We quickly expanded to other cities, running our commercial with the product's release in each new market—and sales exploded.

Pink Chablis became a big hit overnight, thanks to that single commercial. It taught me that a great commercial moves product, and moves it quickly.

AT THIS POINT, THE U.S. WINE BUSINESS was still two-dimensional, consisting of dessert wines, whose sales had peaked and would head perceptibly downward, and the new generic table wines, which were on the rise.

Despite our progress, I was not satisfied. When we considered the tremendous opportunity that still existed for wine in the United States, I understood that we had as yet failed to make a large dent in what could be done. National consumption of wine remained only slightly higher than it had been five years earlier. While wine consumption in some countries in Europe ran as high as 50 gallons per capita, in the United States it was less than a gallon (1961).

To put this in perspective, Americans consumed more than ten gallons of tea per year—a beverage I once facetiously described as "hot water with leaves in it"—but drank just one tenth this amount of wine, a beverage Benjamin Franklin likened to "proof that God loves us and loves to see us happy."

The consumption figures didn't mean that a lot of Americans were drinking a little wine. Probably 15 percent of the people were drinking 85 percent of the wine in this country. At the same time, other alcoholic beverages were enjoyed by a good 70 percent of our population, so the fundamental market was broad enough to accommodate an expansion of the wine business several times over.

The wine market as we know it today was not the same in the fifties and sixties. A "typical American" would come home after work, turn on the new hifi or the new TV, and have a gin martini before dinner. During the evening meal, this "typical American" did not drink wine.

To make wine accessible and pleasing to more people, Julio's and my challenge now was to follow our "Gourmet Trio" and other successful products with more and better wines of consistent quality at moderate prices that the average person could afford.

Ours was a good beginning, but only that.

The real opportunities lay ahead.

BY THE LATE FIFTIES, Americans were showing an increased preference for carbonated beverages. Soft drinks were experiencing steady gains in consumption, and of course beer was the most popular alcoholic beverage in the United States. What we needed was a new, popular wine product that could bridge the gap between sweet soft drinks and beer.

The type of product I had in mind would have a pleasant taste, be low in alcohol, and be packaged in a single serving. Our consumer research on taste preferences also indicated that such a product should taste best when served cold, should continue to taste good after more than one serving, and should, if possible, be carbonated.

The Wine Institute had been able to get the tax law changed in 1959 to allow up to fourteen pounds of carbonation (a measure of air pressure) without the product's being subject to champagne tax, which is levied at a much higher rate. Fourteen pounds of carbonation was considered barely enough to be noticeable to the taste, but not visible to the eye.

In a page and a half, we wrote out the parameters for the new product that we had in mind. It should have a taste and alcohol content that would give it universal appeal. It should be packed in a small bottle. It should be merchandised in every licensed retail outlet in the country. It should be priced low enough to make it affordable to everyone in the market for such a product. And it should be supported by major merchandising programs: floor displays, P-O-S material, and so forth. If we did all of these things properly, I had an idea that the new product could be a very big-volume brand.

Research and Production came up with a sweet, pure grape wine that was slightly carbonated and designed to be served cold. The alcohol content of around 10 percent was low for a table wine, but twice that of beer.

We decided that this product should be sold in one size only: a "tenth" (12.8 ounces). Howard Williams and his merchandising staff developed a novel package design, which had a unique "swirl" design in the glass. The bottle perfectly fit the name we came up with: Ripple.

We launched Ripple in Los Angeles and New York with a major radio and television advertising blitz in January 1960. Williams once explained that not buying enough advertising for a new product was like buying three fourths of a ticket across the ocean. We gave Ripple the largest national kickoff campaign the wine industry had seen up until then. Sales of Ripple were excellent the first year, and peaked at 7.5 million gallons in 1970. Ripple was a major product for us during the late-sixties wine boom but soon faded out of existence.

MY OLDER SON, David, after graduating from Notre Dame with a degree in business administration, attended Stanford's MBA program before joining the winery in 1963.

David had worked part-time for the winery prior to college. He would tell me later that there had never been any doubt in his mind that he would come back to the winery when he finished school. "For as long as I can remember, I never thought of doing anything else," David said, to my great satisfaction.

Given the go-ahead to conduct an intensive study of the domestic champagne business — not only the marketplace but the various ways champagne is produced — David came to the conclusion that we were missing a significant opportunity. At the time there wasn't much of a champagne business in this country. Imports were available, of course, but at high prices only a small segment of the population was willing to pay. Essentially, champagne would be a new beverage for most Americans.

Legend has it that when Dom Pérignon, the Benedictine monk who discovered the champagne "method," first tasted his creation, he called to his fellow monks, "Come, brothers, I've tasted the stars." Champagne came to symbolize celebration.

"There's a big opportunity in this market that we're definitely missing," David told me with the enthusiasm he brings to most discussions. "No one is trying to provide a nationally marketed brand. We ought to get into this business right away, Dad."

He had done his homework, even projecting the number of cases he thought we could sell, what our price ought to be, which segment of the market we should enter, and the costs associated with making champagne by each method: the bottle-fermented *methode champenoise*, the transfer method, and the bulk-fermented Charmat method. He had properly noted that the market for domestic champagne had been small and growth had been stagnant before the mid-1950s. But then the growth rate of sales had begun to increase annually, even without any strong national brands. David thought that the domestic champagne industry was only at the beginning of its marketing potential, and that it could expand at a rate of 25 percent annually for the next several years.

Prior to David's report we had not been considering the champagne business. But by the time I finished reading his report and discussing it with him and others, I agreed that an opportunity existed for a lower-priced domestic champagne. The Charmat style of fermentation, in which the champagne is fermented in large tanks instead of individual bottles, would make possible the vending of quality champagne at prices the average family would find within its reach.

David had broken new ground for us. This wasn't the first or last time that I appreciated the importance of bringing new blood into an established organization. Sometimes the best ideas come from young people. They arrive with fewer assumptions that something cannot be done and are less bound by tradition. Often, one of the most difficult things to get is a fresh outside approach to a situation. Young people so often deliver that, when they see something that is obvious to them but that the rest of us have missed.

About that time, David had to leave to fulfill his military obligation. Before he went, I told him that Julio and I would be bringing in all the equipment necessary and setting it up during his absence. But I decided to hold off releasing our champagne until he came back to help market it. When David returned from the Army in 1965, we appointed him brand manager of our new product, and he immediately went to work on a detailed marketing plan.

Development of our product was the first step. It took a year to come up with a product, with Production and Marketing working closely together. We wanted a quality product, attractively packaged, which we could sell at a reasonable price.

Comparative fermentations in bottles versus larger containers were conducted by Charles Crawford and Dmitri Tchelistcheff. Numerous yeast cultures were studied to select the best performers. Different varieties of grapes were tried too. Follow-up work was done by Dr. George Thoukis to carry champagne production into a commercial operation.

Anyone who came to our house for dinner in those days was greeted with a number of brown bags. In the bags was an assortment of the best-selling American and French champagnes, plus the latest version of our new champagne. I invited guests to sample each once. All happily did so and rendered their verdicts. From these unofficial taste tests, we developed our new champagne.

Since one of the factors that determines the success of a new product is its name, we thought long and hard about possible names for our champagne. Though we had worked hard to convince the wine-buying public that Gallo could make good, dependable wine, we felt that since champagne was seen as a completely different product, consumers would not readily transfer our know-how to champagne. After considering hundreds of names, we settled on André de Montcort and Vintners of Eden Roc, and released champagne under both names.

David had become intrigued by cold duck, a Concord grape–based champagne, after he noticed its popularity at a restaurant in Michigan. A few wineries had started bottling the product. He insisted that we add a cold duck to the André de Montcort line. We did, and we used the opportunity to shorten the brand name to André. We introduced André Cold Duck in the fall of 1967, and followed in January 1968 with André Extra Dry Champagne, André Pink Champagne, and André Sparkling Burgundy. André Cold Duck was a resounding success. We sold 130,000 cases in 1968, 487,000 cases in 1969, and over 2 million cases in 1971. André Cold Duck introduced large numbers of new consumers to the pleasures of sparkling wine.

By 1971 we held 48 percent of the market for California sparkling wines, which had expanded from 1.6 million cases in 1966 to 6.8 million cases in 1971. Since then we have added a number of new sparkling wine products. In 1983, we introduced a slightly sweet sparkling muscat-like product we call Spumante Ballatore, named after our champagne master, Spir Ballatore. It has won us quite a few awards as well as praise from a number of wine writers.

By 1992, we had increased our share of the market for California sparkling wines to 54 percent.

15

THE SEARCH FOR EXCELLENCE

Julio

One of our priorities has always been to find new, improved kinds of grapes, and to incorporate them into our wines. Between 1948 and the 1960s we had experimented in Livingston with more than 650 clonal selections, including new hybrids as they had been released by UC Davis. (In grape growing, "cloning" means selecting individual branches of vines for their specific characteristic and propagating multiple genetically identical plants from them.) In our twenty years of studying grape varieties and making experimental wines in our small "pilot" winery, we had found many varieties new to the area that grew well there and made good wines.

In our own vineyards we had already ripped out all the old tough-skinned grapes so popular for shipping during Prohibition and had replaced them with better wine varieties. But we had trouble getting many growers to follow our example.

Growers were slow to act for a number of reasons. Good wine grapes yield much less per acre and cost more to produce than ordinary

grapes. Would the extra trouble and expense be worth it? they wondered. This kind of skepticism is in the nature of the breed: Some farmers are willing only to produce what there's a market for at the
moment, without looking ahead to the future. They are in a supply-
and-demand business, whether it's almonds, lettuce, or grapes. As long
as the demand exists at acceptable prices, they keep the supply coming.

For most grape growers, switching over to better varieties came
down to a matter of economics. Grafting over or replanting a producing vineyard costs a grower three seasons of income, as it takes that long
for new vines to mature. There's also the capital expense involved in
buying rootstock and vines, and paying for labor and equipment. In
1960s dollars, it cost about a thousand dollars per acre to plant a vineyard. It's never been easy borrowing money from a bank to replant a
vineyard. With reduced income for the next three years, a grower
could have trouble convincing a bank that he would be able to keep up
his payments. And when the new vines mature, how could the bank be
certain that the grower's crop would sell, or would bring a good price if
it did sell?

Even as growers began to see that in the long run it was advisable for
them to plant different varieties, most of them weren't in the financial
position to dig up their vineyards, replace the old vines with new varieties, and then wait three years for a crop. "Maybe next year," I heard
from one grower after another. The trouble was, "next year" never
seemed to come around. Some growers said if we wanted them to replant so bad, maybe we could loan them the money to do so. I hated
the thought of going into the banking business. Still, something had to
be done.

In 1964, the courts had killed the Fermenting Materials marketing
order, which would have helped to improve the quality standards of
grapes going into California wines. We had strongly backed this marketing order.

Our own repeated requests to growers that they support costly replanting were met with little enthusiasm. We didn't feel we could afford to wait around for the situation to sort itself out. A delay could be disastrous for our industry. None of us prospered when inferior grapes went into California wines. If wineries weren't able to supply consumers with the type of table wines they were beginning to be interested in, we might lose the opportunity.

In 1965, we had become the first winery in the state to establish a Grower Relations Department. We hired a professor of viticulture from California Polytechnic to head the program. Field men—eventually more than twenty—were hired and trained and sent around to our growers to suggest techniques that would result in higher-quality grapes. They did this not just for the two-month buying season but year-round.

We had hoped—in vain, it turned out—that through our Grower Relations effort growers would be convinced that they needed to grow better varieties. But in 1967, after two years of hands-on work with our growers, they were still reluctant to graft over their poorer-quality grapes to better varieties, or to plant new vineyards in the varieties that we knew would grow well in their area and make better wines.

My brother and I agreed that something more had to be done. The only way we were going to get growers to replace their vines was to guarantee to make it worth their while.

We shocked the industry by offering long-term contracts to growers who would plant better varieties of grapes. Beginning after the 1967 season, we gave contracts to growers who would pull out Thompson Seedless, for example, and plant fine-wine varieties. We selected the varieties we wanted growers to plant on the basis of which grapes grew best in their viticultural region. All these wine-grape varieties we had first tested in Livingston, and we knew they grew well. This was another instance in which our own testing and research showed us which direction to go.

That first year, our contracts guaranteed growers a minimum price or market price, whichever was more, for periods of ten to fifteen years. These guarantees were tied to quality standards, and the contracts allowed for bonuses based on quality. If the quality was there and we could use the grapes in our best table-wine programs, then growers would be paid top dollar. However, if we notified a grower prior to harvest that the quality of his grapes was sufficient only for our dessert wines or distilling programs, we would pay him a reduced price or he could deliver them to another winery.

There had been nothing like this in the wine industry before. There was a lot of grumbling by other winery owners, though not much of it to my face. I got reports of complaints that we were not "playing fair" and were "giving the growers too much money." Some wineries preferred to keep the growers guessing from one year to the next.

Growers, many of them fearful about more market instabilities, lined up to sign our contracts. The security our contracts offered meant growers could count on having a home for their grapes. They could even take the contract to the bank as collateral for loans that would allow them to replant. They found the banks willing to lend them the money required for vineyard replanting when they could show that they had a guaranteed sale of their grapes at a profitable price for a long time down the road.

The New York Times reported: "The Gallo program will probably be welcomed by most of the rest of the industry. Gallo is saying, 'We're going to help finance you to convert your vineyard to a good wine variety. It will help you to make more money, help us make better wine, and make the consumers happy.' "

That about covered it.

I have heard it said by people inside and outside our company that this was our major contribution to the production end of the California wine industry. They might be right.

Getting the "right" selected varieties in the ground was key, but we wanted more. Our contracts obligated growers to follow the improved cultural methods we had tested in Livingston and were practicing in our own vineyards. In the past, a grower who had been raising grapes for dessert wines had mostly been concerned about tonnage. Grape quality meant very little to him, or to the wineries he sold to. With increased plantings of quality wine grapes, that would have to change. Again, we made it worth the growers' effort. Provided that a grower would follow the viticultural practices we established, he would receive a bonus over the standard price for quality grapes.

Working with our growers throughout the year, our field men let them know, for example, when to prune, when to water, when to pull the water off, when to sulfur, and when to bring their grapes in.

We gave valuable instructions as to how to produce a better crop. Take pruning. Proper pruning is important so vines don't overcrop—produce too many grapes—which causes a loss of grape flavor and intensity. The purpose of pruning is to limit the number of clusters on a vine to what the vine will bear healthfully with quality—in other words, to make the vine give the most of the best. Each variety of grape is different, with some tending to bear much too heavily. Those varieties need to be more heavily pruned. Vines that are allowed to carry too many grapes will produce more tonnage per acre, but the grapes will not be the best possible quality. This could be a source of conflict between growers, who are paid solely by the weight, and wineries, which are more interested in grape quality than tonnage. But with our contracts guaranteeing minimums as well as higher per-ton payments for the best-quality grapes, we had the incentive we needed to bring reluctant growers around.

One long-standing benefit of our grower contracts was that we knew each year where many of our grapes were coming from for the next harvest. Even into the 1990s, as great as our requirements have become, we know every year where we are going to get a sizable portion of our grapes from. Before long-term contracts, we couldn't be sure where *any* of our outside grapes were going to come from until

August or September, or even October sometimes. And then we couldn't always get the grapes we wanted because somebody might rush in and offer more for one particular vineyard that was better than the rest.

I joined our field men in keeping a close watch on every aspect of vineyard operations. We didn't hesitate to reject grapes from a grower if his vineyard had not been well maintained or not adequately sulfured or was overwatered or whose grapes at harvest did not otherwise meet our quality requirements. A few growers even tried to get away with watering just before harvest—the only purpose being to swell the grapes so that they weighed more at the crusher. We had no interest in working with such growers.

The growers began to realize that we meant business. We wanted our growers committed to producing quality over tonnage.

As grapes go, true wine grapes are generally undersized. They can be ill-formed, in small clusters, thin and withered-looking, lightly bearing. The vines do best in dry, rocky soil, putting all their energy into the fruit. Fewer grapes from healthy but stressed vines make the best table wine.

There's an old saying: A grape vine says to the vintner, "Keep me poor and I'll make you rich."

FROM THE BEGINNING OF OUR BROTHER JOE'S work in 1946 managing our vineyards in Livingston, he had bought land and cattle. Sometimes he was able to graze them on unplanted areas of the properties he managed for us.

In 1948 we had sold our younger brother some pastureland adjacent to our vineyards. A couple of years later, Joe bought a nearby ranch that included a dairy. He started a feedlot and, eventually, a business raising heifers for dairy-herd replacements. His "JG" brand became well known at livestock auctions up and down the state.

At the same time as his cattle operations grew, Joe was expanding his vineyard holdings—to more than five thousand acres by the mid-1960s. As his holdings and outside interests increased, I began to notice that Joe spent less and less time at our vineyards. It had gotten so that he was never there when I went to inspect the vineyards. I'd drive around with Joe's superintendent and say, "When Joe comes back, tell him what we talked about."

My patience was tried at times when I found Joe taking winery crews off our property and putting them to work on one of his own ranches.

By 1967 our Livingston holdings were important enough to our business to warrant a full-time manager overseeing our grape-growing operation. Yet I couldn't very well expect Joe to ignore his own businesses to run our vineyards.

Ernest and I talked it over, and agreed that the proper thing to do was to suggest to Joe that he attend to his own affairs and we find another ranch manager.

I went to see Joe.

"I can see you're very busy with your own ranching business and that's fine," I told him. "That's what you've always wanted to do. It's just that we need a full-time ranch manager down here."

Joe agreed.

It wasn't as if he needed a winery paycheck anymore. Joe was well established now—one of the biggest landowners in his county. I was proud of him.

The following year, Joe bought a 1,900-acre ranch near Merced, where he raised cattle feed, and then five smaller, adjacent spreads totaling 2,000 acres and another big 1,300-acre ranch nearby.

Joe seemed to be doing well for himself.

Ernest

Although Julio and I knew we needed a bigger and better building to house our administrative and production offices, we were in no real hurry to sink money into bricks and mortar. Creature comforts never mattered much to us.

Some newly hired employees, I'm told, were shocked by what they found in terms of our offices.

When Ken Bertsch was hired in 1958, his "office" for the first six months consisted of an orange crate in the back of a windowless storage room. When he was finally assigned a real office, it was so small that when he had visitors he would step out in the hallway with them to be more comfortable.

We were in a cramped two-story cement building we had constructed more or less as an afterthought in 1936 when we realized we needed office space. In those days, Julio and I did practically everything. We simply got a carpenter and laid out the shape of the building and even figured out how thick the floor and walls should be. Neither one of us is an engineer, of course, but we checked out some other buildings. If I remember right, the standard concrete building at the time had eight-inch-thick walls with half-inch steel reinforced bars at six-inch centers. We were short of money. So, we figured, well, let's cut our costs and go with seven-inch-thick walls and three-eighth-inch steel. You get the idea. Over the years, we had tacked on one office at a time as needed.

Admittedly, the building was flimsy. In fact, thirty years later, our example of "economy" construction was, according to some of our employees, ready to cave in. Whenever I heard complaints, my stock answer was "Give us another year or two and we'll build a building that we'll all be proud to work in."

One day, Bertsch's secretary became quite upset because something was dripping through the ceiling right above her, staining her sweater. Someone found a spill in the lab upstairs.

The situation became more serious about three months later. One day there was a commotion coming from the first-floor clerical office—women screaming and men yelling. We rushed in to see what in the world had happened. One of our brand managers was sitting at his desk, covered with what looked like blood. It wasn't blood, but wine. A gallon of burgundy had fallen through the ceiling and smashed on his desktop, covering him and everything in the vicinity with red wine.

That afternoon, I decided we had better get started on the new building. We obtained sketches from some highly regarded architects, but none were satisfactory.

Everywhere I traveled I looked at architecture, trying to figure out what it was I wanted. While visiting retail outlets in North Carolina, I happened to drive by the state capitol. It was an impressive neoclassic-style building with columns surrounding it on all sides. During numerous sight-seeing trips throughout Europe, I had kept my eyes open for the right kind of building. But I had found just what I wanted by accident in Raleigh. I pulled over and made a sketch of the building as best I could. Back home, I sat down with Al Fenderson and Howard Williams at a conference table. On a large sheet of paper, I sketched out a building similar to what I had seen in North Carolina. With their help, I added details to the design. We then called in John Bolles, a San Francisco architect who had designed Candlestick Park, and soon had blueprints. Julio was the one who suggested that ground-up chunks of glass—from our Flavor-Guard bottles—be added to the concrete used for the exterior of the building. The contractor told him that nothing like that had ever been done before, but we were willing to give it a try. When it was finished, the building's exterior had a warmer appearance than it would have had if it had been constructed of plain concrete.

Our new administration building was completed in 1967. I keep waiting for a native North Carolinian to say how much our headquarters looks like his state capitol.

Similar to that state's capitol, it has a central atrium bordered by palm trees. Inside the Palm Court are two fish ponds. (We allow local charitable events, such as an annual Christmas Ball to raise funds for the Modesto Symphony, to be held in the Palm Court.) The interior designer we hired suggested that all the executive offices should look alike to give the building a "professional look." I said no. Our people worked long and hard and I wanted them to feel at home in their offices. Instead, I gave them decorating budgets to use as they saw fit. The result over the years has been unique and different executive offices that reflect the personalities of the men and women who occupy them.

What I feel really makes our administration building special is the rolling hillside setting and surrounding grounds. It almost didn't happen. The building would have looked strangely out of place surrounded by the neighboring office buildings squeezed into our original limited space. Yet up to the day before groundbreaking was to take place, it looked as though that's where it was going.

But my son David encouraged us to try one more time to purchase a forty-acre parcel adjacent to our property. This land was owned by Dave Arata, who apparently had long planned to sell it to us and make a killing.

Every time Arata passed the winery—no doubt noticing our constant expansion—he had just smiled. When we had finally called him about buying the adjacent property, he quoted us an exceedingly high price.

Disappointed, we had bought another adjacent property and removed the old buildings on it with the intention of using it as a site for our administration building. The day before the project was to commence, big tractors were brought in for the work.

I asked Julio to call Arata and let him know that we were set to start work in the morning. "Tell him that once we start, we will never be interested in his property again."

We soon had a deal. We contoured the flat, empty land to beautiful rolling hills for our new administration building and planted hundreds of trees.

Julio designed a long footpath that meanders up and around grassy creekside knolls behind the building.

Looking out from the window of my second-floor office, I couldn't figure out what people were doing off in the distance behind the building. When I finally got around to asking, I learned that many of our employees enjoy walking during their lunch and breaks.

In addition to Julio, they have David to thank for that, too.

MY YOUNGER SON, JOE, JOINED THE WINERY in 1965, after completing his MBA course at Stanford. Like David, he had also graduated from Notre Dame with a degree in business administration.

Joe worked a few months in California, then traveled for the next five years, participating in opening all the remaining domestic markets. During that time, he was often away on sales trips for as long as a month at a time.

It hadn't taken long to recognize that Joe's talent and interest were in sales. This worked out fine, as his brother, David, had gravitated to marketing. From the very beginning, my sons were able to function on a daily basis without stepping on one another's toes. The same could be said for Julio's son, Bob, and son-in-law, Jim, on the production side. My brother and I had long ago learned the value in such an arrangement.

In the early 1970s, Joe took over the management of the winery's sales force, which calls on and services our distributors. Joe studied the opportunities offered by a more intensive sales effort. As a result, we significantly upgraded and expanded our sales organization.

He determined the attributes a person must have to be successful in our organization, then instituted a college recruiting program to seek out and employ college graduates. We look for young people who have a strong work ethic and who are willing and eager to learn.

Once our recruits are hired, they are first given classroom training by our top sales-management people in the principles of salesmanship and sales management. This training continues with their calling on and servicing individual retail outlets. Those who prove they have abilities are then given sales-management experience. They are promoted on the basis of their performance, aptitude, and abilities. These young people realize they have the opportunity to advance just as quickly as they can according to the intensity of their application and ability, not seniority.

Today, we recruit sales personnel at about fifty colleges and universities around the country. After going through our training program, those chosen are placed in any one of several of our distributorships for year-long, hands-on training in sales techniques, merchandising, and management. After that, some join the winery directly. Others continue on the sales-management path by being placed in company-owned distributorships or by going to work for our independent distributor network.

For us, the wine revolution began in 1968.

One of our brand managers received a call from a distributor in Delaware who wanted a railroad car of Boone's Farm Apple wine. Our lightly carbonated, 11 percent alcohol apple wine had been introduced in 1961 but had sold very little since then. Our manager thought nothing of this order until the man ordered another carload the following week. When asked what was going on, the distributor explained that unexpectedly there had been a sudden demand by a cross-section of consumers for Boone's Farm.

A few days later, a Houston distributor called and ordered a railcar of Boone's Farm Apple wine—it had become an overnight favorite among his customers. When this was repeated in a day or two by a distributor in Ann Arbor, Michigan, we began to wonder what was happening.

After several years of modest sales, our apple wine had taken off in these markets without any advertising or promotional push from us. Though they seemed too much like isolated events to mean much of anything, Al Fenderson decided to check it out. He came back with a report that he thought Boone's Farm Apple wine could turn into a "really big item" for us.

"Forget apple wine," I told him. "If it sells on its own, that's fine. But I don't have any interest in advertising wines from other fruits. We're in the business of making and promoting grape wines."

If I remember correctly, someone had originally gotten the idea for us to come out with an apple wine because there was a small amount of another brand being sold on the East Coast. Production developed a very good apple wine. I had always liked the story of Daniel Boone, and I suggested naming the brand after him. I thought we could run a picture of the frontiersman in a coonskin hat on the label. Fenderson did not like my idea, so after some discussion, we had decided to use a picture of an old winery on the label and the name "Boone's Farm."

Since its inception, Boone's Farm Apple wine had remained a low-volume producer for us. In 1967 we had sold 28,000 cases. We had written it off in terms of its ever being a significant seller. It had a niche. A small one.

I know now what happened, but even with hindsight I do not know exactly *why* it happened *when* it did. It broke most of the established rules for brand building. This brand exploded the quickest of any brand in wine-industry history, and without any help—in the beginning—from us.

In 1968, we sold 90,000 cases of Boone's Farm; in 1969, 460,000 cases. In 1970, Boone's Farm became the largest-selling wine of any kind in the U.S., with 2.4 million cases sold.

At that point I could not ignore the potential. We decided to promote and advertise Boone's Farm in 1971. We produced a commercial featuring General Bull Apple, a takeoff on a character from the popular TV show *Laugh-In*. That year, sales shot to nearly 7 million cases.

We introduced a strawberry-flavored wine as Boone's Farm Strawberry Hill. Because there was no way we could ever get enough strawberries from which to squeeze the juice to make the wine in any volume, we produced it as an apple-based wine (9 percent alcohol) with a natural strawberry flavor. Right after Strawberry Hill was released, a young brand manager came back from on the road, quite excited: "It'll sell a million cases a year."

He was wrong.

Strawberry Hill's volume in the twelve months following its introduction in May 1971 was 7.5 million cases, making it the most instantaneously successful new product in our company's history. In 1972, we sold almost 16 million cases of Boone's Farm wines.

Our popularization of apple-based beverage wines created a shortage of apple concentrate in the world market. After buying all that was available in this country, Julio traveled the world in search of apple concentrate—to France, South Africa, Poland, and Tasmania. Up to then there had been a worldwide surplus of apple concentrate. But we were using such a tremendous amount of apple concentrate that once we started importing it, prices shot up not only in the United States but also in Europe. Eventually we planted our own apple orchards.

I believe that Boone's Farm attracted numbers of people who had never before tried wine. Everyone studying the beginning of the "wine boom" reached similar conclusions. It was driven by the young-adult market—ages twenty-one to thirty-four—who bought the new wines because they liked the taste, and because the wines were different and inexpensive.

In the years since, I've talked to many wine consumers who told me that the first wine they ever drank was Boone's Farm.

Our Boone's Farm, a product that was turned into an overnight success by consumers on their own, ended up helping to convert the "baby boom" generation to wine.

BY 1971 OUR SALES VOLUME HAD DOUBLED over that of 1968, to 100 million gallons, or approximately 40 million cases. Most of this large increase was in the newly popular Boone's Farm line and in the sparkling-wine category, but our table-wine business had increased by one third, in spite of our having given limited advertising support to our table wines.

As vigorous as the market for refreshment wines was, Julio and I had reservations. Was this just a fad? Wine markets throughout the world were based on table wines. It was true that certain beverage wines and sparkling wines had experienced triple-digit growth in the U.S. in a three-year period. But table-wine numbers for those years were also excellent in comparison to the past.

I didn't want to just pull the plug on beverage wines. But we did decide to refocus our efforts on table wines while pulling back somewhat on beverage wines. Even so, in the first full year of our new strategy, sales of Boone's Farm wines dropped by more than 10 million gallons.

Our consumer research department did some tests. It seemed that even though consumers preferred our table wines in blind tastings, once the label and price were showing they often preferred other brands. One of the product attributes that consumers are willing to pay for is "image," in other words, how they feel about the product. Pricing, advertising, packaging, and public relations all contribute to the image of a product.

We were sure that our quality was better than any of our emerging competitors'. But we did have to make some changes. We developed new packaging for our premium table wines. The new labels were more sophisticated. Our creative services department designed an attractive new half-gallon bottle. We put our ad agency to work developing advertising that would help consumers appreciate the quality of our wines. The new packaging was ready by the fall of 1972, and the new advertising began then, too.

We were also given some help from an unexpected source. In November 1972, *Time* magazine put Julio and me on the cover, featuring us in a story on the American wine industry. It was an interview that I hadn't wanted to give but had been talked into by Harry Serlis, then president of the Wine Institute, who said it would be in the best interest of the California wine industry.

"Certainly the most difficult and maddening part of the reporting," the *Time* reporter was quoted in the publisher's opening column, "was the pursuit of the elusive Ernest Gallo, who guards his private and business life only slightly less zealously than Howard Hughes."

Though I didn't appreciate those remarks, I suppose the article, "American Wine Comes of Age," was in all our best interests. Harry Serlis, for one, was delighted with the magazine's profile of the industry. Equally ecstatic was Al Fenderson, who figured we received "a million dollars' worth of free advertising."

In the article, our Hearty Burgundy was declared "the best wine value in the country today" by the *Los Angeles Times* wine critic, Robert Balzer, who took part in a comparative tasting panel for the magazine. Hearty Burgundy finished ahead of Beaulieu Cabernet Sauvignon and Mirassou Petite Sirah, though both cost more than twice as much as our Hearty Burgundy.

"Gallo Hearty Burgundy is made from more expensive grapes than a number of comparable competing Burgundies," *Time* reported, "but mass production helps keep the price about the same." The following year, sales of our Hearty Burgundy doubled. Fenderson was right.

"It is almost inevitable that more Americans will become wine drinkers," *Time* concluded. "Some converts to the grape will come seeking a change from the burning toughness of gin and bourbon. Others will move up from pop wine to drier, more complex wines. Americans seem to be shedding the nation's raw, hard-drinking past for a new, more subtle way of indulging themselves.

"As Thomas Jefferson said: 'No nation is drunken where wine is cheap; and none sober where the dearness of wine substitutes ardent spirits as the common beverage.' "

. . .

FOR YEARS, WHENEVER MY WIFE AND I traveled outside the country, I would invite Maynard Amerine, then chairman of the Department of Enology and Viticulture at UC Davis, to accompany us. Amerine had gone to high school with Julio and me in Modesto.

No one knew more about fine wines than Amerine. And he had a remarkable memory. Twenty years after we visited Morocco, for example, he could recall the brand and vintage of French champagne we had enjoyed with lunch.

Regardless of where we went, Amerine knew people in the local wine industry. Either they had been his students at Davis, or he had worked in their country while on sabbatical. Wherever we went, his name meant much more than mine.

In Japan, we visited a small winery in a remote area, and when we pulled up, everyone in the winery—including the office staff—lined up outside to greet us. Or I should say: to greet Maynard Amerine.

We received similar receptions in Australia and South Africa, where we found a colleague of Amerine's, Dr. Vernon Singleton, a professor of enology from UC Davis, who was taking a sabbatical to work in a winery laboratory.

In the Soviet Union, which we visited in 1971, Amerine and I toured research centers. They were quite up-to-date and staffed by very competent enologists. Interestingly, this country produced and consumed more wine than the U.S.

The wine we tasted at the research center was very good, but the same could not be said for the wine we had been served at Moscow's restaurants. I asked why.

"We have the technology," a Russian researcher told me, "but we cannot prevail upon the growers to uproot their old vineyards. They have no incentive to do so." Most of their vineyards, he explained, contained very ordinary varieties of fifty and sixty years ago.

To my surprise, I found that I was given equal status to Amerine at the Soviet research centers. I couldn't understand it because we had no sales or marketing presence in that country.

It soon became clear why. At one of the center's libraries, I was shown a thick file of Gallo Winery Research Department technical papers published on a variety of enological topics.

This brought home to me how our researchers are sometimes a little too fast in publishing their findings the moment they had found or developed a better process or technique. On the one hand, we were proud of our accomplishments, but on the other, I really didn't like giving proprietary information away.

Over the years I had told Julio, "Why don't we at least delay publishing technical papers for a year to give us a longer advantage? After all, these guys have developed these advances while on our payroll and working for us."

Julio replied, "Well, you know a scientist. That's their life. Their biggest satisfaction is to develop something new and be first in telling the world about it."

I have always had the same concerns about UC Davis, which I consider to be the most advanced enological university in the world. I think Davis is sometimes too quick to share technology developed with money supplied by the taxpayers of California. Why should professors on sabbatical travel the world and get paid to teach other countries everything they know about our technological breakthroughs?

Outside of the U.S., the wines of the world have improved greatly because of UC Davis, and it only costs foreign vintners the price of a round-trip airplane ticket for a UC Davis professor and a few months' salary.

Some of the countries so enlightened now export a large volume of wines into this country under favorable tariffs.

Our taxpayers helped make them stronger competitors to U.S. wines.

Julio

In 1968 we blasted to rubble and removed the last of the concrete storage tanks that we had built in 1936 and replaced them all with new stainless-steel tanks—the latest wine-storage technology available.

Besides using good grapes, there are only two other basic rules for making sound wine: Avoid high fermentation temperatures and excess exposure to air. Our new stainless-steel tanks helped us achieve the latter by allowing us to hermetically seal them to keep air out. Nobody can make good wine out of bad grapes, and we weren't anxious to make bad wine out of good grapes.

That year, our projections showed that within five years we would need at least 40 million gallons' more cooperage in Modesto to keep pace with our markets.

Expansion was necessary in spite of our 50 million gallons of cooperage in Modesto, 31 million gallons in Fresno, and another 15 million gallons at contracted wineries. As each year went by, we continued to add cooperage, trying to keep pace with sales. But every year we struggled not to sacrifice quality because of a lack of cooperage. It wasn't an acceptable situation.

Our engineering department calculated that to build 40 million gallons of new cooperage we would need considerably more acreage than was available at or near the Modesto winery. We just didn't have the room, what with the winery, offices, laboratories, glass plant, bottling operation, and millions of existing gallons of storage.

It was then that we started thinking about building a modern winery at Livingston. It made sense, given the thousands of acres we had in vineyards in Livingston, to build a crushing and distilling operation there, while continuing to do all our blending and bottling in Modesto. We drew up plans.

With the completion in 1970 of our new, big facility at Livingston—16 million gallons of capacity that first year—we stopped crushing and distilling in Modesto. Though we were not inside city limits, the town had grown right up to us.

There were other benefits in moving our main crushing operation to Livingston. We would no longer have to haul pomace out of Modesto for disposal. In Livingston we had 5,000 acres available for winery disposal, and before long we began dehydrating the pomace and selling it as a chicken-feed mix. Also, Livingston was nearer our vineyards and those of many of our growers. Crushing closer to the source means savings in transportation costs, plus the grapes arrive in better condition, which makes for better wines.

Our expansion included adding winery capacity at Fresno, as well as a new research laboratory and additional bottling lines in Modesto. We had the facilities, now, to take us into the next decade and beyond.

IN FRESNO WE HAD GONE THROUGH FOUR OR FIVE winery managers since rebuilding the old Cribari plant. We had hired graduates of this and that college, but none had worked out.

In 1971 we were again looking to make a change. I was advised to hire from the outside in order to get the most qualified person, but that went against my grain.

"What's wrong with this Slayton fellow?" I asked.

It had not escaped my attention that during my visits to Fresno, Bob Slayton, a shift supervisor, always had the right answer to any question.

When we had bought the winery back in '52, Slayton had been on the Cribari payroll working in the fields. Since then, he had worked his way up to supervisor and shop steward—he was 100 percent a union man. He knew the plant's operation backwards and forwards.

Slayton was my kind of guy. I'll take a down-to-earth hard worker who is a little rough around the edges over someone with plaques on the wall any day.

After I put Slayton in charge, Fresno ran smoothly from then on.

In 1978, we had similar management problems in Livingston, which by then we had expanded to 93-million-gallon capacity. At one point, the manager was requiring our Modesto winemakers to make appointments to be let inside the facility. If they weren't expected, they weren't allowed inside.

"By God, the winemakers are responsible for every drop of wine in your plant," I told the manager. "They can go in any time night or day to take samples or check whatever they want to check. Is that clear?"

In the meantime, Slayton was doing a terrific job in Fresno, which had a somewhat smaller storage capacity than Livingston but crushed more grapes. I called Slayton in Fresno.

"Bob, I'd like you to keep doing what you're doing in Fresno and take over the Livingston plant too."

"If you think I can handle it, Julio."

"I think you can."

Though either plant was a big enough job for one person, I put Slayton in charge of both plants—which were then crushing in excess of half a million tons of grapes annually and totaled 160 million gallons of storage capacity.

Livingston and Fresno are sixty miles apart, but Slayton hasn't let that stop him from doing a great job at both plants ever since. I tell him he was the best part of the Cribari deal. We tore down and replaced the Cribari plant.

But we still have Bob Slayton.

16

CHAVEZ AND THE UFW

Julio

By the mid-1960s, farm laborers needed a leader.

Since the late 1950s, the established rate had been around $1.00 an hour for field work. There was plenty of labor available, no question about that. But the hourly wage hadn't increased much, even though the cost of living was going up all the time.

We eventually broke away from other growers and raised the rate. I got a call right away from Harry Baccigaluppi of California Grape Products in Delano, south of Fresno.

"What's the trouble, Julio?" Baccigaluppi asked. "You having a hard time getting labor up there?"

"No, we're not having trouble getting labor."

"But you raised the rate."

"Yes, we did. We thought it was time. Don't you?"

"Oh, I don't know," Baccigaluppi said. "We're turning labor away over here. Why raise it?"

"Labor isn't a commodity. They're people, Harry. Their cost of living is going up. We feel we're doing the right thing."

"Well, down here we think they're doing all right. We don't see any reason for raising their pay."

"I tell you, Harry, if we don't do what we can, someone is going to come in and organize these people."

That's exactly what happened a few years later: Cesar Chavez went to work in Delano right in Baccigaluppi's backyard.

My brother and I may be in the minority among growers and winery owners because we believe that Chavez's stepping forward in 1962 to form the National Farm Workers Association was great for the farm labor movement. Increases in pay and benefits for farmworkers were overdue.

When Chavez tried in 1967 to organize our farmworkers—already the best-paid in the state—he found nothing standing in his way but the Teamsters, who also wanted to represent our laborers. Dealing with unions was nothing new to us. Our winery workers had been unionized since 1943. Our glass-plant workers had been unionized since the first day we fired up the furnace. We also employed union truck drivers. Our relationship with unions had been good.

The dispute between the two unions over our farmworkers was soon settled. State officials oversaw an election in 1967 and our farmworkers elected Chavez's union, reorganized under the AFL-CIO as the United Farm Workers of America (UFW), as their bargaining agent. We signed a three-year contract with the UFW—one of the first growers to sign with Chavez's new union.

Some of the conditions that the UFW had haggled over with other growers we had already covered:

• Since the UFW did not then have a medical plan for its members, we volunteered to continue covering our farm laborers on the medical plan we had in place for our permanent employees.

- We had always been cautious about pesticides. Our standards for worker safety when pesticides were being used in the fields were stricter than those of the state.
- We did not use child labor; minors worked in the vineyards only in accordance with state law.
- The workday was nine hours, except under very unusual circumstances.
- Our farmworkers were eligible for membership in our company credit union.

Not long after, Ralph Duncan, of the state Department of Labor Relations, was quoted as saying, "This agreement represents on the part of E. & J. Gallo Winery the most enlightened and liberal view of the status of agricultural workers that has been forthcoming from any of the negotiations taking place."*

Dolores Huerta, the UFW's chief negotiator, also appreciated the way our negotiations had been handled. "We found the Gallo people to be very cooperative. Their attitude creates a healthy climate for their workers. . . . They have been altogether different from almost any of the [other growers] we have dealt with."†

In the spring of 1970, we renewed our labor contract with the UFW for another three years without incident.

By that summer, Chavez had brought several big table-grape growers to their knees through a nationwide boycott that brought the union and its leader lots of publicity. Chavez was able to get a great deal of media coverage and attract many volunteers—particularly from churches and colleges—to walk picket lines.

Some of the tactics used in the UFW movement were disturbing. When some table-grape growers called for union elections in 1970, the

*Modesto *Bee*, September 24, 1967.
†Modesto *Bee*, August 8 and September 14, 1967.

UFW refused. Chavez insisted that they sign their workers up with the UFW, whether the workers were in favor of the union or not.

By 1971, after a four-year relationship with the UFW, our previously good working arrangement with the union began to sour. We started having problems with the union "hiring hall," as Chavez attempted to take control of our work force away from us. Until then, the hiring hall had been located at one of our ranches, which acted as an extension of our personnel department. But after the UFW moved the hall to Livingston, they insisted we hire only through them at the hall.

We found the situation unsatisfactory, primarily because the hiring hall couldn't regularly supply all the workers that we needed when we needed them.

My son, Bob, who had added personnel matters to his duties, became involved in talks with the union. Now, Bob is very people-oriented. He has great patience with personnel matters—much more than I do—and he took on this assignment with the attitude that we could get along amicably with the UFW.

Our second contract with the UFW expired in April 1973. After one negotiating session in March, the union was unable or unwilling to meet with us until after our contract expired.

Even though the UFW wanted to rewrite the entire contract, which is extremely unusual in contract negotiations, we quickly agreed on about two thirds of the contract provisions. In our view, economic issues were not a problem. We stayed committed to cost-of-living increases for our workers. Medical benefits were not an issue either. In fact, Bob had worked so closely with the UFW in helping them come up with their first medical benefits plan in 1968 that the union made him a trustee of its Robert F. Kennedy Health Plan.

From our standpoint, a major stumbling block was the UFW's insistence on keeping the union "hiring hall." We wanted more say in hiring the workers when we needed them. Also, we did not like the punitive measures the union had included in our contract. They wanted to keep any union member not in "good standing" with the UFW from working. Under the union's definition, a member could be found not in "good standing" for forgetting to pay his union dues or failing to attend a demonstration or man a picket line or for about any other reason that the union chose.

We had already had troubles with this "good standing" clause in our 1970 contract. In September 1971—during the middle of our harvest—the UFW requested that ten of our workers be excused for a day to attend a demonstration in Sacramento. Since it meant losing a day's pay, several workers refused to go and were placed in "bad standing" by the union. Under the rules guiding every other union, good standing was strictly defined as nonpayment of union dues and initiation fees. This was not the case with the UFW, who did not operate under the National Labor Relations Act. We refused to suspend or fire the workers and told the union we would assist our workers "in legal action against the union" if necessary.

One of the issues in our negotiations with the UFW was: Who had the say over a worker's activities during the workday? Did it rest with the employer, who paid his salary, or with the union, which was supposed to serve him? When the union told a worker to slow down, should the worker slow down and risk being fired? Or should he continue working and risk being placed in bad standing?

Bob described our "sit-down staring sessions" with UFW negotiators in which our people tried to reach a mutual understanding on unresolved issues, but left each time thinking that the UFW was more interested in mounting slowdowns and demonstrations than it was in negotiating the nuts and bolts of a union contract.

When we'd first signed with the UFW in 1967, the union had very little experience in contract administration. But instead of taking advantage of the opportunity to learn how to run a union, they kept their attention on organizing and boycotting campaigns.

Bob had met face to face with Chavez a number of times on different issues. He described Chavez as quiet, shy, and uncomfortable in one-on-one discussions. "But he's very effective when he's speaking to a group," Bob said. "You should see him then, Dad."

After one all-morning meeting in San Francisco, Bob took Chavez and some of his people up to the executive dining room on the fifty-second floor of Bank of America headquarters. Their entrance was quite a sight—Chavez in his parachute jacket with his two big German shepherds, Huelga and Boycote ("strike" and "boycott" in Spanish) at his side. Bob figured that it was the first time dogs were allowed to dine with some of San Francisco's leading business executives.

The point I want to make is that we tried very hard to reach an agreement with the UFW to extend our contract with them. There was no question but that we had every intention of negotiating a third contract with the UFW. However, we wanted the UFW to make some concessions. The hiring hall, seniority, and union discipline were the primary unresolved issues. But the UFW wouldn't budge and broke off talks.

"We are ready to talk," Bob wrote the UFW two months after our contract had expired, "so will you call me if there is any change in the union's position on these items?"

The UFW didn't contact us.

In the meantime, the Teamsters Union had intensified its effort to organize farm labor throughout California. The Teamsters called to let us know they were interested in representing our workers. As I recall, they phoned a month before our contract had expired with the UFW. The Teamsters made it clear that they had no intention of "pirating" any contracts, and the matter was left there. But after our UFW contract expired and negotiations bogged down, Teamsters organizers started talking to our workers. That didn't bother us, as long as they didn't do it during working hours. In fact, we probably couldn't have prevented union officials from talking to our people even if we had wanted to.

On June 25, 1973, the Teamsters sent us a letter claiming that they

The *New Yorker* cartoon (April 14, 1973) that Ernest has on his office wall. The caption reads: "Surprisingly good, isn't it? It's Gallo. Mort and I simply got tired of being snobs." *(Courtesy of The New Yorker Magazine, Inc.)*

Julio pouring E & J Brandy in the Himalayas a few miles from the border of Tibet, 1986. "I was surprised to find our brandy," Julio admits, "in a prized spot next to a French cognac at the end of the world in such a remote place." *(Photo courtesy of Ernest and Julio Gallo)*

Bob and Julio at Gallo Sonoma, 1986. Together, they helicopter weekly to Sonoma County to visit their vineyards. "Nowadays," Julio says, "I am primarily interested in seeing that my winemakers have a source of good varietal grapes." *(Photo courtesy of John Harding)*

An advertising agency presentation, 1993.
From left, Cliff Einstein of Dailey &
Associates (leaning over table), Gerry
Glasgow, Albion Fenderson, Debbie
Jepsen, Ernest, and David Gallo. "I do not
make decisions single-handedly about
what advertising to run," Ernest says.
(*Photo courtesy of Ernest and Julio Gallo*)

Gallo print ad, Dailey &
Associates, 1993. (*Courtesy
of Ira Brill*) "Right from the
beginning," Ernest explains,
"we wanted to market wine
with food."

Julio and Aileen on
their fiftieth wedding
anniversary, 1983.
(*Photo courtesy of Ernest
and Julio Gallo*)

Julio and Aileen in the garden of their vacation home in Carmel, 1986. *(Photo courtesy of Ernest and Julio Gallo) Below:* Julio's daughter, Susann, and her husband, Jim, center, with their children, their children's spouses, and their grandchildren, 1993. *(Photo courtesy of Ernest and Julio Gallo)*

Julio's son, Bob, and his wife, Marie, with their family, 1993. *(Photo courtesy of Ernest and Julio Gallo)*

Amelia and Ernest, on the occasion of their sixtieth wedding anniversary, 1991.
Amelia passed away on December 22, 1993. "Amelia was a great wife, mother, and
grandmother—and a truly great lady. While her loss is very, very difficult for me,
I feel fortunate and thankful that I have had her for sixty-two memorable years."
(*Photo courtesy of Ernest and Julio Gallo*)

Amelia and Ernest on their sixtieth wedding anniversary, 1991. Behind them,
from the left: Stephanie, Ernest, Christopher, Mary, David, Joe, Ofelia, and Joe.
Theresa Gallo is not pictured. (*Photo courtesy of Ernest and Julio Gallo*)

Ernest and Amelia with their catch at Rancho Las Cruces, 1956. Fishing is a hobby of Ernest's. *(Photo courtesy of Ernest and Julio Gallo) Below:* Ernest and Amelia with sons David, at left, and Joe, at the Grand Canyon, 1966. Ernest joined the fight to prevent the construction of two dams on the river in the Grand Canyon. *(Photo courtesy of Ernest and Julio Gallo)*

Ernest at the helm, 1990. *(Photo courtesy of Ernest and Julio Gallo)*

Ernest with David and Joe, 1994. *(Photo courtesy of Ernest and Julio Gallo)*

Ernest's son Joe and his wife, Ofelia, seated, and their children, Stephanie, Joe, and Ernest, 1994. *(Photo courtesy of Ernest and Julio Gallo)*

Ernest's son David and his wife, Mary, with their son, Christopher, on the occasion of his high school graduation, and daughter, Theresa, 1992. *(Photo courtesy of Ernest and Julio Gallo)*

Dr. Ivan Diamond, director of the Ernest Gallo Clinic and Research Center at the University of California, San Francisco, and research scientists Dr. Laura Nagy (center) and Dr. Adrienne Gordon. The Center, which is affiliated with UCSF's Department of Neurology, was established by Ernest in 1982 to conduct basic and clinical research into alcohol-related neurological disorders. Ernest has also endowed a chair in the name of Dr. Maynard Amerine in UC Davis's Department of Viticulture and Enology. *(Photo courtesy of Ernest and Julio Gallo)*

From left: Julio, Aileen, Amelia, and Ernest, on Easter Sunday at Bob's ranch, 1993. (*Photo courtesy of Ernest and Julio Gallo*)

Julio and Ernest receiving *The Wine Spectator*'s Distinguished Service Award at the Fairmont Hotel, San Francisco, 1983. (*Photo courtesy of* The Wine Spectator)

represented a majority of our workers. The next day, we informed our workers of the Teamsters' claim. At that time of the year, we normally have about two hundred farm workers, but our work force swells to five hundred during the peak of harvest. The following day, about seventy workers went on strike in support of the UFW. The UFW, we found out, had been telling workers that anyone who signed with the Teamsters would be fired when the UFW signed us to a new contract.

Bob immediately sent an open letter to our workers: "You are in the middle of a contest between two unions. I hear some people have threatened you with loss of your job if you do not sign up with them. The company does not take sides in this dispute.

"Here are the facts:

"No one can force you to sign a union card against your will. You will not lose your job for signing, or not signing, a union card.

"No one has the right to threaten you. If anyone does, tell your supervisor at once and we will take proper action."

Farmworkers are specifically excluded from coverage under the National Labor Relations Act. We strongly disagreed with that exclusion because it meant that farmworkers had no legal right to be consulted about which union, if any, could represent them. It also meant that they didn't have the right to conduct secret-ballot votes on union matters. This was particularly unfair to the workers.

The Teamsters sent us signed authorization cards from our workers. The results showed that a clear majority wanted to join the Teamsters. Though we were not obligated by law to go along with our workers' choice of unions, we strongly believed that they should have a voice.

We had experience negotiating with the Teamsters because of our trucking operation. We had found it to be a tough union that lived up to its contracts.

We entered into negotiations with the Teamsters. After seven sessions we reached an agreement. Again, economic issues were not stumbling blocks for us, as we were committed to continued cost-of-living raises as well as health-care coverage. The Teamsters did not insist on a union hiring hall, agreeing that we could go back to hiring the workers ourselves.

We signed with the Teamsters on July 10, 1973.

After our workers heard the terms of the proposed contract with the Teamsters—Bob insisted that each worker be given a copy of the contract written in the worker's native language—they ratified it by a huge margin.

The UFW began picketing our vineyards, making it difficult to harvest the '73 grape crop.

That season, we ended up hiring about a thousand pickers over the course of the season, way above the usual number. Many of them lasted only a few days, because they were harassed so much while coming to and going from work that they were afraid to come back, even though they needed a job to support their families.

Visiting the fields myself, I was shocked at the verbal abuse our workers were taking from the UFW pickets. Although I was proud to see how our workers stood up to this harassment, it was very difficult to watch our workers having to take this kind of treatment.

Ernest

Initially, we considered the UFW's unhappiness to be largely a jurisdictional dispute between two powerful unions. I could understand the UFW's frustration. After representing our workers for the past six years, it had lost out to the Teamsters. No union likes losing contracts.

In the beginning, I had thought Chavez's objective in forming the UFW was a good one. He spoke of wanting to increase the living standards for farmworkers. Like my brother, I was in sympathy with farm laborers' receiving more money and better working conditions, which was why we had always paid more for farm labor than any of our neighbors. I viewed Chavez as a gutsy man with a good cause, and wished him success.

We became disappointed, however, with the UFW during our second three-year contract. The people Chavez had administering our contract were very difficult to work with on a day-to-day basis. I knew that if Bob, who had more patience than most people, found them so tough to deal with, anyone would.

Our workers apparently became disillusioned with the UFW, too, as they were willing to listen to Teamsters organizers when they came around. A majority of our workers decided to leave the UFW and sign with the Teamsters. That year (1973) the Teamsters won a number of new contracts in the Valley.

We all hoped things would cool off. I felt that the UFW would move on to more pressing matters, such as properly administering the contracts they already had, and also working to sign some of the thousands of big growers in the state that had no union contracts at all. We would no doubt hear from them again in three years when our contract with the Teamsters expired. They could at that time call on our workers about representing them. If they succeeded in convincing our workers to change unions, then we would stand ready to negotiate with the UFW.

With the benefit of hindsight, I can see that what Chavez wanted more than just another grower under contract or even more than building a reputation as an efficient administrator of union contracts was to find a recognizable national brand against which he could mount a widespread boycott. He wanted the headlines, volunteers, and donations it would bring him, in order to turn his cause into a political movement. Chavez turned out to be a very talented tactician in public relations.

One of the UFW's favorite tactics was the "secondary boycott," boycotting retail outlets, even though the latter were not directly involved in the labor dispute, solely because they carried certain growers' products. The UFW had used secondary boycotts against the table-grape and lettuce growers.

In 1969, there had been a serious attempt to amend the law so that agricultural workers would come under the protection of the National Labor Relations Act. Among other things, the NLRA protected the rights of workers to organize for the purposes of collective bargaining, required employers to bargain collectively, and guaranteed secret-ballot elections for workers who wanted to be represented by unions. This proposed amendment had the full support of organized labor.

Julio and I also favored mandating this protection to farmworkers, believing very strongly that they should have the same rights as workers in our unionized plants and shops. To the surprise of many, including George Meany of the AFL-CIO, Chavez came out in opposition to the amendment. If the NLRA were expanded to cover farmworkers, their unions would be bound by the provisions of the Taft-Hartley Act, which specifically excluded secondary boycotts. Obviously, Chavez realized the importance of keeping those boycotts in his arsenal.

The UFW's boycott of California lettuce and table grapes had been difficult to enforce. Some growers had signed UFW contracts, others hadn't. How could the shopper at Lucky's tell the difference between UFW-approved grapes or lettuce and boycotted ones?

Chavez must have come to the realization that a boycott would work best if aimed at a nationally known brand name: one that was available in virtually every state; one that would keep their organizers busy and the media interested; one that people could easily spot and boycott. A recognized brand like Gallo wine.

In October 1973, the UFW began a national boycott of our products. Accusing us of signing a "sweetheart" deal with the Teamsters, Chavez, a man of considerable charisma, was able to obtain extensive media coverage to air his side of the story. We became the symbol against which Chavez mounted his campaign and built his national movement. It seemed like we were on the nightly news with monotonous regularity, and I doubt that there are many observant Americans who didn't see or hear the reports.

I remember my deep sense of frustration and injustice at the time over how we were mischaracterized to the public. We had been pioneers in voluntarily improving the lot of farmworkers in the California wine industry. Yet we found ourselves caught in an accident in history.

In the beginning, I had believed that any attempt to respond to the UFW's campaign against us would be a mistake. Chavez was seen by many as a saint, and one cannot attack a saint and succeed.

The UFW publicly charged that we had paid our workers 77 cents per hour before signing a UFW contract (untrue); provided no toilets or drinking water in the fields (untrue); did not protect our workers from pesticides (untrue); and illegally used child labor in the fields (untrue).

We were being falsely charged with a litany of misdeeds. I finally decided that we had no choice but to answer them. There are, after all, two sides to every story, including this one.

At the time, our public relations skills were nonexistent. We knew how to make wine and sell it at a fair price. The distributors in turn sold our product to their retail accounts on the basis of profitability for the retailers. I had never before seen a need to develop a public relations capacity.

Now I did. I hired a former public relations executive, Dan Solomon, who was very familiar with the workings of the news media, to coordinate our response to the trade and the public.

"Stay rational and calm," I told Solomon, "and stick to facts that can be proved." I was determined that we would never put out anything inaccurate or inflammatory.

Solomon helped us communicate our position on the labor dispute to the trade and to consumers; by mid-1975 we sent out more than

21,000 letters to consumers who had written the winery about the boy-cott. Staying in close touch with our field personnel on boycott-related matters, Solomon received daily field reports of UFW activity from salesmen, retailers, and distributors. He reviewed UFW material that was being distributed in various markets and provided timely responses to the press.

Whenever a top UFW official spoke at a neutral gathering, we made sure someone from the winery was at the podium to state our position clearly and accurately. The speech made by a UFW leader at the Unitarian Universalist Convention in New York City on June 26, 1974, provided a telling comment on the tactics we were up against. The UFW spokesman made the often-repeated charge that we exploited child labor and to prove the point held up a picture of a young child supposedly laboring in our vineyards. When our representative, George Frank, was finally able to get a closer look at the picture, he sailed it into the audience and urged everyone to take a good look before passing it on. "You'll see a child working in an onion patch. Gallo does not grow onions."

We also responded to stories in the press, but for the most part it was an exercise in futility, since the charge was always more newsworthy than the denial.

In early 1975, the UFW marched on Modesto. With Chavez coming to our home turf, I decided to make myself available to the press. So, after his speech in Graceada Park, I held a press conference—my first ever—at a nearby restaurant, the Chuck Wagon.

I walked into a meeting room at the Chuck Wagon and approached the podium. A group of fifteen to twenty reporters who had been covering the march were seated in a horseshoe around the podium, waiting for me.

Starting with some opening remarks, I was cut off by a frenzy of questions from the reporters:

"Do you still use child labor?"

"Is it true you pay your field workers less than other big growers?"

Not about to be put on the defensive, I stood silently until the reporters quieted down.

"You ladies and gentlemen have the advantage over me," I said calmly. "You know who I am. I do not know who you are. Would you please introduce yourselves?"

One by one, the reporters introduced themselves and announced their affiliation.

From then on, with none of us covered by the cloak of anonymity, we had a very reasonable exchange and I answered every question put to me that afternoon.

Perhaps naively, I hoped that some of the reporters left that day having given at least some thought to our position.

In time, the boycott faded and our brand survived. The legislature in California passed the landmark California Agricultural Labor Relations Act—which we supported—and Chavez moved on to target other companies.

In view of the unfairness of it all, some people might think I carry bitterness or anger in my heart. I do not. With the benefit of hindsight, and perhaps due to my age, I have quite a different perspective on those times.

Chavez taught me a valuable lesson about the power of symbols. He was a master propagandist, with great skills in shaping public opinion. Truth was not the issue. In this respect, it probably wouldn't have mattered what we did to defend ourselves. What mattered was public perception. Chavez understood this more clearly than I did at the time.

I also believe that in the larger historical sense, Chavez's capacity to impassion the public may have come along when it was most needed by farmworkers. He crystallized—you could say riveted—the farm-worker issue in the public mind as never before, and his legacy is obvious.

I regret only that we became to a large extent the symbol for needed reform, and that we were never able to effectively get our side of the story before the public.

17

EXPANDING THE BUSINESS

Julio

In the early 1970s, I took a drive out to the Snelling area, about thirty miles southeast of Modesto. A Wells Fargo banker had telephoned me about some ranch land that would soon be coming on the market in an estate sale.

The property was located southeast of us, near where the foothills rise into the gold country.

"It's mostly grain country out there," the banker had said, "but I'm told it would be suitable for grapes."

I wasn't so sure, but I was willing to take a look. We were anxious to plant more grape varieties—types that we knew made good wine and grew well in the Valley but were not yet readily available.

I was out in the middle of a field using a soil tube to make sure the topsoil had the necessary depth, when a pickup came out of nowhere.

"What are you doing?" the driver yelled.

"Testing soil," I hollered back.

"Not on my ranch you don't, mister."

I had unintentionally crossed onto the next-door property—not the best way to meet a neighbor.

The sale property—totaling some 3,000 acres—was divided into 300- and 400-acre parcels that for years had been rented out to dairy farmers. The homes and buildings were abandoned and in bad shape. Most of the fencing was broken down. The weeds and brush were out of control, and tules filled muddy sloughs along the banks of the Merced River, which cut through the property. But in terms of soil, it was very fertile, with a fine, river-bottom silt that would grow grapes or just about anything else.

Back in Modesto I told Ernest I thought we should consider buying the property. He came out with me to see the land. Sealed bids were due at the bank in three days.

Though we could hardly walk or drive through the overgrown property, Ernest quickly saw its potential. But what should we bid? Even in such bad shape, we figured it was probably worth $400 an acre. Once it was cleared and had drainage ditches to keep the surface water from flooding lower fields, the property could be worth twice that much. But we doubted that many people would be willing to make that effort. We thought we might be able to pick it up for a bid of $400 an acre.

A few hours later, Ernest called me at home. "I don't know, Julio. It's the only large piece of its kind so close to us. Maybe we should bid more."

We decided on $450 an acre.

Early the next day Ernest called again. "We agree it's an excellent piece of land. If we lose it to a bid that's twenty-five dollars an acre higher, we're going to feel shortsighted. What do you say we go to five hundred?"

When the bids were opened the next day, it turned out that we had submitted not only the highest bid but the *only* bid. Even though we had outbid ourselves twice to get the Snelling property, Ernest and I weren't upset. We don't like to second-guess ourselves, and we did have the land. Later, we would agree that it was one of the best buys we ever made.

With sales of Boone's Farm going so well at the time and causing a growing need for apple concentrate, we decided to plant apples instead of grapes.

Apples generally need cooler climates. When I had heard about a warm-weather apple grown in Australia, I decided to check it out. When I got there I headed for the island of Tasmania and found big orchards of Granny Smith apples doing well in a climate very similar to ours.

I returned from Australia with all the Granny Smith wood stock I could buy—enough to plant about 300 acres. I ordered more wood stock as it became available. We ended up with 1,500 acres of Granny Smith, and 1,000 acres in Royal Gala, Summer Red, and Golden Delicious.

The market in this country for table apples took off so much that most years we have ended up selling our Granny Smiths to the fresh market for top dollar, then buying apple concentrate for a lot less. Because growing apples was a new project for us, Bob took an interest in it right away. He made deals with packers for them to ship our apples to the fresh market as long as prices held. Whenever prices dropped, our apples would be diverted to the winery for concentrate. It's a very nice arrangement to this day.

We did more than just plant fruit trees at Snelling. Along the five miles of our Merced River frontage—our riparian water rights are the oldest on the river—we drained the sloughs and planted grass. We created lakes out of brush-choked swamps, and left islands for wildfowl nesting areas. When we were finished, it was spectacularly beautiful—a place where I've always liked to go to get away. We built an employees' community of modern, air-conditioned triplexes, and created recreation and picnic areas for our workers to enjoy.

One of the things I like best about the Snelling project is that we returned major portions of the land to its natural state. Wood ducks, swans, geese, blue heron, beavers, and other native species that hadn't been seen in the area for years returned.

I call this our "give-back" program. We cultivate those portions of the land we need for business, and give back the rest to nature and the environment.

I confess: I wish I could live there.

WE HAD BEEN buying grapes and bulk wines from Napa and Sonoma counties since the 1930s and were among the largest purchasers of grapes and bulk wine in both counties from the mid-1950s on. During that time, I became familiar with vineyards and wines in these two viticulture regions.

There's a long-standing debate that won't end any time soon about which region produces the best grapes and finest wines. Napa gets the most publicity and so it's better known by consumers.

We could have increased our commitment in either region, of course. At one point in the late 1950s, we were buying the entire output of bulk wine from both the Napa Valley Co-op and St. Helena Co-op wineries to blend into our Hearty Burgundy and Chablis Blanc. These two co-ops, which made their wines under our supervision, represented some 3.5 million gallons, about 50 percent of Napa's total wine production at the time.

At the same time we were purchasing about 40 percent of all the grapes grown in Sonoma County. After years of such grape and wine purchases, we decided that Sonoma is the better appellation. My experience is that Sonoma produces wines of more intense flavor than Napa; climate has everything to do with it.

To produce grapes for quality wines, vines do best in a soil base of gravel, limestone, or soft shale. These soils give good drainage and allow the roots to dig far for nourishment. From a soil standpoint, that's all you need for vines to do well. It's the weather, much more than the soil, that gives you the mouth feel you want in a wine.

The climate should be moderate, with warm days and cool nights. The presence of nearby bodies of water helps ensure these conditions. The heat is what gives the grapes the sugar, and the change in temperature gives you the high acid you look for in premium wines.

I'm convinced that Sonoma's weather, cooler because Sonoma is 20 to 30 miles from the coast while Napa is 40 to 60 miles away, allows grapes to ripen gradually and more evenly. Summer highs in Sonoma get into the 90s and sometimes near 100 degrees, but it cools off at night when a layer of marine air moves in. In the summer, the night's low will often halve the day's high. This is great for grapes. It allows them to mature more slowly, giving the grapes added flavor and making for a heavier-bodied wine that requires longer aging.

I had from the very early days bought wine from Frei Brothers winery, located in Sonoma's Dry Creek Valley. It was one of many small North Coast wineries I called on, meeting their owners and sampling their wines.

I had first discovered Frei back in 1934. It had been started by Andrew Frei, a San Francisco furniture-store owner who had purchased his small winery in 1895. After Andrew died in the early 1920s, his sons, Walter and Louie, took over. Expanding their vineyard and winemaking operations, they crushed for local growers and sold the wine in bulk. We bought a lot of wine from them — in fact, from 1948 on we took their entire output. Walter passed away quite some time before his brother, so most of my dealings were with Louie. On the basis of a handshake, I would tell Louie what I wanted to pay for grapes and he would go out and buy them from local growers, crush them, and deliver the wine to Modesto.

After Louie died, in 1960, I began dealing with his son Andy. Louie had another boy, Tom, with whom I had no real dealings. The two brothers didn't get along, and in 1971 Andy called and said they were breaking up their partnership. He wanted to know if I would be interested in buying Tom out. We ended up doing that. Several years later, in 1977, when Andy had to change climates for health reasons, he sold his half to us for the same price we had paid his brother.

That was our first major acquisition in Sonoma County. As partners with Andy Frei, we had already expanded the capacity of his grandfather's old winery to about three million gallons and modernized it with new equipment and technology. In addition to the winery itself, located in Dry Creek near Healdsburg, the property involved in the transaction included 345 acres adjoining the winery—of which about 250 acres were planted in grapes—and a 415-acre apple orchard at Laguna Ranch north of Sebastopol near the Russian River. Laguna, which Andrew Frei had purchased in 1882, had been a vineyard before Prohibition. Frei must have thought there would be no market for wine grapes; he had dug up the vines and planted apple trees.

With our requirement for apple concentrate through the 1970s, we left the orchards alone. Then, in 1980, as we expanded our line of varietal wines, Bob and I decided to get busy replanting all of the Frei properties.

The old vineyards had never been properly leveled, making them difficult to cultivate. The vines had suffered through the years. We pulled them all—as well as the apple trees at Laguna—let the land lie fallow for a year, then reshaped and replanted on a scale that had never before been attempted in Sonoma. Because of soil conditions and the danger of phylloxera, a root louse that destroyed European and California vineyards in the late 1800s, all the vines we planted were grown on a pest-resistant rootstock. Our objective was to develop the finest vineyards with the best grapes in that region.

At Laguna, we planted white wine grapes that I knew would do well in that cooler region: Gewürztraminer, Johannisberg Riesling, and

Chardonnay, a choice wine grape grown throughout the wine regions of France that was now in great demand in California.

At the vineyards adjacent to the winery—in the warmer Dry Creek region—we leveled and filled in the land, then planted mainly Zinfandel and Cabernet Sauvignon, red grapes that like the warmer climate.

Ernest

Sales of beverage wines—low-alcohol wines, usually flavored— peaked in 1972. Now, with millions of new consumers introduced to wine—largely because of the Boone's Farm phenomenon—our challenge was clear. We needed a variety of new products on the market when they were ready to move up. Whether we would be able to keep them as wine consumers depended upon the wine industry's success at making certain the right products were on the market at the right time.

As part of our strong emphasis on table wines, we decided to take our Carlo Rossi Red Mountain line national. We had developed this line a decade earlier as a response to several wineries' going after the "price" business. Petri and my in-laws, Franzia, were being the most aggressive. We countered with a competitively priced line called Red Mountain, the name of the first winery in Stanislaus County. The words "Red Mountain" couldn't be trademarked. So we made the brand a namesake of our longtime employee Charlie Rossi, who also happened to be married to a cousin of my wife's.

For years, on the label the words "Red Mountain" were larger than "Carlo Rossi." ("Carlo" sounded more like the name of an Italian winemaker than "Charlie" did.) When we decided to expand the brand's distribution, my son David suggested it would be a good idea to focus on the name of the "winemaker" rather than on the name Red Mountain. We began transitioning the label: "Carlo Rossi" grew larger and "Red Mountain" shrank until it disappeared altogether.

We needed to find someone to serve as a commercial spokesman. After a number of suggestions, I said, "Why not Charlie?" After all, the wine was named after him.

Rossi, who had been at the winery since 1953, had a great personality. I knew him to be a smart, charming, entertaining guy who smiled a lot. Everyone liked Charlie—what better spokesman could we get?

Rossi was quite content with his work in the sales area. In fact, his first reaction was that he did not want to serve as spokesman for Carlo Rossi wines. "I'm not an actor," he said. "I can't go on radio or television."

We had two young brand managers who had faith that Charlie Rossi was the perfect Carlo Rossi. They coached him, discovering that he did much better if he did not have to memorize a prepared script. They went to a local radio station, recorded a thirty-second commercial, and bought time on a San Francisco Giants baseball broadcast. They set up a radio in a conference room, and when the fifth inning came, they called me in.

Now, I like baseball, but I was annoyed at being summoned to listen to a game in the middle of the workday. It wasn't even the World Series. Not telling me what they had up their sleeves, they asked for my patience. Before long, Charlie Rossi's voice came over the airwaves. I knew at that moment we had found our Carlo Rossi.

We ran radio commercials featuring Rossi, and in 1975 we decided to launch a TV campaign. Radio was one thing, but looking into a TV camera was something else. "You put an amateur in front of a TV camera and he'll freeze up," I was told. Rossi's first TV commercial proved the detractors right. He was stiff and self-conscious before the camera.

"Look, let's give this assignment to someone who will work with Charlie and get him to relax and be more natural," I said.

We put him to work with an experienced TV commercial producer named Hal Tulchin. Things went a little roughly at first. One night, when they were winding down over a good dinner and some Carlo

Rossi wine, Rossi declared, "I'd really rather drink it than talk about it."

The next day on the set, Tulchin put Rossi in a back-porch scene, handed him a glass of wine, and rolled the cameras. The result was advertising history:

> Hi, I'm Carlo Rossi. You know, to make really good-tasting wines, you need to know exactly the right time to pick the grapes, and that's when experience makes the difference. We get the grapes to the winery when they're at their peak. That's why folks like our Carlo Rossi wines, like our Burgundy. It's soft and mellow. I'm sure you'll taste the difference experience makes. I like talking about Carlo Rossi Burgundy, but I'd rather drink it.

The commercials were a big hit, and Charlie Rossi became a celebrity. When he walked down the street anywhere in the country, people came up to him to shake his hand. He was in demand for parades and shopping-center openings, where women often came up to kiss him.

To our surprise, not only did the older generation like our graying, balding spokesman, but so did the younger adults. They also liked the wines.

By 1980, the Carlo Rossi line was the number two–selling brand of table wines in America—right behind the Gallo-brand wine.

THE WINE INDUSTRY EXPANDED RAPIDLY during the 1970s. Many consumers came to know that wine was a pleasant, good-tasting, even romantic beverage steeped in history.

As more and more Americans became interested in and were enjoying wine, successful people from all walks of life—lawyers, doctors, engineers, airline pilots, machinists, etc.—who were looking for a change of profession and for new experience invested their life's earnings in the wine business by acquiring small wineries or building them from scratch. Some succeeded, some did not.

At the time, the prevailing expectation in the industry was that as people became more knowledgeable about wine, they would not remain content with generic wines but would experiment with the more complex wine tastes that could be achieved in varietal wines. Although it was accepted that wines made primarily from grapes of a single variety were the highest form of California winemaking, great demand for these products did not yet exist.

To advertise our first release of varietals, we decided that stage and screen actor Peter Ustinov would be an ideal spokesman. Our ad agency's research showed he was regarded as "a man of culture" who also had appeal to young people.

Ustinov was a wine lover, and himself raised wine grapes in Switzerland. He agreed to do a commercial for us on the condition that he taste our wines—and *like* them.

We brought him to Modesto. "I'm not used to making commercials at all," he explained, "because I've made it a rule never to do a commercial for a product which I don't approve of or use myself."

We prepared a tasting of our varietal line for him. He paid careful attention to each of the eight wines.

It might have been a scene from one of his movies for all the drama of the moment. The actor carefully held up each glass to inspect the wine's color. He sniffed the aroma. Slowly, he tasted each one before saying a word.

"I'm impressed," he finally announced. "These wines are extremely true to the grape."

We all breathed a sigh of relief.

The commercials were shot on a set that was an exact reproduction of the set of the Broadway play *Sleuth*. We thought the commercials were almost as good as our wines.

Consumers, however, were not as impressed with our wines as Ustinov had been. Not even the great Babe Ruth hit a home run every time. Our varietal line simply did not meet with the kind of acceptance that I had hoped for. Sometimes when a product line doesn't succeed, the best thing to do is to abandon it. In the case of our varietal wines, that wasn't an option. They were so important to the future of the company that Julio and I didn't even consider the possibility of failure. He would go back to work on the products, and I would keep working on the marketing. Whatever changes we ended up making, the name on the label had to be Gallo.

Julio

By 1976 or '77, I was convinced that our growers had vineyards bearing sufficient quantities of quality grapes for us to produce more varietal wines—wines whose label bears the name of the type of grape principally used to make the wine. Many of these grapes came from vineyards planted as a result of our long-term contracts with growers, stemming from the initiative our Grower Relations Department had begun in the mid-sixties to broaden the choice of grape varieties and improve the quality of grapes that growers could plant. Now, Sales and Marketing were interested in expanding our varietals. (At the time, federal law required varietals to be made with at least 51 percent of a single grape variety. Today, it is 75 percent.) They were projecting that sales of varietals would soon overtake all other table wines. I had slowed them down some, wanting to be certain that our popular generics, like Hearty Burgundy, wouldn't be hurt by allocating so many good grapes to another program.

It was because of the success of our long-term contracts with growers that I would eventually be able to look anyone in the eye and say that the varietal grapes our growers delivered to us were among the very best to be found anywhere in the world.

The varietal line we released in 1974 was our first line of cork-finished wines. I had resisted going to cork because I believed that corks were not the best closure. In fact, I still believe that wine deserves a better closure in order to keep the wine fresh and avoid spoilage.

None of our early varietals were aged in oak. Oak makes wine different, and not necessarily better. Ernest and I agree that since wine is made of grapes, it should taste like fruit, not wood. But we came to recognize the need to oak-age future varietals for those consumers who like that flavor—though I am careful not to allow it to mask the varietal characteristics of the grape. Also, wood aging does soften wine, and I have no objection to using it for that purpose.

Construction on our oak-aging cellars began in November 1976. After considering and rejecting many designs, my son, Bob, said, "Let's go underground."

Everyone was very fuel- and power-conscious after the 1974 Middle East oil crisis and long lines at gas stations. Bob conducted some tests and found that in the heat of the summer, when the temperature often exceeded 100 degrees outside, it stayed 65 degrees six feet underground. The air-conditioning necessary to maintain year-round cellar temperature (65 degrees) in a large building aboveground would have been costly and wasteful.

We didn't want to tunnel into and scar up the hillside next to our administration building. So we sent the bulldozers a couple of hundred yards to the southeast, digging far enough down to construct an underground cavern approximately the size of two football fields, or about two and a half acres. The concrete walls and twenty-foot-high ceiling are a foot thick. The 100,000-square-foot structure is covered on top with a six-foot layer of compacted soil. Aboveground the surface was planted to lawn and trees. Unless you know where the entrance is located, you can pass the cellars without ever noticing them.

After much consideration of wood characteristics from various regions of the world, we decided that one quarter of our casks would be of French oak, for white wines, and three quarters of Yugoslav oak, for reds. We had enough European wood—from France and from Yugo-slavia—for 650 big, upright casks shipped by train to Italy to be constructed there. After the casks were constructed, all the staves were individually numbered for refitting later. The casks were then disassembled and shipped to Modesto. At the time, the wine trade called it the largest purchase of imported oak cooperage ever recorded in U.S. wine industry history.

Reassembly of the casks in our cellars would require a high degree of skill. When we set out to find someone who could handle the job, we discovered that handmade coopering was nearly a lost art in this country. So we brought over from Spain an experienced cooper, José Lopez, and his apprentice son. They stayed two years.

When our cellars were finally finished, we had custom-made oak casks that could hold a total of more than two million gallons of wine—at the time, the largest collection of oak cooperage anywhere in the world. The temperature stayed a constant 65 degrees, varying no more than two or three degrees no matter what season. Though we had no air-conditioning, we did install huge humidifiers to keep the air inside from getting too wet or too dry.

The first wines to be aged in oak in our underground cellars were two of our red varietals, Zinfandel and Cabernet Sauvignon. They were sterile-filtered into the tanks so that no bacterial changes would take place inside the oak casks. The casks had domed wooden tops with expansion chambers; each was filled to the top so that none of the wine could be exposed to air.

Depending on the grape variety and cask size, we aged the wine from one to three years. In the case of the reds, especially, we would let the wine tell us when it was ready. After bottling our varietals, we aged them additionally for at least four to six months before release.

This was a turning point for our company.

18

QUALITY,
QUALITY, QUALITY

Ernest

In 1972, the Federal Trade Commission filed an antitrust complaint against us, charging "exclusionary marketing policies." The government's target was our distributor network. At the same time, the FTC filed complaints against the parent corporations of two other wineries, United Vintners and Franzia.

The FTC had become interested in the wine industry in 1969, when Heublein, a giant in the distilled spirits business, acquired United Vintners, the nation's second-largest winery. Franzia had been purchased by the Coca-Cola Bottling Company of New York in 1971. Coke–New York also purchased the popular Mogen David label. This operation, called the Wine Group, became the fifth-largest wine marketer in the United States. (The Coca-Cola Company, the beverage manufacturer, was also about to enter the wine business in a big way.)

I thought it best to try to work out a compromise with the government. Engaging the FTC in a protracted legal fight would have taken up valuable time and resources. Furthermore, since 1966 it had no longer been necessary, in antitrust cases involving restraint of trade allegations, for the prosecution to show that the consumer had suffered as a result of the alleged practices.

At one point, FTC lawyers suggested we agree to limits on our sales and advertising. Such proposed constraints were unacceptable to us, especially given the competition: well-financed, multinational corporations that were entering the wine business.

At the time, the FTC was proceeding under an enforcement philosophy that gave little or no credit to the efficiency of companies or the degree to which they were serving consumer needs. In other words, if a company was gaining market share because it produced better products at lower prices and presented them to consumers with better services, the interest of consumers should have dictated that the government not interfere. Regrettably, in the early 1970s the FTC was excessively suspicious of success and had an unfortunate tendency to try to handicap more capable companies so that they would not be able to outpace less efficient companies who were not as good at meeting the needs of the consumers. In a manner of speaking, it was just like a racing secretary handicapping horses with weights in a race meeting. The racing secretary assigns extra weight to the best horses in the hopes that it will slow them down and provide for a closer and more exciting race. That makes for good sport in horse racing, but it makes no sense as an economic policy. In the wine business, the FTC's policies led to such unfortunate effects as discouraging price competition and impeding suppliers in seeking to maximize distribution services for their brands.

Nevertheless, when we couldn't make our case with the government, we agreed to sign a consent order with the FTC in 1976. We did not admit to any wrongdoing. In the order, the FTC acknowledged that we had made progress since 1970 in changing our "practices and methods of competition" to conform with antitrust laws.

The key provisions of the consent order closely regulated our relationship with distributors for the next ten years. We could not prevent distributors from taking on a competitor's wine line. We could no longer require distributors to handle certain Gallo products if they wanted to carry our other products. We could no longer guarantee any loan for a distributor, or assume any capital expenses to help a wholesaler's business. We could no longer require distributors to submit financial statements unless they asked us for management counseling. And we had to stop "floor stocking": increasing prices for products already in their inventories or in transit to them. We had instituted this practice to discourage distributors from overstocking in anticipation of a price increase. Overstocking had disrupted our shipping, with some distributors ordering a few months' supply of wine to get the drop on an increase.

The role of the distributor is particularly important in the wine industry. Distributors are the most familiar with local laws. They obtain retail distribution, sell and deliver on a regular basis, set up displays, and in general do whatever they can to increase sales.

We always insisted on intense effort by our distributors; we want their undivided attention. We have built our company through paying close attention to our distributors, and they have prospered.

In the early 1980s, I asked our new general counsel, Jack Owens, an experienced civil attorney and graduate of Stanford Law School, to review the FTC consent order, which also stipulated that we had to allow FTC investigators monthly inspections of our transactions with distributors. Several factors led me to believe that we should try to convince the government to lift the consent order or, at least, ease some of the restrictions that had been placed on us.

After our FTC order went into effect, much economic research and scholarly work demonstrated that the earlier 1970s approach of the FTC was seriously flawed. Experts in the field of antitrust law had come to realize that the last thing the government should do is discourage companies who are doing their level best to produce better products at better prices and to maximize the distribution services for such products. It became increasingly clear that our FTC order was in direct conflict with developing economic and antitrust concepts. When we brought that to the attention of the FTC, they rescinded the order, stating: ". . . the broad scope of the Order's prohibitions appears to hinder unnecessarily Gallo's ability to utilize many of the marketing devices that are freely employed by its competitors."

This action reflected a sea change at the FTC, which had come to realize that its primary focus should be on consumer benefits rather than on protecting less capable firms. We were one of the first companies in the U.S. in the 1980s to take advantage of the change that had occurred in antitrust thinking and to move to rescind an outmoded, anticonsumer order from an earlier era. After the FTC rescinded our order, many companies followed in our footsteps, and many of them cited the approach we used in our petition.

I believe we have always treated our distributors fairly. I still think it is to the advantage of both our winery and the wholesalers for them not to take on competitive wine lines. We have a list of wines—generic table wines, varietals, sparkling wines, beverage wines, dessert wines, coolers, and vermouth, as well as brandy—that compete in each category, and I do not feel it is feasible for a distributor to sell and service two different brands in the same category effectively. We simply will not accept any distributor treating our wines as an afterthought.

We did not go back to "floor stocking." Now, if we suspect a distributor is trying to overstock to avoid price increases, we simply say, "Look, we'll sell you only a month's supply."

We do continue to help our distributors build their business and help guide their sales force.

Thus, we both succeed.

COCA-COLA, ONE OF THE MOST SUCCESSFUL MARKETING STORIES in U.S. history, is huge and well financed. The titan of the soft-drink market and the holder of the world's best-known brand, Coca-Cola made no secret of its intention to teach the wine industry how to market its products.

"Coke's strategy is to engulf and devour," commented one industry leader in a trade publication. "Coke has the money and the endurance to wear others down, then step in and claim the market."

Potentially, Coca-Cola was the greatest competitor we ever faced. We knew we were in for a fight.

In the mid-seventies Coca-Cola bought the Taylor Wine Company of New York, followed by Sterling Vineyards and Monterey Vineyard. Coca-Cola grouped these wineries together in what they called The Wine Spectrum, which immediately became the fourth-largest U.S. wine company, edging out the fifth-place Wine Group, owned by Coke's New York bottler.

The Wine Spectrum created a new brand, Taylor California Cellars. The head of this company told the *Los Angeles Times* that they were going to become major competitors without getting into a direct confrontation with Gallo. "We don't want to be second to anyone in this market," he added.

Television ads for Taylor wines did something the wine industry had always avoided. The spots showed wine authorities and tasting groups tasting the new Taylor wines and preferring them to Almadén, Paul Masson, and Inglenook. This type of "taste comparison" had long been used in soft-drink commercials, but wineries had been careful never to disparage a competitor's product.

Gallo was not included in Coca-Cola's television wine-taste tests. If the executives running The Wine Spectrum thought that by not confronting us in their advertising they could avoid a battle, they did not know us.

Obviously, Coca-Cola knew all about consumer products distribution. This huge marketer apparently figured it would be easy to transfer its experience to the wine industry. But distribution of soft drinks throughout the United States is far different from that of wine.

For the most part, Coca-Cola sells its syrup to local bottlers. There are certain guidelines from the supplier that bottlers must follow in regard to keeping their plants clean, bottling a sound product, and so forth. The finished product is delivered via a truck driven by a driver-salesman on a regular route. The driver-salesman, who is primarily an order taker, has a 50 percent chance of making a sale before he leaves the garage, as most consumers drink Coke or Pepsi. In addition, Coca-Cola spends hundreds of millions of dollars advertising that Coke tastes better than Pepsi. "How many cases do you want?" is often the extent of the driver-salesman's pitch to the retailer. He is supposed to push for cold-box space, which is easy because it's also in the retailer's best interest: People like buying Coke chilled.

In the wine business you are competing for shelf space against not only more than five hundred wineries, but hundreds of distilled spirits and beers as well.

We concentrated our sales efforts and at every turn did Coca-Cola one better. In some markets, Coke's Taylor California brand engaged in deep price-cutting in an effort to take market share away from us, but we were more than ready to beat Coca-Cola, or any other publicly held company.

Julio and I are spending our own money. We do not have the pressure from shareholders to make the most return on their money. We always take a long-term view.

Julio is convinced to this day that Coca-Cola—not unlike the distillers in the forties—never really understood that by entering the wine business they were also getting into farming. "This business is a lot different than putting syrup and water together," my brother said. "You can't sit in some office in Atlanta and set up a program for buying grapes and crushing on a certain date. You have to be ready to make an instantaneous switch, if need be. We're dealing with Mother Nature here. Every growing district is different from the standpoint of quality.

This takes experience to deal with. You've got to put your boots on and go out and take a look."

I agreed. Our organization was able to make quick, sound decisions based on conditions we observed close at hand. This was a real advantage for us.

Coca-Cola sold The Wine Spectrum to Seagram in 1983.

On balance, having Coke in the business did us good. It energized the entire industry. During Coke's six years (1977–83) in the wine business, industrywide advertising expenditures tripled.

If you are not challenged, you seldom do your very best. There is nothing like strong competition to push you to maximum effort.

At lunch one day, one of our executives was commenting on Heublein's entry into the wine business. He was pointing out that they had developed the Smirnoff Vodka label, and that they are a great marketing company and were going to be a major competitor for us. All this was true.

Everyone around the table voiced an opinion. Many obviously were concerned.

"I don't agree with your pessimism," I said. "Heublein will not cause any major problems for this company."

"Why do you feel that way, Ernest?"

"Because I know us and have confidence in us."

BY 1980, WITH CALIFORNIA WINERIES HAVING IMPROVED their wine quality and marketing efforts, yearly U.S. wine consumption had risen to 480 million gallons—from 33 million gallons back in 1934.

As wine appreciation and consumption increased in this country, wine imports from France, Germany, Spain, and Portugal, and especially Italy, started to increase dramatically in volume. By 1984 foreign wines accounted for 25 percent of the U.S. wine market.

There was great concern among U.S. vintners, inasmuch as most of these countries subsidize their wine industries. At the same time, the

U.S. government was permitting these foreign wines to come into this country with very low tariffs, while foreign governments retained restrictive tariffs for U.S. wine products. It was not a level playing field.

My brother and I knew how other American industries, such as the automobile, steel, electronics, and textile industries, had been rapidly losing volume to foreign producers. We were not willing to let the same thing happen to the U.S. wine industry.

Being a private company and not answerable to anyone helped us again. We were free to do whatever was necessary to aggressively compete. This required not only narrow margins, but also the advantages of large volume.

We went on a program of increasing our production, intensifying our sales and marketing effort, and narrowing our margins. Along with other U.S. wineries, we vigorously competed against the influx of foreign wines.

Foreign wines imported to the U.S. peaked at 142 million gallons in 1984, and declined steadily until 1992, when they again started to increase, primarily from Chile and Argentina.

In Chile today, wages are around $8 to $10 per day with few, if any, fringe benefits. Here, for the same type of work, wages are $7 to $14 *per hour* and workers receive liberal fringe benefits. Good vineyard land in Chile can be purchased for $900 to $2,000 per acre, versus $3,000 to $20,000 per acre in California.

Sadly, the threat to the U.S. wine industry from foreign wines is, once again, very real.

Julio

I long opposed vintage-dating our wines.

Vintage-dating had started in Europe because of the adverse growing conditions there. Many years they would have difficult vintages: Bad weather would prevent the grapes from maturing properly to make a fine wine. With alternating good and bad years, there was reason to let consumers know the vintage. Generally speaking, of course, if people knew a good year they would stock up on it and stay away from the poorer vintages.

In this country we have some seasonal variations, but nothing like those they have in Europe. It has been said before: In California, every year is a vintage year.

I pride myself in knowing that we can bottle wines of consistent quality. To do that, we carry over a big inventory from one year to the next, and blend. We also use grapes from the North Coast, Central Coast, and San Joaquin Valley, avoiding as best we can the whims of nature in any given year or region. *Continuity* is what I'm talking about, and what I'm always striving for.

Vintage-dating, however, became a marketing necessity. Wine writers and wine buffs want to be able to refer to one vintage as being better than another. The serious wine drinker looks forward to discerning the differences in wines from the same winery.

I admit that vintage-dating does make some sense because of the consumer's desire to know how old the wine is before buying it. For example, consumers who prefer a newer wine with a fresher taste can buy more recent vintages.

I fought vintage-dating our wines, but eventually gave in to the Sales and Marketing departments. We released our first vintage-dated varietal in 1983. It was a 1978 Cabernet Sauvignon, made from 100 percent Sonoma County Cabernet grapes, aged in oak for thirty-five months and bottled-aged another eighteen months. It was a full-bodied wine, rich with ripe Cabernet flavors and complexities framed with an oak character. I was proud of it.

One production standard I insist on is accepting the responsibility of keeping our wines until they are ready to drink. I think it's unfair to the consumer when a winery sells wine before it is ready and depends on the consumer to do the aging. We release a wine only when it is ready to drink. From the beginning of our vintage-dating program, we re-leased red wines several years older than the same varietals from other wineries. That is true to this day.

When other wineries were putting out their 1989 Cabernet Sauvi-gnon, we were releasing our '84 vintage.

WE RELEASED E & J BRANDY NATIONALLY IN 1977. It became the number one–selling brandy in the U.S. six years later.

Our brandy is made from seeded grapes. It contains no added flavor-ings. Its smoothness is the result of longer aging: four years or more in oak barrels.

Aging is the difference. While we soften our brandy by aging it for at least four years, many producers put out two-year-old brandy and soften it by sweetening it. That's where you get the hot-sweet taste in so many brandies.

It costs more money to age brandy many years, and you certainly need a lot more barrels. But we think the extra smoothness is worth it.

I like our brandy. I especially enjoyed a nip when I found myself on a mountaintop in the Himalayas one afternoon in 1986. . . .

Aileen and I had taken a trip to Nepal and stayed at a hotel in Kat-mandu for three days. One day we took a tour bus with about twenty other people and went up almost to the border of Tibet. We were on a steep, winding road going up the side of the Himalayas, when we stopped at a small inn. Out in the middle of nowhere, it was the only place around for miles.

Before lunch, I wandered into the little bar and took a look around. There were three or four bottles each of whiskey, bourbon, scotch. At the very top of a mirrored cabinet, in a prized spot, were a bottle of French cognac and a half-full bottle of E & J Brandy.

I was surprised to find our brandy at the end of the world in such a remote place. I invited our fellow travelers over, showed them my brandy, and invited them to join me.

The bartender didn't speak English. I signaled that I wanted to buy brandy for the house. He started lining up these little shot glasses, but I pointed to regular-sized glasses.

After the bartender lined up the glasses, I started pouring brandy. We emptied the bottle pretty quickly.

Everything went fine until it was time to pay up. The bartender got visibly upset, but I couldn't understand him. Our guide came over to translate. The bartender didn't know how much to charge for the brandy. He only knew the price per shot glass. Trying to help, I said that the bottle had been half full.

The guide translated for the bartender. "He says it was more than half full and it is imported brandy. Very expensive."

I reached into my pocket and took out a roll of the colorful local currency. It was all the money I had on me. Without counting it, I put the entire wad on the bar.

"That should cover it," I said.

The bartender was all smiles.

To this day, I don't know how much I paid. But it was worth it—the best damn "imported" brandy I ever had.

19

GALLO VERSUS GALLO

Ernest

On a sunny June day in 1983, Amelia and I took the company helicopter down to my brother Joe's large commercial dairy near Atwater, thirty-fives miles south of Modesto.

A hundred or more visitors were gathered near a new structure adjacent to the cow barn. It was my youngest brother's new cheese plant.

Joe was happy to see us at the ribbon cutting. I knew he would have liked for Julio and Aileen to make it too, but they were traveling and unable to attend.

As Amelia joined some of Joe's family, Joe ushered me through the crowd. We both greeted guests as we passed.

Gallo wine was being poured. In the center of a long table sat a forty-pound block of Joe's Cheddar, which was being sliced up and served on platters by waiters.

Joe started showing me all the cheese-making equipment and various work stations. It was unusual, he pointed out, for a cheese plant to be on the same premises as a dairy. Most had to ship milk in by tanker trucks. His setup would reduce transportation costs, he explained.

The plant had been in operation for several months. I saw how the milk was delivered via underground pipeline from the dairy, and how the cheese was made in 3,500-pound vats, then pressed into large molds. Forty-pound blocks were shipped in cardboard boxes marked "Joseph Gallo Cheese Co., Plant No. 06-77, Atwater, CA."

Joe had told me previously how dairy profits were razor-thin in spite of federal government price supports. A year earlier, the government had begun reducing its price supports because of a huge supply of surplus milk, forcing many smaller, family-owned dairies out of business. "The milk industry is really hurting," Joe had explained. "I can get a higher price for cheese than for fresh milk. With this big dairy sitting here, it made sense to go into cheese."

I asked Joe if he was involved in the actual plant operation.

"I have people running it," he said. "I hired a cheese maker from Wisconsin."

"You're selling it wholesale?"

Joe nodded. "Forty-pound blocks to customers who cut it into smaller pieces and package it for retail sale under their own brand names."

"So you won't be selling to consumers under the Gallo name?"

"No, I sell only to commercial buyers. Chain stores, mostly. They package it under their house labels."

I nodded. "Good. We can't have consumers thinking the winery is in the cheese business. If you ever change your mind about only selling in bulk, you shouldn't use our trademark. You know, we signed our settlement with Gallo Salame just a few days ago."

Joe had been aware of our trademark dispute with the owners of Gallo Salame.

An Italian family named Gabiati in San Francisco had started to produce dry salami around 1941. In the late 1940s, they renamed their product Gallo Salame. I first became aware of this Gallo brand while purchasing salami at our favorite delicatessen in the North Beach area of San Francisco sometime in the 1960s. At the time, I did not think too much about it, since it was a family trying to make a living selling locally to corner delicatessens. One morning in 1979, I read that Gallo Salame had been sold to Consolidated Foods (predecessor to Sara Lee Corporation). I immediately thought: *What would this giant conglomerate want with a small San Francisco salami manufacturer if they didn't intend to capitalize on the Gallo name?* The very name that we were spending millions of dollars a year to advertise and promote on television and elsewhere. I telephoned Consolidated's chairman of the board, who assured me that they had no intention of exploiting the Gallo brand name. I immediately wrote to him demanding that they discontinue using the Gallo brand. Consolidated refused, and started to expand the line and its distribution. We had filed a lawsuit to protect our trademark.

I now told Joe how under the terms of our recent out-of-court settlement, in exchange for Consolidated's assigning their Gallo Salame trademark registrations to the winery, we had given them an exclusive license to sell processed meats and cheeses under the Gallo name. Consolidated agreed that after a four-year period it would not distribute Gallo Salame beyond the eleven western states. Under the agreement, we were obligated to control their product quality and protect the trademark.

Joe seemed unconcerned. "I don't want to get involved in marketing. I'm too old for that."

We returned to the party.

I was expected at a wine function in Napa that afternoon, so after the tour of the plant, Amelia and I stayed only long enough for a few slices of Joe's cheese and a glass of Gallo wine.

Though I wouldn't hear about it until later, after we left a plane circled overhead towing a long banner. The plane had lost the "Joseph" part of the sign on takeoff, and the message read GALLO CHEESE.

I also didn't see the eleven o'clock news that night, which showed footage of the cheese-plant opening, or hear about what the TV newsman said until later. He reported: "Gallo, already known as the largest winemaker, may soon become a big name in the cheese business. Wine and cheese—a popular combination. The Gallo wine folks may think so as they open their own cheese factory. Why not? Wine and cheese go hand in hand."

About a year later, I returned from lunch one day to find an eight-ounce package of "Joseph Gallo" Monterey Jack on my desk. It had been purchased that morning at a Modesto supermarket, I was told. The cheese had been part of a floor display featuring several of our varietal wines.

I held the package of cheese, looking at the label. This was all wrong. I still remembered Joe telling me: *I'm selling only in forty-pound blocks to commercial buyers. I'm too old to get involved in marketing.* What had happened since then? Why in the world hadn't Joe been in touch with us?

I called Joe right away. "I've got a package of your cheese here. I'm surprised—shocked, really—to see this consumer packaging. You assured me you weren't going to sell in this manner under your name."

"Times are tough," he said. He expained he was having trouble selling his cheese.

"I thought you understood the obligation we are under to Consolidated regarding Gallo Salame. You'll be creating great problems for us because it will seem we're permitting our brother to sell cheese under the Gallo brand after we've licensed it exclusively to them for salami and cheese."

"It's my name too," Joe said impatiently. "I have a right to use it."

I knew something of the complexities of trademark law. Someone born with the name Joe Ford could no more use his name on a new line of automobiles than someone named Anne Coke could use hers on a new soda pop. Ford and Coke were protected trademarks, and so was Gallo. Back in 1949, in fact, we had won a trademark-infringement suit against an Ohioan named Mary Gallo who had started her own "Gallo Wine" brand.

"Please do us all a favor," I told Joe. "Go see a top trademark lawyer and have the law explained to you. Trademark law is very complicated and does not give anyone the automatic right to use his name."

I was certain that any competent trademark lawyer would tell Joe that he didn't have the right to use the Gallo name on his cheese products.

"I have my *own* lawyers," Joe bristled. "They tell me I have a right to use my name on my cheese."

"If they tell you that, you should look for better lawyers, because you're being badly advised."

We were required under our licensing agreement to notify Consolidated if we discovered any possible trademark infringement. After sending Joe a copy of our licensing agreement with Consolidated and a list of law firms experienced in trademark matters, I gave some thought to the situation.

In February 1985 I phoned Joe. "Tell you what. We'll try to get Consolidated to let us license you. I'll tell them that you're our brother and that we'd like you to be able to use the name. If they agree, we'll license you."

Our general counsel, Jack Owens, contacted Consolidated. I asked him to find a way Joe could keep selling his cheese with Gallo on the label. "Make it clear that we want to work out a licensing agreement with our brother."

After many discussions and considerable persuasion on our part, we succeeded in getting a green light from Consolidated to prepare a licensing agreement for Joe.

Julio and I were pleased.

We asked our attorney to draft a "minimal" licensing agreement for Joe's cheese brand—meaning that weight would be given to familial trust and goodwill.

For starters, the license would be royalty-free; we did not want to receive a dime from Joe's cheese sales. Also, we downplayed our right to inspection. We presumed that Joe would be concerned about keeping high standards. After all, if there were any problems with his cheese, his name would be besmirched too. Our attorney included a clause that forbade Joe from selling his brand name with his company to outsiders, thereby ensuring that the name would stay in the hands of his heirs, the extended Gallo family.

Joe balked at the no-sale clause. He insisted he needed to retain the right to sell his cheese label and business to whomever he wished.

That changed the picture greatly. We could find ourselves dealing with who-knows-what conglomerate next month or next year, a real "arm's-length" type of relationship that would bear no resemblance to the bonds of kinship. If that ever happened, it would be prudent for us to have a stronger licensing agreement like the one we had with Consolidated Foods for Gallo Salame, which gave us an ironclad right of regular inspections to assure sanitation and quality control.

ON FRIDAY, JUNE 14, 1985, the *Los Angeles Times* broke this front-page story: "Bacteria Kill 28 in Southland; Recall of Cheese Ordered."

Many more news stories followed throughout that month and into the next, as the tainted-cheese calamity received widespread national and even worldwide attention. Cheese produced by the Jalisco Mexican Products Company eventually resulted in the deaths of forty-eight people. The source of the problem was found to be "leaky equipment and faulty pasteurization."*

For us, the news of the Jalisco cheese tragedy and needless loss of

*Los Angeles Times, June 22, 1985.

life was especially unnerving. So, too, were the ramifications for the winery if something similar should ever happen with cheese bearing the Gallo name.

From time to time, we send an inspection team into the three Gallo Salame plants in northern California. Included on the team are hygienists highly trained in food safety and Food and Drug Administration procedures. Solely at our expense we have employed the most highly skilled food safety experts in the country; two of them have worked with NASA on food safety for the astronauts in space. These experts wrote the food-safety procedures for Gallo Salame and devoted many hours to working with and advising their personnel on implementing the procedures and on upgrading their plants and operations. When the team recommended upgrading Gallo Salame's recall system, we designed a new one at our expense, even though we weren't obligated to do so. We are that committed to ensuring the quality of their products being produced under the "Gallo" label.

In our minds, whether the process is the manufacturing of salami or cheese or wine, cleanliness and proper sanitation are paramount.

IN MARCH 1986, Joe called for a meeting.

When I showed him into my office, Joe said he had a solution. He explained how he needed an identifiable brand in order to sell his cheese in supermarkets. He said if we would undertake to build him a new brand "as strong as Gallo" that he would change labels and "get off your trademark."

"Build you a brand as strong as Gallo?" I asked.

"I'll have to get your assurance," Joe said, "that you'd build a brand that is just as acceptable to retailers and consumers."

I was flabbergasted. "As much as I'd like to help you, we cannot undertake to build a new brand for you that is equal to Gallo. Don't you understand, Joe? We've spent hundreds of millions of dollars and a great deal of time and effort in the past fifty years to build our brand."

It was completely unrealistic.

I explained how we were committed by the licensing agreement with Consolidated to enforcing protection of the trademark for its cheese. As we'd been able to get them to go along with us licensing him, it was now imperative to come up with something that would work for all of us.

After I had a revised draft of a licensing agreement for Joe in front of me, I telephoned him.

Joe had received the same document a week earlier. It seemed very straightforward to me, containing adequate protection for all involved. There would be no interruption of Joe's business and he could keep his name on his cheese. It would be royalty-free, and Joe would retain the right to sell his cheese operation and brand name to anyone he wanted. We had adequate inspection rights to police quality and sanitary standards. Consolidated had already given preliminary approval to the agreement. I was pleased that all concerns had seemingly been addressed.

"It's not acceptable," Joe said immediately.

"Why not?" A small point here or there, I thought, could easily be recast.

"I can't give you the right to inspect."

"What?"

"I just can't do it, Ernest. Look," he said angrily, "I know what you guys would expect. You would expect me to run the place on the same sanitary basis you run the winery. Nobody alive can do that besides you guys."

I was stunned.

Of course Julio and I would expect Joe to operate his cheese plant in the most sanitary manner. And why not? It wasn't just Jalisco that had problems; every few months there was an article in the paper about someone getting sick because of the careless handling of a food or beverage product.

"Joe, it's in your own best interest for you to run a top-notch, sanitary operation. How can you suggest otherwise?"

"I won't let you inspect," Joe said, sounding more adamant by the second. "You'll have to take it out."

If he didn't keep his plant standards high and if something terrible happened like what had taken place in Los Angeles, Joe would be risking not only his own cheese brand but the Gallo name as well. He might be willing to take that chance but I wasn't. I knew that Julio wouldn't be either. More than any man alive, Julio was responsible for upgrading the quality-control and sanitary practices of the California wine industry. We were not going to agree to remove the inspection clause.

Long after our conversation ended that day, I kept rolling over in my mind this obvious but nagging question: *Just why was Joe so opposed to our quality-control inspections?*

Throughout our drawn-out negotiations with Joe, he continued to build his retail cheese brand. Retailers were aggressively promoting and selling his cheese, often in a manner suggesting a connection to our wine. Typical were newspaper ads placed by the Albertson's chain that promoted our wine, Joe's cheese, and Gallo Salame jointly.

Joe sold $16.5 million worth of cheese in 1984. At year's end, he inaugurated a new product under his label that flew directly into the face of Consolidated's Gallo Salame brand: a combination salami and cheese product.

According to our licensing agreement, Consolidated could force us to take legal action at our own expense to stop the infringement.

I realized that if we were unable to license Joe, we'd have to sue him for trademark infringement or Consolidated would sue us.

Suing a brother was not a prospect I wished to consider. But as time went on, I felt that I needed to make clear to Joe the ramifications of our not reaching an agreement.

"This can't continue," I finally told Joe. "You'll just end up making us all spend a lot of money on legal fees for you to learn about trade-mark law. If you keep refusing our license, we'll have no choice but to bring a lawsuit against you."

"Have at it," Joe said.

My brother had dug in his heels.

Julio

We bent over backward to try to resolve the problems by giving Joe a royalty-free license, but it was impossible to get him to see reason. He didn't want to be subject to an inspection of any kind, or at least not inspections by us.

We later found out just how unsanitary his operations were. State inspectors found a lot of things at his cheese plant that weren't up to standard, including excessive "insect and fly problems."* This certainly didn't surprise me. Who ever heard of building a cheese plant so close to a few thousand cows?

We later learned that periodic USDA inspections continued to find problems at Joe's cheese plant during the time Joe was refusing our license agreement containing an inspection clause.

At the time, Ernest and I knew nothing of Joe's troubles in keeping his plant operation up to minimal government standards. When we

---

*In October 1983, the U.S. Department of Agriculture (USDA), whose personnel made regular inspections of the nation's dairy and cheese operations, assigned an "Ineligible Status" to the Joseph Gallo cheese plant due to "mold found in the processing areas" and a number of other "deficiencies" in the operation. This disqualified any cheese made in the plant for USDA grading until another inspection confirmed that the problems had been corrected. In September 1984, a regional supervisor of the USDA's Dairy Grading and Standardization branch wrote to Gallo Cheese Co. advising that a number of maintenance and housekeeping deficiencies had been found at the plant. "We are especially concerned with the poor sanitary conditions found. . . . [T]his will have to be corrected before the next inspection is made in order to retain USDA approval." As a result, the plant was eventually dropped on the USDA's rating system to the lowest rating possible.

found out, we knew why Joe had been so adamant in refusing to allow us to inspect. In the end, Ernest and I agreed that we had to have a licensing agreement with a strong inspection clause.

It was a painful decision for us to authorize a lawsuit. On April 17, 1986, the winery filed suit in U.S. District Court, Fresno, against Joe's cheese business (for trademark infringement, trademark dilution, and unfair competition). We asked for no monetary damages, only for the court to order Joe to stop using "Gallo" on his cheese.

In August 1986, as our case was pending in court, a USDA inspection team found ongoing unsanitary conditions and practices at Joe's plant. These included a "lack of effective screening and other protection against birds, rodents and flies." They also discovered a "compromise of pasteurizing procedures." The plant was put on notice.

A "compromise of pasteurization" had been found to be responsible for the Jalisco cheese tragedy.

Ernest

A month after we filed suit against Joe, he asked for a meeting with Julio and me. The three of us met in a small conference room at the winery. We were alone.

Without any explanation, Joe said, "Shouldn't we get to my third of the winery before we get any older?"

At first, I thought he was kidding. But he looked so serious, I realized it wasn't a joke at all. He must think he owned a third of the winery. "Joe, where did you get such a crazy idea?"

"You know," he said.

Julio looked perplexed, too.

"You don't own any interest in this winery," I said. "You know that. You've had nothing to do with building the winery. Where did you get such an idea?"

"You know," Joe repeated.

"Stop talking in riddles," I shot back. "Where did you get the idea that you own a third of the winery?"

"It's all there in black and white," Joe answered. "Right there in the courthouse in Modesto. It's plain as day. The records of the guardianship proceedings prove that I own a third of the winery. Send somebody down there and they'll find it."

"Joe, I don't understand this at all," I said. "You know you did not inherit any interest in the winery. You know there was no winery when Father died."

"This is ridiculous," Julio interjected. "It is pretty well known who in the hell built this business."

"Send somebody down to the courthouse," Joe said, standing up. "Have them look at the guardianship files. Then maybe you can tell me what it all means."

With that, Joe turned and left.

Julio and I remained seated. Neither of us said anything right away.

I thought of the times I had offered Joe an interest. Once, when he had been in the Army, and again, when he returned home after his discharge. At the time, we were desperately looking for managerial people to come into the winery. I remembered making it clear to Joe that I was concerned about Julio's health and how much we could have used him as a partner. But Joe had turned me down both times. I even recalled his exact words: "I'll have no part of it. Anytime I do anything right I never hear from you. Anytime I do something wrong, you holler." His rejections had hit me hard at the time. Joe was the only person Julio and I ever wanted as a partner.

"I'm shocked," Julio said after Joe was gone.

"So am I."

I remembered how happy we had been to find a good piece of land for Joe when he was in the Army, and how we had developed it into a fine vineyard, without charging him, so he would accumulate property while in the service. We had been glad to help him in other ways. We had encouraged him to invest in our tartrate recovery business while he was in the Army and he had doubled his money in a few years. When we set up the glass plant in 1957, we had urged Joe to invest in the plant for his children as we were doing for ours. Joe put in a little over $50,000, which gave his children a 10 percent interest in the glass company. In 1965 we cashed out Joe's stock in order to merge the glass plant with the winery, and paid into trusts for his three children a total of $650,000.

We had always retained close personal and business ties to Joe. Years earlier, Julio and I had been trustees for his children's accounts, and a signatory to the articles of partnership when Joe set up his cattle company.

"For him to even think of such a thing . . ." Julio's voice was barely audible. "I asked him more than once to join us. Told him how much we would like to have him in Modesto as a partner, but he wasn't interested."

I picked up the phone and dialed the extension of Jon Shastid, our vice president of finance. Explaining as best I could Joe's bizarre claim, I asked Shastid to go down to the courthouse and check Joe's guardianship files.

A day or two later, Julio and I met with Shastid, who had spent hours reviewing courthouse records. All the old legal filings seemed in order and offered no hint as to Joe's purported "inheritance." That is, not until Shastid came to the document "First and Final Account of Guardians." The accounting, filed after Joe turned twenty-one, listed all his assets. Among his "undivided one-third interest" in various properties was this entry: "E. & J. Gallo Winery . . . $16,492.26."

I had no idea what the entry meant.

"It took me a while," Shastid said, "but I finally figured it out. This was an account receivable. The winery had been buying the estate's grapes every year."

I nodded.

"This was the amount the winery owed Joe for his one-third interest in the estate's grape crop," Shastid went on. "He was credited with this amount and it was included in the assets he received when the guardianship terminated. Joe's lawyer must have jumped to the conclusion that the probate court had awarded Joe one-third interest in the winery. But it had nothing to do with any equity or ownership in the winery."

Of course it had nothing to do with winery ownership. How could Joe have inherited a piece of our winery from our parents when Julio and I didn't start our business until after their deaths?

Also, had someone calculated the value of one-third interest in the winery in 1941—seven years after we had started in business—it would have been a figure considerably higher than $16,000.

"Jon, I'd like you to call and arrange for a meeting with Joe's attorney," I said. "Explain what you found and what it really means."

I fully expected this would make it clear that Joe had not inherited an interest in the winery.

Joe's attorney rejected Shastid's explanation of the $16,000 entry in the court records. He was threatening to sue on Joe's behalf, claiming that the entry proved that Joe inherited one-third interest in the winery.

I phoned Joe at home, asking that we meet.

I drove to his place in the rain.

When I got there, Joe took me through the house and out to the back porch.

I summarized what Shastid had found in the court papers and how this had been misinterpreted by his attorney. "That 'one-third interest' did not mean you had a one-third interest in the winery, Joe, but that your guardianship account was due a third of the money the winery owed the estate for its grapes that year."

"I don't agree," Joe responded.

"That was the amount of money you were *owed*. And the court records show you were paid it."

"If it meant that, why didn't it say so?" he asked. "Our father's estate included his business. The business that some court document says you continued, and which I should have inherited one third of."

"The business we continued was Father's grape-growing business. The fact is, Julio and I saved the estate. If we hadn't made it solvent, you wouldn't have inherited anything. Father didn't have a winery. Come on, Joe, you know that. You were there."

I had never talked much to Joe about our father. There had not seemed to be any reason to. Perhaps that was a mistake. There were very painful memories associated with what had happened to our parents. It had seemed best to try to put it behind us, and go on with our lives.

"You heard Father talk," I said. "You know that he was only in the wine business as a small-time peddler before Prohibition. You know he was never in the wine business after that."

"Look, I don't want a part of the winery," Joe said softly. "What I want is my debts paid off."

"What are you talking about?"

Joe explained that he was greatly overextended.

Though Julio and I had, at times, been concerned about how quickly Joe had expanded his ranch holdings, I had no idea the extent of his financial problems until he detailed them for me.

On the surface, Joe had done well for himself. Grape grower, cattle rancher, dairyman. His 8,000-head dairy herd was one of the largest milk-producing herds in the state. He was the largest landholder in Merced County, with 25,000 acres in his name. For ten years he had owned California's biggest and best-known dairy replacement herd, consisting of 13,000 heifers known as "springers." And come each harvest, Joe sold his wine grapes—2,000 acres' worth, or about 20,000 tons—usually to us for top dollar.

But I now heard how rapid growth and extensive land development had not paid off. Not only did he have virtually all his land mortgaged, he had taken on new debt to build the cheese plant. His agribusiness empire was shaky and in need of increased capital, Joe explained.

"Joe, I would be willing to help you as a brother. Julio would too, I'm sure. We could loan you something—"

"I don't want to borrow more money. As it is, I owe the Federal Land Bank millions of dollars. If you pay off my debts," he said evenly, "I won't pursue my ownership claim."

"I can't believe I'm hearing this. You are threatening to sue us if we don't pay off your debts?"

He nodded.

I fought to regain control of my emotions. "In other words, you are perfectly willing to take a third of the winery if you can get away with it."

I wouldn't have expected Joe to do this to a stranger, let alone to a brother.

I needed to stay calm and logical.

"Lawsuits cost a lot of money," I continued. "You know you don't own an interest in the winery. You're going to end up losing, and you'll have to pay attorneys' fees."

He shrugged. "I've found lawyers who will take my case on contingency. I've got nothing to lose and you guys can't afford to take the chance."

It was a long walk back to my car.

Julio

Though Joe had kept us pretty much in the dark about his growing financial problems, I was not really surprised to hear of his troubles. I knew he had made some bad business decisions through the years. I recalled a ridiculous claim Joe had filed not long before against the Federal Land Bank, alleging that the bank had loaned him more money than it should have.

In the mid-1970s we were interested in 3,000 acres in Livingston that came on the market. It was about a mile from our winery operation. We were looking at it not for vineyards, but as additional land for disposal of distillery waste. Next thing we knew, Joe had bought it out from under us, apparently assuming we intended to plant it in vineyard. On one of my next trips to Livingston, I ran into Joe. He told me he was going to plant grapes on at least 1,000 acres of the property that year.

"That's quite a big undertaking," I said. "We think we're pretty big operators, but I've never planted more than five hundred acres any year. This wine boom can take a turn, you know."

"White wine will never take a turn," Joe said. "It'll always be in demand. I'm going to get as many vines in the ground as quickly as I can."

"Well, I don't agree. Things can take a turn."

He ended up planting 1,000 acres that year. Unfortunately, he didn't check the soil first. It had large areas of alkali where the grapes didn't do well. It turned out to be a very marginal vineyard, with low production. And when the demand for the types of grape Joe had planted in such quantity—primarily Chenin Blanc and French Columbard—did end, there was a big surplus, causing prices to go down. Eventually he kept 500 acres of vines and turned the rest back into pasture for his cows. That was one big investment that just didn't pan out. Joe took fliers that way.

We had struggled with Joe over the quality of his grapes. Once I was called by one of our winemakers at our crusher. He had pushed aside several truckloads of Joe's grapes because they weren't up to our standards. "What should I do about them?" the winemaker wanted to know. Now, how could I train our winemakers to carefully and fairly grade grapes, and then go and tell them to do something different for my brother's grapes?

"Downgrade them," I said—meaning Joe would not be paid top dollar for them because they would be going into one of our secondary programs.

I refused to allow any double standards. There was no excuse for Joe not to grow top grapes, even if he was distracted by his cattle and dairy operations. I heard immediately from Joe's son, Michael, who was involved in his father's business.

"How dare your winemaker tell me our grapes aren't good enough," Michael said angrily. "What does your winemaker know about growing grapes?"

It's true our winemakers aren't growers, I granted—"But you don't have to be a chicken to judge an omelet."

Some years Joe and Michael sold their grapes to other wineries, but I noticed that they always came back to us.

I certainly thought that Joe was getting bad advice from his lawyers. Not long after Ernest's talk with him, I met privately with Joe, hoping to talk some sense into him.

"You must know in your heart that you don't have an interest in the winery," I told him. "Maybe you think this will be some kind of leverage in the trademark suit. But you can't possibly believe you own any part of the winery. The folks died before we went into the wine business, so how in the hell could it be part of their estates? There was no winery until Ernest and I started it over on Eleventh and D streets. You turned down every opportunity to join us, so how in the world can you claim a third of it?"

"I'm not claiming I do," he said, "but my attorneys say I do."

I looked at him for the longest time. I was hurt and angry. Sad, too. "Joe, you know, the last time I talked to our mother, she said she didn't care what happened to her as long as she knew that us boys would be able to get along." I felt a lump in my throat. "I hope we can, Joe."

I knew Joe to have a strong will of his own. He listened to advice, like we all do. But this was *his* decision. I considered him responsible for the senseless claim that was filed against us in July 1986. Joe's lawyer in his suit against us was the same guy who had handled Joe's unsuccessful action against the Federal Land Bank. Looking back now, I shouldn't have been too surprised. I should have figured that people who would sue a bank for loaning them too much money would sue just about anybody for anything.

In his lawsuit against us, Joe claimed that we had deprived him of his rightful inheritance of a one-third interest in the winery Ernest and I had built.

Joe's action was one of the biggest disappointments of my life. After being close to Joe through the years, my feelings about him would never be the same again.

All of it was pretty hard to take.

From that moment on, I knew there was a good chance I would never speak to my brother Joe again.

Ernest

In August 1988, after numerous court hearings, a federal judge dismissed Joe's claim to one-third ownership of the winery. The judge wrote that he based his decision on confidence in the records of the court in the 1941 guardianship proceedings, which showed that Joe had been treated fairly in the matter of his inheritance.

At the same time, the judge ordered that our trademark suit against Joe's cheese brand proceed to trial.

Two months later, on October 9, 1988, the *Los Angeles Times* carried the headline "23 Stricken by Food After Wedding Fete." The following day's headline in the *Daily News*: "Market Pulls Cheese from Shelves." The story reported that a Panorama City grocery store had voluntarily pulled five pounds of Joseph Gallo's Monterey Jack cheese off the shelf after the bride told authorities she had bought ten pounds of the cheese at the market. The following day, however, it was reported that unrefrigerated food was to blame for making the wedding guests ill. Happily, no one was seriously ill and Joe's cheese was not to blame. Still, such stories continued to point up the potential for a trade-name disaster if there ever was a serious problem with Joe's cheese.

In November 1988, the court trial began. I attended daily.

In testimony by a marketing consultant who had been hired by Joe at one point, it came out that Joe had originally suggested the trade names "California Natural" and "California Farms." When the consultant first suggested using "Joseph Gallo" as the brand name, Joe seemed uncomfortable with the suggestion but did not say why.

A food broker consulted by Joe testified that he had also recommended "Joseph Gallo." With "Gallo" on the label, he explained, the new cheese brand could capitalize on the reputation and selling power of Gallo wine. Retailers would be much more receptive.

"I can't use 'Gallo,'" Joe had reportedly answered, no doubt recalling my admonition. "My brothers won't let me."

The food broker explained to Joe that retailers would be reluctant to make shelf space available for a new line to compete with Kraft and other well-advertised cheese brands "unless it carried a famous name like 'Gallo.'"

Joe eventually told his consultants to go ahead with the "Joseph Gallo" label.

According to what came out at trial, the "Gallo" label worked just as the experts predicted. Joe's sales representatives, who had been warned not to officially connect "Joseph Gallo Cheese" to the winery, couldn't resist doing so. Some even wrote to prospective customers implying that Joe's product was produced by a division of the winery. Joe's advertising agency concluded that shoppers would associate Gallo cheese with Gallo wine, no matter what. They recommended that Joe "capitalize on the Gallo name and image, and flirt with it as much as possible." Similarly, Joe's retail customers promoted Gallo cheese as another Gallo product, tying it not only to our table wines, but to Gallo Salame's products as well.

I testified that our Gallo brand name would be harmed if Joe's cheese suffered an incident such as the one that had befallen Jalisco.

Our lawyers introduced evidence that showed substandard conditions at Joe's cheese plant.

Also, we introduced the results of a consumer survey that had been conducted under the personal supervision of pollster Mervin Field. The survey showed "extensive evidence of consumer confusion" as to whether Joe's cheese was a product of Gallo Winery.

When called to testify, Joe defended the quality of his cheese. He claimed that the use of his name on cheese was no different than putting his name on his ranches or grapes.

On June 19, 1989, the federal judge ruled that Joe had tried to capitalize on the use of a name that had been developed and built up in the retail marketplace by us and to which he had not contributed.

The judge's language could not have been more blunt. He noted the "willful exploitation of the fame and advertising value of the Gallo brand" by Joe's cheese business. This exploitation involved "their disregard of Plaintiffs' demand that they cease and desist despite mounting proof that the Joseph Gallo mark is confusing to consumers."

The judge chastised Joe's side for trying to "bury" evidence—notes involving marketing of Gallo brand cheese—so that winery lawyers wouldn't find them. Eventually, they were located in an unrelated tax file. The "Cheese Notes" were "cogent, independent evidence of the likelihood of [brand] confusion," the judge said. "Defendants' obvious attempt to forestall Plaintiffs' discovery of such evidence is indicative of a conscious purpose to conceal the truth."

The judge gave Joe 120 days to stop infringing on our trademark. On his label, Joe would be allowed to show himself as the producer of the cheese, but his name would have to be smaller and placed below a new brand name.

It was a sweeping victory, but one in which neither Julio nor I took any joy.

When I left the courtroom for the final time, Joe was also on his way out. Without looking at each other, we went our separate ways. I headed down the hallway in one direction, and Joe went the other way.

Time heals all, I used to think.

Now I am not so sure.

ON FEBRUARY 7, 1992, the U.S. Court of Appeals for the Ninth Circuit upheld the judge's decision that Joe did not have any ownership claims to the winery. They modified only very slightly the ruling on the trademark matter.

After the federal court of appeals upheld the rulings for us, Joe requested a rehearing. This request was made to all of the judges in the appellate court—more than two dozen.

Not one of the judges voted to rehear the case.

Not a single one.

20

FRANK AND ED
AND HAL RINEY

Ernest

Wine spritzers and coolers had long been enjoyed by Americans who mixed these refreshing drinks for themselves, usually over ice on warm summer days.

Bottling wine coolers was not new either. In the 1960s we came out with one of the first. We originally blended hard cider with pure fruit flavors, though later we changed it to a pear wine base. Called "Scotty," this and all future wine coolers were possible because of a change in the law that we helped to get enacted that allowed "special natural" flavorings to be added to wine products.

We packaged Scotty in a six-pack of "stubby" beer bottles. Supported by local radio spots, we launched the new product in a few test markets. When Scotty didn't show much strength, we abandoned it.

Twenty years later, two young men working out of a garage in Lodi, California, came up with a cooler made of fruit juice, carbonated water, and wine. Their product, California Cooler—below 7 percent alcohol—provided consumers with a tasty and enjoyable new beverage.

At first we took a wait-and-see attitude.

In 1982, California Cooler sold 80,000 cases. The following year, sales reached nearly two million cases, turning the small company started by the two young entrepreneurs into the tenth-largest wine company in California. They achieved this with just one product, and without any advertising or national distribution.

Wine coolers had broad appeal. More of the mostly young-adult customers tended to be female than male. They came from all races, income levels, and life-styles.

Coolers were a refreshing wine drink with a low alcohol content, but clearly they were transitional. Could this parallel the success of Boone's Farm, which saw many of those consumers eventually turn to table wines?

By 1984 we had concluded that we should release a wine cooler. We were more interested in doing it right than in just jumping in. I knew that our production department could create an excellent product. I also knew that we could handle the advertising, merchandising, and selling required to get our fair share of the cooler market.

By that summer, we had our cooler.

Hal Riney, who headed Ogilvy & Mather's San Francisco office, was handling our advertising. Around 1980, Al Fenderson had mentioned to me that he was impressed with some of the Riney commercials he had seen. He suggested that we talk with Riney. He had some great ideas that we bought, including the "All the best from Ernest and Julio Gallo" theme for advertising our line of premium varietals.

At the time we began talking to Riney about wine coolers, the industry considered the targeted consumers to be young adults. As a result, all the producers were working on "young" brand names and "young" advertising campaigns. We did our share of that early on. With our new product ready to go—waiting only for the labels to have the brand name added—we considered a lot of "young" names. One I remember was "Route 66," after the famous highway that had inspired a popular hit song and TV show.

At some point we realized that with a couple dozen other wine coolers set to come out at the same time, all reportedly with "young" brand names and advertising campaigns, we wouldn't stand out from the crowd if we did the same thing. Plus, I wasn't convinced that the cooler market would be strictly under-thirty adults. I had an idea that there would be plenty of people in their forties and fifties who might enjoy these beverages.

We needed something different.

One idea was to hire "Crocodile Dundee" as our spokesman. But the Australian actor Paul Hogan was already advertising Australian beer, and as much as he would have liked to take on the assignment, he felt it would place him in the position of seeming to be unfaithful to Australian beer.

We saw merit in another of Riney's ideas, which was based on using American "country humor." Riney used terms like "tongue-in-cheek," "whimsical," and "offbeat" to describe what he had in mind. "Two old codgers who look like farmers sitting on a porch talking about wine coolers can do all kinds of things typical advertising can't do," he explained. "It will be very difficult to ignore these guys. We could have them talking about the product, and getting different messages across every time."

Riney came up with the name "Bartles and James." Fenderson suggested adding a "y" to "James" to make it more distinctive.

Frank Bartles would be a rough-around-the-edges marketer—the product's spokesman—and silent Ed Jaymes, the production guy.

We bought the idea. Riney was cutting across the grain, but I liked that. I am never willing to be one of the pack. I always want our advertising to be innovative and our agencies unafraid to be daring.

Riney wanted "real people" instead of polished actors for the commercials. He sent his wife, Liz, who ran her own casting company, around the country looking for our spokesman, Frank. She interviewed and photographed hundreds of farmers and other ordinary folks in small towns in Oklahoma, Nevada, Oregon, and Washington. She eventually found a local fellow hanging around a grange in Alfalfa, Oregon. His name was Dave Rufkahr, and he was a small-time cattle rancher. Rufkahr became Frank. Ed was cast closer to home: Richard Maugg, a construction contractor from Santa Rosa, California, and an old school chum of Riney's.

We tested the commercials in Phoenix and a few other markets. Initially, many viewers thought the two older guys were kind of strange, but most of them soon became quite fond of Frank and Ed. In a few weeks, "Bartles and Jaymes," a citrus-flavored white-wine cooler sold in four-packs of 12-ounce bottles, had gained 50 percent of the Phoenix cooler market.

Bartles and Jaymes went national in 1985. "Ed took out a second mortgage on his house, wrote to Harvard for an MBA, and now we're preparing to enter the wine-cooler business," explained Frank in the first commercial, which ended—as they all would—with him humbly thanking the viewers for their support.

A lot of people believed that Frank and Ed made Bartles and Jaymes themselves. We received letters sent to them empathizing with their entrepreneurial effort. Some of the envelopes even contained dollar bills. (We returned the money, of course—with appreciation for the thought.)

That first year, we sold 7.5 million cases of Bartles and Jaymes, slipping into second place behind California Cooler.

The following year we jumped into first place with 17 million cases sold—about 25 percent of the U.S. cooler market. At that point, coolers represented nearly a third of all California wine shipments. Industry-wide, wine-cooler sales peaked at 56 million cases annually in 1987.

Many of the smaller cooler marketers who had moved so quickly into the category were weeded out by the explosion of brand advertising. Even California Cooler was not immune, suffering a 72 percent volume loss in 1989. The two fellows who had invented the product did just fine, though. By then, they had sold out for $63 million cash, and further payments depending on the future profitability of California Cooler. The brand quickly disintegrated against tough competition.

We were among three or four major competitors left to fight it out in what would soon become a shrinking market for coolers.

One day I had Rufkahr and Maugg for lunch at the winery. All of us found it very amusing that in a bit of reverse casting, "Ed" talked a blue streak while "Frank" was the shy and quiet one.

"Frank and Ed" won Riney numerous awards. His work could be popular, witty, and sophisticated, all at the same time. He has a real talent for humor that sells. Bartles and Jaymes was the most effective campaign Riney ever did for us.

The little jokes "Frank and Ed" made weren't meant to last long. Like the time "Frank and Ed" visited New York City, a place that really baffled them. When they saw lox and bagels for the first time, they were amazed by the big doughnuts with fish on them. We made a point not to keep a commercial on for long. Instead, Riney did fifty to sixty spots a year.

Some experts estimated that the cooler market would reach 130 million cases by the year 2000. Though the category proved not to have that kind of staying power, coolers are far from dead today: Approximately 34 million cases were sold in 1993.

WHEN IT CAME TO ADVERTISING our "Gallo" brand wines, Riney was trying to dispel a myth. "There are many people who don't believe Ernest and Julio Gallo are real people," he had told us soon after he started working with us. Apparently, people thought our names were a trademark, like Smith Brothers and Betty Crocker.

Riney proposed to try to humanize the winery in every way possible in our advertising, and also to work toward upgrading our image.

I agreed with Riney that it would be beneficial to project the personal care and dedication that went into making our wines. But how to do that?

The first suggestion made by virtually every advertising agency we have ever hired has been for Julio and me to appear in commercials. In this way, we were told, we could show consumers that we are real people, and that we carefully watch over the making of our wines. I've seen a dozen such proposals, but Julio and I never considered going on television. Neither of us wanted that type of personal notice. Besides, I don't like the idea of being on television for a given product when we have such an extensive line and are always coming out with new products. Pretty soon, we would wear out our effectiveness as pitchmen. In the long run, it would lose its uniqueness.

For our premium line of wines, Riney wanted a campaign based on "emotion." He said it could be just as effective as any "rational appeal" for a product. "Most clients think the rational appeals for their products are much more important than the consumer thinks they are," Riney said. We were well aware, though, that if we were going to attempt an emotional appeal, we had to deliver. We couldn't hold anything back, including expense.

This would be a much different campaign than Bartles and Jaymes, one not based on humor. It would have to be well composed and aesthetically pleasing, while still containing a message that sold the product.

After we heard many ideas that didn't click for us, Riney's right-hand man, Bruce Campbell, brought to us the music of Vangelis, a Greek composer who works in London and composes music on a synthesizer. Campbell thought Vangelis's works, popularized in the film *Chariots of Fire*, could be the backdrop for a series of great commercials.

We were willing to try it. Campbell flew to London, where for several days he sat beside Vangelis at his control panel in a room full of electronic equipment. Vangelis rearranged his enchanting piece "Hymne" to fit thirty- and sixty-second spots.

In one commercial, with "Hymne" playing softly in the background, various scenes were depicted: a man driving a tractor in a vineyard, a cooper at work, the harvesting of grapes, winemakers tasting the wine. Bottles of several varietals, including Cabernet Sauvignon and Chardonnay, were shown. Riney, doing the voice-over himself, delivered this simple message:

> There are no better ways to make wines.
> No better land to grow wine.
> No better wines than Gallo wines—today.
> Today's Gallo—all the best a wine can be.

Another in the Vangelis series has Riney saying:

> To all the people who grow the wine
>   and to all those who enjoy fine wine,
> Ernest and Julio Gallo give their best.
> Today's Gallo.
> All the best a wine can be.

The Vangelis spots—there were several of them all using the same piece of music—and other advertising Riney did for our premium line were thoughtfully developed and beautifully produced. Fenderson called them "works of art," and I couldn't disagree.

These commercials proved to be very popular with the public. In the first twelve months that we ran them, we had over fifty thousand letters, telegrams, and telephone calls asking for the name of the music and locations where it could be purchased. The commercials could bring a lump to your throat, but how many people remembered the name of our product? When I voiced this concern to Riney, he smiled. "How did they know where to write or call, Ernest?"

While the commercials certainly got the viewers' attention—the first thing any advertising must do to be effective—we detected no movement in sales. I began to think that the music had vamped the product. People liked and remembered the music but were not persuaded to buy. They came away entertained but not sold.

We all thought the commercial Riney did for the introduction of Tott's champagne was great. It opens with a shot of an attractive woman in front of a château that serves as a backdrop for what appears to be a European love story told in a series of short, almost abstract visuals as a voice is heard singing the beautiful Puccini aria "O mio babbino caro." It cost around $700,000 to make this commercial with enchanting music, splendid scenery, beautiful people, magnificent buildings. Again, we got an enormous amount of mail from people who wanted to know the name of the music, the singer, and information on where they could buy the album. Again, it just didn't convert into consumers going out to buy our product.

The main problem with these "beautiful" commercials was that they didn't sell hard enough. Which is to say that they didn't accomplish the prime purpose of advertising: to sell product. A great commercial moves boxes.

In addition to Hal Riney and Partners, we have worked with many outstanding agencies in the advertising business (sometimes concurrently)—BBD&O; Doyle Dane Bernbach; Leo Burnett; Needham, Harper and Steers; J. Walter Thompson; Young & Rubicam; Erwin Wasey; Ogilvy & Mather; and Dailey & Associates, among others. We have told them all—and repeatedly—their job is not to win awards for their advertising but to sell our wines. The advertising industry would better serve clients and in the long run earn more money for itself if, in judging commercials for awards, it simply used the criterion of how effective a given commercial is in selling the product.

Just because a marketer spends money on commercials doesn't mean it is really advertising.

When we are paying a lot of money to produce and run a series of commercials, we want results quickly. One advertising agency complained that after working weeks preparing a commercial, I had not given it a real chance to work. They claimed that after running the ad on television on Friday night, I called stores on the weekend to see how many bottles of wine had sold. That is not true.

I waited until Monday.

It is true that I am not willing to wait a year to find out whether or not a campaign has worked. In that period, millions of dollars could be wasted and time lost.

It is customary for our brand management to meet regularly with our advertising agencies to pass on the direction and strategy we have for a specific product. The agency, knowing our objective, then goes to work. When the brand managers think the proposed advertising has merit, the agency makes its presentation.

The president of the American Association for the Advancement of Advertising made a speech several years ago in which he said that brand managers were a hindrance to the development of good advertising. They just got in the way, he claimed, and ad agencies shouldn't have to deal with them at all. I disagree.

I can understand how it can be irritating for a very good creative director from a top agency to have a junior brand manager, fresh out of business school, sit there and comment on his creativity. But the team process is that important at Gallo.

When we discuss advertising for a particular product, the marketing director and everyone under him or her, as well as my son David, Al Fenderson, and consultant Skip McLaughlin, participate. This makes for an especially strong team. I feel we get much better advertising by having an interchange of opinions.

After an agency presentation, we go around the table, starting with the most junior person present, usually an assistant brand manager. I don't want anyone to be put in the position of having to contradict his or her boss. My objective is to give these young people a chance to develop, as well as to give us a way of appraising their potential. Too, the entire process helps to stimulate everyone's thinking. I believe that this results in better decisions.

My grandmother had a saying that I have tried to follow through life. *Devi sentire tutte le campane a suonare.* Translated from Italian: "You have to hear all the bells ring." Literally, this means don't accept the first version of anything you are told, but wait and listen to differing opinions before a decision is made.

We advertise more than any other California wine company, and usually rank among the top one hundred clients in the country for dollars spent on television advertising.

However, we have also been ranked as "one of the worst clients" by advertising trade publications. In articles quoting many anonymous sources who claim to have worked on our advertising, stories are told to illustrate just how demanding we are.

Some years back I was given the opportunity to comment for an *Advertising Age* article entitled, "How the 'Gallo Experience' Wears Agencies Down."

"Our present agencies—Ogilvy & Mather and Needham, Harper & Steers—are two of the most creative and successful agencies in the business," I said, "and they are currently taking our advertising to new creative and effective heights.

"As to what we expect from an advertising agency, we simply expect effective creativity. We do not look for or require all of the other services that an agency normally supplies." I listed those services we do not require, but handle ourselves: media planning, market research, copy testing, participation in brand planning, and involvement in marketing strategy, packaging, and P-O-S design.

"The challenge that we give to our agencies is that which Leo Burnett himself said twenty years ago: 'Develop advertising as good as the product.' This is, and has been, a challenging and rewarding assignment for many of the best creative minds in the business."

In another article in the same trade publication, entitled "How Gallo Earned Tough-Client Title," I was criticized for my "unusual" practice of watching the television on weekends to see our scheduled spots. The article went on to explain how I would demand a refund from the network if our advertising didn't run, or if our spots had portions of the audio or visual missing.

Though I have been known to watch our commercials, we hire a monitoring service that spot-checks our advertising and reports any problems. If a network misses our spot, or cuts it short, or if the audio isn't clear, the next day our Media Department asks the network for a "make good" spot in the same time slot. In other words, we insist on getting what we pay for.

What I expect an advertising agency working with us to provide is advertising that will switch a consumer from buying a competitor's wine to buying ours, and induce people who are not drinking wine to try ours. This is necessary if the commercial is to sell more than enough wine to pay for the cost of the advertising. This sounds obvious and should be.

But here is the problem: Agencies do not get paid on the basis of creating successful advertising. They get paid on the amount of advertising their client runs—whether that advertising is productive or not.

A sound agency understands that its own long-term profit is inextricably linked with the profit of their client, and that no client can or will continue to run unproductive advertising for very long. As with some other businesses, the need for an agency to keep its short-term profits up can get in the way of its best long-term interest.

Unfortunately, this problem is sometimes taken to ridiculous extremes. One agency complained to us that we were "too demanding" because we turned down a number of their storyboard presentations. From where I sat, I thought we had been extremely patient. It didn't seem to matter to the agency that the advertising they presented was not effective in our view. What apparently mattered most to them was that since they had brought so much stuff to us, we should have run *something*.

In this situation, not just the agency lost. First, we wasted our time. My marketing team and I looked at each one of those presentations of unacceptable advertising. And second, we lost the sales of wine that we could have made, had we been presented with advertising that would work, and that we could have been running in the marketplace.

I believe a good agency welcomes a client who is "demanding." Demanding clients encourage and stimulate an agency to produce better advertising, and both the client and the agency profit from such work.

Additionally, when other clients see good, productive advertising on television or in magazines, they want to know which agency did it. The best advertising for an advertising agency is their own good work.

After the many years we have been advertising, and trying to improve the effectiveness of our advertising, I have become convinced that there is no real way of knowing whether a commercial or campaign is going to be effective until you actually run it in a test market and count the boxes sold. We have, over the years, used all the latest testing procedures—focus groups, copy, recall, and persuasion tests—with some very misleading results.

I have come to believe that the collective judgment of our marketing team—from those assistant brand managers on up—may be a better guide to effective advertising than the results of any kind of test other than a market test.

AFTER PRICING, more than any other action, advertising creates the consumer image of a product and of a company. Unfortunately, some advertisers fail to act responsibly.

The wine industry has long been aware that we must advertise in a socially responsible manner. As long ago as 1949, the Wine Institute adopted a strict and responsible advertising code for the industry.

The result is that wine is advertised in a socially responsible manner, and the wine industry is justifiably proud of its advertising code. In 1985, Senator Paula Hawkins told the Senate that the wine industry's advertising code was "exemplary in its provisions and practice. As an example of private initiative, the code stands as a model of social responsibility which deserves wider support and recognition."*

The provisions that Senator Hawkins considered the most important were:

- Subscribers to the Code shall show food available to be used or intended to be used in ads where wine is served.
- Any attempt to suggest that wine directly contributes to success or achievement is unacceptable.
- Any advertisement that has particular appeal to persons below the legal drinking age is unacceptable. (For example, Code subscribers shall not feature traditional heroes of the young, such as cowboys, race-car drivers, rock stars, or use amateur or professional sports celebrities, past or present, or anyone else engaged in pastimes and occupations that have particular appeal to persons below the legal drinking age.)
- Wine advertising should in no way suggest that wine be used in connection with driving.
- Wine advertising by Code subscribers shall not appear in or directly adjacent to television or radio programs or print media that dramatize or glamorize overconsumption or inappropriate use of alcoholic beverages.

*Congressional Record, February 18, 1985.

313

One night in 1989, I was watching a news program on television at home, when it showed a derelict lying on the street with a bottle of Thunderbird in his hand.

That unforgettable sight crystallized my thinking: I did not want our company to be associated with anything that catered to such unfortunate individuals.

The next morning, I issued a directive that went out to all our distributors: They were to halt distribution of Thunderbird to any retail accounts that served derelicts.

I HAVE NEVER ASKED an employee to retire.

Quite the opposite—I always regret when someone who has ability and experience wants to retire. Usually, I try to talk them out of it.

But I did not succeed in dissuading Jon Shastid and national sales manager Ken Bertsch from retiring in the summer of 1989. At that point, we faced the loss of two employees who had helped build our company. (Howard Williams, our very capable advertising manager, had died in 1978.)

"Working with Jon has challenged all who worked with him into better thinking," I said at the dinner party I gave both men at my home. "The result has been many very good decisions for the winery, making it a better company."

"Ken was a great salesman who became a great sales manager," I went on. "He did a very good job in laying the foundation for a sales force that was to become the acknowledged most effective in the entire alcoholic-beverage industry today."

It is true that we are constantly recruiting young people and bringing them up in the organization. This keeps pressure on us to remain open to new ideas. Individuals who can't keep up the pace soon reach the conclusion that they would be happier elsewhere.

When I hear the word "retirement," I envision a fellow who has worked hard all his life going off to Florida, buying a condo by the beach, sitting in a rocking chair with his shirt off showing his red suspenders, his feet on the veranda rail, twiddling his thumbs while counting the gulls.

That isn't for me.

Not as long as I am having so much fun at what some people would call "working."

"WHAT ROUTE have you laid out for me?" I asked.

"None," answered Denny Despars, our winery representative for the Los Angeles area. "We'll take you anywhere you want to go, Ernest."

Despars had been with us for twenty-five years. He knew my habits when it came to surveying stores.

For many years I have spent Memorial Day in Los Angeles. Not for a holiday, but to survey stores. For this particular survey trip in May 1991 I was joined by my sons, David and Joe.

I have turned over to Joe and David many of the day-to-day responsibilities for running my side of the business, Joe in Sales and David in Marketing. I have a lot of faith in them. Of course, I still put in full days at the office. In fact, I'm so busy at the winery that I take my mail home with me to read after dinner.

Soon after landing at Santa Monica airport at nine A.M. we split into two teams. David, Al Fenderson, and I were on one. Joe went with another group that would cover different territory. We would all meet back at the airport that night.

I asked Despars to take me to where we were having problems.

We visit retail accounts to determine the effectiveness of the distributor's effort to benefit the retailer's interest, the distributor's interest, and the winery's interest. If any one of these interests are neglected, it calls for a session with the wholesaler. A brand cannot succeed unless all these interests are satisfied.

Do distributors get worried about such an inspection tour? Generally not. I would hope they would want us to come to town to see what we can do to provide additional support. They want to do a good job. They want to be number one in their market, if they aren't already. If they are on top, they want to stay there. We are really all in a partnership: winery, distributor, and retailer.

We drove down Sherman Way in Van Nuys in a gray van. On a day when many Americans were attired in shorts and sandals, looking forward to a picnic or barbecue, we were dressed in suits, visiting stores.

In this area, Despars explained, there were 150 retail accounts handled by our distributor.

To ensure that our calls were productive and that we all were focused, I began by asking: "What are we going to look for?"

Despars gave me specifics about the monthly "program" for this area.

A typical program focuses on eight or nine items from our line. Two or three will be cork-finished table wines. A couple of sparkling wines. Coolers and generic wines. Maybe brandy and vermouth. The idea is to focus the local sales force's resources and effort on those targeted products that month. The following month we highlight a fresh lineup of our products. As Joe says, "Our whole secret to selling is specialization and focus."

"Let's also look for tie-ins," Despars said.

Despars was concerned that some competitors were cross-merchandising to move their products—pairing them up with other types of products—and he thought we should be considering our own tie-ins with products such as flowers, meat, and fish.

I was cool to the concept, though I knew that the industry was going more in that direction instead of spending money on advertising. Ideally, fine wines are sold by effective advertising and/or point-of-sale, and/or packaging based on their quality, not with tie-ins or coupons that give the customer a refund on a pound of spaghetti or a geranium for every bottle of wine they purchase.

"Let's also be considering Tott's," I said, "and whether or not we should be bringing Eden Roc into this market."

Eden Roc was a new champagne we were developing that would be priced between our two existing champagnes, André and Tott's.

The first store we went into was a chain. Someone went over to introduce himself to the manager and let him know all these "suits" were from the Gallo Winery and not from the FBI.

First we checked our prices, comparing them to our competitors'. I suggested raising a couple of prices to improve our image long-range, not a recommendation that would come from a sales force. A salesman is generally happiest when his price can be the cheapest, because he can sell more.

Next, we compared packaging on table wines.

"What about our label?" I asked.

"Too traditional," Despars said.

At a Tott's display, there was quite a bit of missing stock—a good sign, as it meant there had been sales. But should the display and stock be expanded?

"You know what they say about out of stock?" David asked no one in particular.

"Out of business," two or three voices answered.

"Most brands of White Zin are fifty cents to a dollar a bottle under us," Despars said. "They're getting to us. We need to lower our price."

"Give it time," I said. "Our quality advertising and higher price, along with our product, will raise our image. As that happens, our share will increase."

After each store visit we sat in the van and discussed what we had seen. I asked everyone for a summary.

"Our biggest opportunity in this store is to have more Tott's," said our area sales manager for chain stores. "We could also move more brandy."

We don't talk about having "problems" in our organization. Instead, we talk about "opportunities" to improve our position.

When considering our labels against those of the competition, David was concerned. The label on our varietal wines has our administration building on it. "Our label is cold and forbidding," he said. "We want sophistication but we also want labels that are user-friendly. We need to warm up our labels." That was to became a top priority of his.

No one can more quickly evaluate our position in a store than David. He can instantly detect a bad display location, the absence of our wines from the cold box, insufficient shelf spread, or any other "opportunities" that can give us a chance to better our position.

We went into small mom-and-pop stores too, of course. Back out in the van after several more hours of surveying, I asked our chain manager how long he had been with us.

"Four years, sir."

"What college?"

"Northwestern, class of '87. I was recruited on campus."

I was pleased. Joe's college recruitment program has paid off by attracting bright, aggressive, motivated young people to our firm. We offer our recruits the chance to be part of the number one team in the industry. Helping us remain number one seems to be a challenge they really enjoy. If, for their reasons or ours, they leave, their Gallo experience usually proves to be a valuable asset to their careers. Many of those in the wine industry today refer to themselves as graduates of "E & J University."

At lunch, I told a story about making a market survey in Florida a while back. We were hustling from store to store, as usual. We inadvertently left behind at one stop a slower member of the team, but no one noticed. At a store three hours later, the distributor's sales manager, who was with us, was called to the phone. He came back to ask if we should backtrack to pick the guy up. "No," I said. "How valuable can a guy be if he wasn't missed in three hours?"

That afternoon, I noticed none of these guys slowed down a bit.

One of our first stops after lunch was a family-owned-and-operated liquor store. Most of the family was behind the counter. When one of our group started his usual spiel—"We're with Gallo wine on a market survey . . ."—the young guy behind the counter interrupted.

"So which one of you is Mr. Gallo?" he asked, trying to be funny.

I stepped forward and offered my hand.

The man's jaw dropped open in surprise.

I asked if we could look around his store.

"Please," he said. "You are very welcome."

Other family members wanted to shake hands.

"How's our distributor's service?" I asked.

"Fine," the retailer said. "Very good."

I made a point of picking out a couple of higher-priced wines and took them to the register. When I realized I didn't have any cash on me, Despars came to my rescue.

At a chain store, I noticed a display card on one aisle that was about fifteen feet in the air.

"People do not look up at the ceiling when they are shopping," I said, upset that a basic tenet had been broken. "*Eye* level is what we're after. We've been saying that for years and years. *Eye* level."

Eye level is not difficult to find. Since most of the population is between five feet and six feet six inches, eye level falls within only an eighteen-inch space. That's where *all* the point-of-sale pieces should be located.

"The salesman should be embarrassed," our chain manager admitted. "I'll talk to him personally."

The assistant manager of the liquor section was working on the holiday. We were introduced.

"How often do our guys come in?" I asked.

"Every week."

"I want to thank you for your support," I said.

21

THE LAND THAT HAS DONE SO MUCH FOR US

Julio

We bought 1,000 acres of land near Asti in 1989. The property, some of it already planted in grapes, had once belonged to Italian Swiss Colony. This brought to about 4,000 acres our land holdings in Sonoma County.

The vines already in the ground were so old and unproductive that we pulled them out, then fumigated the soil to clear it of insects and fungus before replanting. We had intended to keep the surrounding hillsides, covered in oak and brush, as watershed. But when I went out and started to dig around up there, I found some of the finest soil I had ever seen.

Below the topsoil were pebbles, rocks, even big boulders. This type of material is the key to good drainage, which keeps the soil dry and light and leaves the vines with dry feet. The soil was ideal for growing grapes. We started to have other ideas about just what to do with this land.

Our new property was located in the northern Alexander Valley, where it is warmer than at our Russian River vineyards. Alexander Valley provided the perfect climate to grow grapes for many red-wine varieties. We decided to grow Merlot, Cabernet Sauvignon, and Cabernet Franc—varieties I wanted to try blending for a Bordeaux-style wine. Also, Petite Sirah, maybe some old-time Italian favorites such as Nebbiolo and Sangiovese, and of course Zinfandel, still my favorite. We would conduct the same type of viticultural experiments as we had at Livingston to find which varieties grew best in the region.

My son, Bob, along with his twenty-seven-year-old son, Matt, went out with our engineering experts and figured out how best to reshape the terrain so we could expand our grape acreage into the hills.

We had to clear the land, and we would need well-designed sloping for proper runoff. It would necessitate reworking and moving hills. Not wanting to overdevelop, we decided to plant 600 acres and leave 400 acres in watershed and greenbelt.

Buying cultivated land can be a problem. Often it is worn out. Most of the time, you are better off buying virgin soil. It has the potential for more vigorous growth. Also, it is usually less expensive. People tend to want a lot of money for existing vineyards, even though more than half the time you end up pulling out the old vines and replanting. We were fortunate that Asti had so much uncultivated acreage that we could plant.

Asti was the biggest development project we had ever undertaken— and the biggest anyone had ever attempted in Sonoma County. We knew it would take several years and cost a great deal of money. But that's the nature of winemaking and grape growing. They are long-term investments.

I was seventy-nine years old the year we started in Asti. At the time, I was aware that these new premium vineyards would benefit our descendants more than Ernest and me.

Once the land was ready, we would be planting at most two hundred acres a year. The new vines wouldn't give us a commercial crop for three seasons. I don't like to rush the rootstock that wine grapes are grown on. The roots are the heart of the plant. I like to give them two full growing seasons before grafting the varietal vines to the disease-resistant roots.

Phylloxera, a louse that attacks the root system of a vine by sucking nutrients from the tiny ends of the roots and injecting toxins, has become a big problem in Napa and Sonoma counties. This pest has been around for centuries. Everyone thought the problem was under control with the use of rootstock believed to be resistant to infestation. But in recent years, a new strain of Phylloxera has developed that prefers vines planted with a type of "resistant" rootstock called AXR-1, which was widely used in Napa and Sonoma. Phylloxera doesn't wipe out a vineyard overnight, but comes on slowly, eventually affecting the quality and quantity of grapes. The only economical way to fight the infestation is to replant. This can be very expensive—up to $20,000 an acre. Some growers can afford it, others can't. Marginal growers will be forced out of business. It all results in higher grape and wine prices.

During our own research on rootstock, we discovered years ago that other rootstocks provided better grape/wine quality, so we stopped using AXR-1 around 1986. We divided up our new plantings among ten other types of rootstock. Our ongoing research program and our concern for quality are paying us major dividends in this regard.

Some years earlier and well before we had made any decision on developing Asti, Bob had bought at auction some surplus earth-moving equipment, huge machines that had moved mountains up on the Alaska pipeline project.

"I got them for a good price," he explained at the time. "We'll find something to do with them, Dad."

He was right, and his foresight paid off. We had already found several good uses for them before the Asti project.

One reason Asti took three years to develop was because we could work only between the last spring rains and the first fall rains. We knew better than to work the ground when it was wet. Ernest and I had tried that back in the winter of '29.

That first fall at Asti we cleared the land, chopping down trees, which would be used for firewood. I don't like to cut down trees. Unfortunately, a lot had to go at Asti, but I walked those hills myself marking the ones to be left, like a particular big oak or a line of redwood midway up a ridge. We left as many as possible, just as we do whenever we take out orchards to plant vines. It's true that vines that are thrown into the shadow of trees during the afternoon will not do quite as well. And yes, we are in the grape business.

The real work on Asti didn't begin until early summer. The first two feet of topsoil was scraped off and put to one side, then hilltops were smoothed out and gullies were filled. When the shape, height, and slope were just right, the topsoil was put back on, plowed and mixed in, and the hill smoothed over. Then, trenches were dug so that pipe could be laid for drainage systems, drip irrigation, and in some areas, sprinklers for frost protection. We designed it so that groundwater would run no more than ten rows before hitting a drainage ditch. That way there would be no erosion, and we wouldn't silt up the rivers, creeks, or neighbors' properties.

Bob and I visited Asti every week during the summer, taking the helicopter over from Modesto. Though we had rolls of schematics drawn by engineers, we liked to climb over the hills ourselves. My grandson Matt usually accompanied us. In fact, by now Matt was in charge of vineyard land development in Sonoma.

In some cases, to get a nice 12-degree slope, as much as sixty feet of soil had to be taken off a hill—the equivalent of moving a six-story building. In one summer (1991) alone, a million yards of dirt were moved.

If, after all that work, a slope looked too steep, we had it reworked, even if it added a few days to the job.

"Fifty years from now," Bob said once, "I don't want this to look man-made."

I couldn't have agreed more.

I LOVE BEING OUTDOORS. I visit our own vineyards at least once a week.

Though I can't visit all of our growers anymore—we have almost a thousand now—I do spot-check some now and then. Our Grower Relations Department, headed by Phil Bava, now has a dozen viticulturists stationed between Sonoma and Fresno. This effort is more important than ever in terms of keeping in touch with our growers.

Not long ago I stopped at a Sonoma County vineyard and was chatting about weather and soil with the ranch manager when the owner, whom I had never met, drove up. I was told later that after I left, the owner asked the manager who I was. When he was told, the owner said, "Why, he looks like a farmer."

I look like a farmer because that's exactly what I am.

During the harvest, when you have to keep one eye on the weather and one eye on the rising sugar and acid levels, I am still at it eighteen hours a day, seven days a week.

At this point in the growing cycle, it's a real judgment call. Bob says it's like going to Reno every year. If you guess wrong, you can lose big. For example, if you keep the grapes on the vine to try for more sweetness and it rains, you can end up losing much of the crop to mold.

Or if it's unusually hot in early fall in a normally cooler region like Laguna, do you irrigate? It's best to avoid watering that late in the season because you'll get more intense flavor in the grapes if you don't. But if the vines look overly stressed and you think they may not make it, you have to do something for them.

In late July 1991, Bob and I made the rounds of our Sonoma County vineyards, now totaling approximately 2,000 acres. We have another

2,000 acres in watershed for irrigation purposes and "set aside" for wild-life habitat.

At our 150-acre Chiotti Ranch in Dry Creek, not far from our winery at Frei, we had mostly Cabernet planted, along with some Zinfandel. Like Alexander Valley, this is a warmer climate ideal for red wines. I could tell just driving by that the vineyard was overcropped.

"I wouldn't buy a grower's crop that looked like this," I told Bob and Matt. "With so many grapes, you're going to lose some intensity in the fruit. You have to take some off."

An hour or two later, at our Laguna Ranch vineyards, we had a different type of problem: small "shot berries" mixed in among bigger grapes. The foreman called them "pumpkins and peas," and he proposed thinning the "peas." He thought the smaller grapes might be more susceptible to rot in case of late rains.

"Taking grapes off now will not reduce rot," I said. The more I looked at the vines, the less I liked the idea of thinning. These vines were carrying the right amount of fruit. I thought there was a good chance the smaller grapes would reach maturity by harvest time.

"Let's not thin," I said. "These vines can support the new growth. They look fine."

At times like this, experience pays off. I can't always explain *why* we should do something, but I usually have a pretty good idea of *what* we should do. I guess this comes from doing the same thing for almost sixty years.

These vineyards are very important to our future. The best grapes in California are grown in this region. And here is where we are raising the grapes for our estate wines. Estate bottling will be one step further for us, something we have never done before.

The designation "estate-bottled" may be used only on wines produced from grapes grown within a single viticultural area. They must be harvested from vineyards owned or controlled by the bottling winery. And the winery itself must be in the same viticultural area and must make and bottle the wine in that winery. We plan to do this at our Dry Creek winery with grapes from our "northern Sonoma" vineyards.

When we started out, Ernest and I made a commitment. We would give the consumer the best wine and price possible. In fulfilling this promise, our winery became the largest in the world. Now, I look forward to dispelling the idea that fine wines can't be made by a company like ours that puts out volume.

Before, Sales and Marketing had been interested mostly in products that could develop into a big market. But with our premium estate wines, Ernest and I want to prove a point. We want to show that Sonoma's vineyards are among the best in the world, and that we have the know-how to produce some of the world's finest wines.

Wine is not manufactured. It is grown. It is a living agricultural product. It is born and matures naturally during the growing cycle. The winemaker guides the entire process. Ultimately, wine is a result of the winemaker's sense of smell, taste, and of the "feel" of the grape in his hand and on his palate. It is a matter of personal taste and style.

Who makes the best wine in the world?

Who knows? Who is to judge? Anytime you get more than two wine drinkers together, someone will like more body in his wine and someone wants it a little lighter. Someone wants more fruit, someone wants it drier.

I still taste wine daily over at Research with my "tasting panel." My son, Bob, and son-in-law, Jim, join me—they have each been with the company now for 35 years. Jim and Bob run Production, having taken over all the day-to-day operations I used to handle. Nowadays, I am primarily interested in seeing that my winemakers have a source of good, varietal grapes to fill their programs.

If someone were to ask how important the daily tasting sessions are, I would say, "It's the most important thing that we do." No wine is shipped out unless it is approved by our tasting panel, and I am very involved in that. I want to see that each lot of wine that is shipped has a continuity of quality. I pride myself in knowing that our consumers get the quality they deserve.

Besides Bob and Jim, other longtime members of my senior tasting panel include winemakers George Thoukis (with us for 33 years), in charge of champagne and, along with Guido Croce (32 years), all dry wines, and Peter Vella (30 years), who heads the division for special natural and dessert wines, coolers and brandy. Others show up depending on which products we're considering. All of the people on the panel have extensive wine-tasting experience, which is important. Each of them has an excellent memory for the recognition of flavors and aromas.

In all, we have seven head winemakers, and each has from two to four assistants, depending on which type of wines they make. When the winemakers come in for a tasting—they always attend a tasting of their own wines—they usually bring an assistant winemaker with them. Everyone joins in on the discussion, as I encourage each person to express an opinion. I want to hear why they prefer one wine or blend over another. Every opinion is considered, and the group works very well together. Nobody gets offended if they happen to be in the minority. Generally speaking, there is always a majority and pretty much we go with that. If the group is split and they can't agree, someone has to make the final decision. In those cases, I do. At that point, the winemakers are directed as to how they should change the blend or whatever other course of action we have approved.

Professional wine tasting is hard work. We are usually in there for an hour. I like to schedule tastings late in the morning just before lunch, when the appetite is strongest and the senses most alert. Samplings are done "blind" with numbered bottles, so the tasters don't know what they are tasting until afterward. We keep the temperature in the tasting room at a constant 68 degrees. The air is humidified with all foreign odors extracted. The glasses we use are thin-walled, narrower at the mouth than the base to concentrate the fragrance of the wines.

We begin a session by inspecting the wine's color and clarity.

Next, we swirl the wine around in the glass to release its aromatic components and inhale the wine's fragrance. We do this rapidly because nerve endings fatigue quickly. Smell, of course, is the most important part of taste. After nosing the wine, we taste it. Holding the wine in the mouth, we draw air over the liquid to vaporize the more elusive aromas. Finally, a drop or two is allowed to trickle down the throat to judge the wine's "finish." We spit the rest out in one of the line of stainless sinks behind us. To drink more would affect the taste of the next wine, and eventually, drinking twenty or more wines before lunch would catch up with anyone. To rest the taste buds between wines, we sip water and munch on unsalted crackers.

After the tasting, we consult the chemical analysis made by our laboratory of the various wines. From time to time, I will disagree with the lab's report of a wine's makeup and ask that the wine is reanalyzed. Sometimes, it turns out that my nose and tongue were right, and the scientific equipment wrong. I figure in more than fifty years of professional tasting I've probably sampled more than half a million wines. As I said, experience counts.

The way we run our winemaking operation we are really a number of small wineries, with specialists who work only with their wines and nothing else. I am very thankful for the loyalty and effectiveness demonstrated over the years by our production team.

We bring people up from within the Production Department. The young employees coming up are trained with our methods and come to understand our routine. We take these graduates of UC Davis or Fresno State, start them at the bottom and let them work themselves up to a position of assistant winemaker, and finally to a winemaker position. There's no doubt we have some of the top winemakers in the industry today.

As far as new products are concerned, my son-in-law, Jim, meets with the Marketing Department once a week. The purpose of these meetings is to communicate between Marketing and Production as to changes in packaging or suggesting new types of wine they think have potential and which they would like us to work on. Jim then comes back and we take a look at these ideas. Are the grapes available for the new wine? If not, sometimes we have to wait before we can move. If we do have the grapes and wine available, then we'll turn the idea over to the Product Development Department, and they will usually come back with several different proposals.

My panel always tastes new products first. If we like it, we send it up to Marketing. If they like it, then they will do the necessary market research. After that, they come back to us and tell us whether it has potential or not. All this takes time. It is not like it used to be. Years ago, I would develop a product and Ernest and I would make the decision. We didn't spend a lot of money developing products in the old days. Of course, we didn't have it to spend.

Nowadays, there are more people involved in coming up with new products, and it takes a lot of back and forth discussion between both sides of the company. There's a good reason for that because today it takes an enormous amount of money as well as sales and marketing effort to release and promote a new product. It is quite a commitment, and you need to be very sure that there is a market out there.

All in all, I'm very satisfied everything is working the way it should on the production side. I don't worry too much these days because I know I have experienced, well-qualified, dedicated people on the job.

Every Christmas Eve, Ernest and Amelia come to our home for a special dinner: *bagna cauda*, a traditional Piedmontese dish that is like a single-pot fondue made up of chopped garlic and anchovies cooked in olive oil and butter, in which you dip fresh vegetables. Ernest always brings a special bottle of wine for us to try. One year, it was a $450

Bordeaux. We all tasted it, then opened our own Hearty Burgundy. At the end of the meal, our bottle had less left in it than the French one.

You see, we make wines we like best.

IN FRESNO, MY DAUGHTER'S OLDEST SON, Greg Coleman, now 35 years old and a Fresno State graduate with a degree in viticulture, manages our Madera vineyards. He also deals with our growers in that part of the Valley.

At last count, I have eight grandchildren working full-time for the winery. That's not to say a few of the younger ones won't be coming along when they finish school.

Greg's brother Brad, 33, a Fresno State agricultural business graduate, manages our vineyards at Livingston and Modesto. Their sister, Caroline, 28, a USC graduate in communications, works for us in San Francisco. Chris, 36, a graduate of the California College of Arts and Crafts, and Joan, 31, a USC graduate, are mothers and homemakers. Their two younger brothers are headed our way, though. Ted, 25, graduated from USC and went on to Fresno State to receive a degree in enology. He is working for the winery. Tim, 23, is majoring in ag business at Fresno State. Anne, 21, just graduated from St. Mary's in Moraga with majors in English and philosophy. And their mother, Sue, is a dealer in fine English antiques.

As you can see, a number of my grandchildren have attended Fresno State. I came to prefer Fresno State over UC Davis for viticulture because it has a more practical, hands-on approach, while Davis emphasizes research.

Working at the winery on Bob's side, in addition to Matt, a UCLA graduate, we have John, 32, who graduated from Santa Clara University, managing our Purchasing Department; Tom, 29, a graduate of Cal Poly at San Luis Obispo, manages our family-affiliated printing company; Amy, 23, who attended Modesto Junior College, works in printing; and Gina, 26, who graduated from the College of Notre

Dame (Belmont), is learning winemaking. Julie, 35, a Santa Clara University graduate, is now a homemaker, and the youngest, Mary, 22, attends Loyola University in Chicago. (Bob and Marie tragically lost a son, Mark, to leukemia in 1978.)

I don't know if it was at school or later, but somewhere along the line Greg became very interested in reducing the use of chemicals in farming. My first grandson, he was the newborn baby I had held in my arms for a nighttime stroll back in 1959, along the edge of our vineyard.

Our company had always sought to minimize chemical use, especially commercial fertilizers and herbicides. As a hobby I had long enjoyed organic gardening at home. I needed no convincing that fruits and vegetables grown naturally tasted much better.

Still, like other grape growers, we had become involved in the pesticides cycle. It seemed the more everyone sprayed, the more pests we had, which meant we had to spray even more the following year. Forty years ago we didn't have all the problems with pests like mites and leaf hoppers.

Greg and I had several discussions about this. He thought part of the reason we had so many more pest problems these days was because every time a farmer sprays he is also killing the beneficial insects that eat the harmful ones. And whenever he sprays for weeds, he kills the ground cover that the good bugs need to survive.

I had come to the conclusion some time ago that spraying to control weeds was irresponsible. The chemicals saturated the soil and soaked into the roots. I had made us cut back on herbicides, favoring the old-fashioned way of dealing with weeds by plowing them under as "green" fertilizer.

I asked Greg how he thought we could get off this chemical treadmill.

"By eliminating all spraying. Someone has to start. We could help Mother Nature along by buying good bugs from insectories and releasing them into the vineyard."

I liked the sound of it, but was it practical?

Under Greg's leadership, Fresno became our organic testing and proving ground.

In 1988, using only a forty-acre test plot, Greg eliminated synthetic fertilizers, and reduced herbicide and pesticide use. He then carefully monitored fruit quality.

"I always figured if I got into too much trouble," Greg admitted to me later, "we would spray."

But he didn't have to.

The following year, he expanded his program to four hundred acres. He also put the rest of the ranch on "low-input maintenance," meaning that he used chemicals that were less harmful to the beneficials, or "good bugs," he was releasing. He cultivated "cover crops" between the rows of vines that were conducive to the beneficials.

Each year he expanded the program: more acreage, more beneficials, and less spraying.

I was pleased with Greg's progress, but the scope of his "beneficials" program didn't hit me until one summer day in 1990.

Greg and I had been taking a drive. He was showing me the vineyards. "I haven't sprayed," he said.

It was hard to believe. The vineyard looked great—better than ever.

"Wait a minute. You haven't sprayed?"

He nodded. "We sulfur to prevent mildew, but that's it."

"Stop the car. Let me out."

The vines were exploding with new growth. There were no signs of pests. This time of year—even when we had been spraying—vines were often covered in leaf hoppers and other damaging insects.

"Let me get this right," I said. "You haven't sprayed this vineyard *at all?*"

"That's right, Grandpa. No fungicides, no pesticides, no herbicides, no synthetic fertilizers. Nothing chemical at all. It's clean."

Greg said he had succeeded in creating a natural balance between pests and beneficials that eliminated the need for spraying.

The final test, as always, was in the grapes and wine. Both were better than ever.

I told Greg we needed to sign up our growers for this program. "Bring them over here and show them how it works," I suggested. "Let them know they'll be saving money by not spraying."

Though there were so many other advantages, I knew the cost factor alone would help convince many growers. It didn't seem too farfetched to hope that organic vines would not only produce more and better fruit, but also keep costs in line and possibly even reduce grape and wine prices. Organic growers could also look forward to eliminating worker-safety concerns regarding the use of chemicals, and avoid complex pesticide reporting regulations.

We had made a good beginning.

Recently, Greg has gotten the state to certify us as "organic growers." In fact, his vineyard is the largest "certified organic" vineyard in the state.

Another grandson of mine, Brad Coleman, has started his own "sustainable agricultural practices" program for our vineyards in Livingston and Modesto. We have since expanded the program to other vineyards, including Sonoma. Every area has its own problems—different types of weeds, insects, and so forth. But we are learning how to handle them.

We have to bring nature back into balance.

It's the least we can do for the land—the land that has done so much for us.

22

STRIVING FOR
PERFECTION

Ernest

My son Joe invited me to speak to members of the Young Presidents'
Organization when they visited the winery in May 1991. This is an international group of company presidents and CEOs, all under the age
of fifty, which Joe had belonged to for some time.

I began by explaining the advantages of a privately held company.

"Because we are a family-owned company, all our actions are influenced by what is best for the long range.

"Speed of decision and action is another advantage. We want things
done right away. No waiting. No dawdling. As soon as we make a decision, we do it and do it now, before a competitor gets it done. If a better
piece of equipment comes on the market, we buy it. If another building is needed, we construct it. If competition increases, and more salesmen or more advertising or more competitive pricing is indicated, we
do what is required. We do not give a thought to what our profit will be
for the quarter, or for that year as compared to past years. All that matters is: Does it make sense long range?"

I explained that our board of directors consists of Julio, his son and son-in-law, my two sons, and me. "We never have a formal board meeting, but you might say we are in constant sessions. We are all instantly available to each other by phone.

"Another advantage in being a private company is that because our own money is at stake, if an error is made, the moment it is discovered it is corrected. In some public companies, before an error is revealed and a change can be made, a scapegoat must first be found. Such a delay can be costly, both in money and in market share.

"And I am glad we do not have to divert energy to what public stockholders think of our management, our future, or the value of our stock. It is amazing to me to see some press releases—and reports of security analysts—where corporate officers describe new products to be introduced or how successful new ventures are. They are trying to increase the market price of their stock or their ego requires they try to impress others at the expense of giving competitors useful information.

"Also in most public companies, there is a constant drive to program earnings, so as to show an increase each quarter. All too often this is at the expense of what is best for the business long range.

"If you have a private firm, stay private. If you are public, buy it back."

In our nearly sixty years in business, I explained, I never once tried to steer our company to a predetermined profit for the year. "I have read repeatedly about the importance of long-term budgeting. Several times we wondered whether we should try this, but as quickly as the idea came to us, we dropped it."

We could not make meaningful projections for any given period when there are unknown factors: what wine consumption will be; what new products will be accepted and rejected by consumers; what new products competitors will introduce; what the pricing policy of our competitors will be; how much our competitors will spend in advertising; whether their advertising will be effective, and what new excise taxes may apply to wine.

"I always have felt we didn't really know what was going to happen next year," I admitted, "let alone in the next five years or the next ten years."

I had guessed that the young company presidents wondered just how Gallo had become the largest winery in the world with such an obvious lack of planning by its owners.

"The reasons are that we are constantly unhappy, and constantly striving for perfection. We are unhappy:

"Because we could always use more fine wine grapes.
"Because we want to improve our winemaking technology even faster.
"About the effectiveness of our advertising.
"That our sales force—good as it is—is not even better.
"That our relationship with our wholesalers—good as it is—is not better.
"That our relationship with our retailers—good as it is—is not better.
"That our wines do not have the image with the consumer that they deserve.
"That we are not selling all the wine in the country."

It was that continuous striving for perfection, I explained, that helps keep us ahead of our competition. "And now my advice, which will cost you nothing, and that is probably what it is worth:

"Don't go public. If you already are, go the leveraged buyout route.
"Hire good people.
"Never be satisfied.
"Strive for perfection.

"Don't plan too far ahead.

"Develop a sense of urgency.

"Work like hell.

"Be lucky."

Later, at dinner that night, I fielded a lot of questions from YPO members. One fellow, looking very concerned, wanted to know if I was really "that unhappy."

I had to laugh because I don't know of anybody who is happier than I am. My point, of course, was that I am not satisfied with our accomplishments when I think we can do much better.

"Every day I see waste," I explained, "things slipping through our fingers. But we are aware of them and we try to improve and keep it from happening again. People who fail in business either didn't see the missed opportunities, or if they did see them, it didn't upset them enough for them to work harder to take advantage of them. The day that you are satisfied with your business is the day that your progress comes to a halt and you start to slide downhill."

Although at present we are by far the largest winery in the world, we sell only 37 percent of all the wine produced in California. We are not at all happy with this. If we were not unhappy, it wouldn't take long before we began to lose market share.

Considering that we have more vineyards than anyone else, some of which are certainly equal to the very best in the world; facilities that are second to none; the best winemakers in the business; a marketing department that is head and shoulders above our competition's; a sales department that rivals that of the largest consumer products companies in the U.S.; unlimited capital; and that we are the only wine company making its own bottles and closures—we *must* be unhappy with only 37 percent of the volume.

Experts say that in a consumer-products business you always remain vulnerable, even if you have more than 50 percent of the market. For example, Gillette remains a fierce competitor in razor blades and Anheuser-Busch in beer, even though these brands dominate their markets. As soon as you become happy with your performance, you start becoming soft and competitors can find niches in which to grow, making them stronger and you weaker.

THE CURRENT GLOBAL ANTI-ALCOHOL MOVEMENT includes a real challenge to vintners, retailers, and wine consumers alike.

We endured a similar anti-alcohol experience in this country seventy-five years ago. Prohibition didn't work then. Yet the movement led by today's neo-Prohibitionists is picking up increasing momentum worldwide.

World consumption of wine peaked in 1978 at 7.7 billion gallons. Since then it has declined 20 percent, a loss of 1.5 billion gallons in just fifteen years. This decline reflects the efforts of a powerful coalition dedicated to reducing the consumption of alcohol, including wine, by any and all means possible — higher taxes, restrictive legislation, warning labels, and a barrage of public messages that alcohol threatens health and fitness. This campaign has been increasingly successful in inducing governments to adopt punitive measures against alcoholic beverages, including wine.

The wine industry and consumers are faced with formidable opponents who have many allies in high government positions working to eliminate or drastically curtail the consumption of wine. If they are successful, the result will be to put out of work millions of men and women involved in grape growing, winemaking, distribution, and related industries (glass, railroad, trucking, etc.). They would reduce government tax revenues from this source, and they would deny the pleasure of wine to humanity.

The anti-alcohol movement would treat wine as if there were no difference between Cabernet Sauvignon and cocaine. The goal is to strip wine of its centuries of tradition, history, and culture and to convince the public to regard it as a harmful substance.

There is, of course, an irony to this attempt to equate wine with drugs. Historically, wine has been understood to be a robust complement to the family meal—not a "toxic and dependence-inducing drug," but a means of strengthening communal and familial bonds.

The irony of our predicament is further underscored when you consider that while all this is going on, the weight of medical and scientific evidence regarding the health benefits of responsible wine consumption is expanding to the point of irrefutability.

Serious health researchers—none of them supported by the alcohol-beverage industry—have built an increasingly credible case that moderate alcohol consumption is good preventive medicine, especially as it relates to reduced coronary artery disease.

For example, in May 1992, Harvard University Medical School researchers writing in the *New England Journal of Medicine* (vol. 326, no. 21) included moderate alcohol consumption as one of nine scientifically supportable ways to reduce the risk of heart attacks.

Other recent studies have confirmed the positive correlation between moderate alcohol consumption and reduced risk of heart disease. Among them are a report by Dr. Arthur Klatsky published last year in the *American Journal of Cardiology* (February 1993). And in the June 1993 issue of the *Journal of the American Public Health Association*, researchers from Harvard's School of Public Health concluded that "light to moderate drinkers have substantially lower rates of cardiovascular mortality and mortality from all causes than do non-drinkers or heavy drinkers."

It is no surprise that many doctors support wine. Many are joining together to establish chapters of the organization Medical Friends of Wine. Who ever heard of doctors forming an organization called medical friends of tobacco, or butter, or red meat?

For the first time, Americans became broadly aware of the health benefits of wine when a CBS 60 *Minutes* broadcast in 1991 explored the so-called "French paradox": heavy fat consumption but relatively few heart problems among the wine-drinking French.

While I have always believed in the health benefits of moderate wine consumption—and even think I am a good example of it at a youthful eighty-five years of age—I resisted the efforts of some members of the wine industry to seek a change in federal regulations that would allow our promoting the health values of wine to the public.

Recently, I have had a change of heart. Given the steadily accumulating body of scientific evidence concerning the contributions of a moderate use of wine to a healthy life-style, I am now convinced that we should seek a change in the regulations that would permit us to state the true facts.

First, the public has a right to know about anything that can improve health, and we have an obligation to inform them of it. Secondly, it makes economic sense to extol the proven benefits of a product—that is just plain good business.

If wine is permitted to be falsely seen as a "toxic" and "dependence-inducing drug," it automatically changes public perception of the traditional role of wine. Instead of being seen as an integral part of daily life, the enjoyment of wine becomes undesirable.

No one would deny that wine must not be used in excess. By the same token, excessive consumption of salt can cause high blood pressure. The excessive consumption of fatty foods may promote cancer. Obviously, educating consumers about the health effects of what they consume and in what amounts is an appropriate activity.

I believe pregnant women should abstain from all alcoholic beverages. Although it has not been established what, if anything, moderate consumption of wine has to do with fetal alcohol syndrome, why take a chance?

I was on a jury many years ago for a drunk-driving case. The defense attorney seemed pleased that I was on the jury. Perhaps he thought I would go easy on his client because of my involvement in the wine business. He found out otherwise. We returned a quick and unanimous guilty verdict. Driving drunk is a crime. There is no in-between and no excuse. Drive drunk, go to jail.

The point, however, is that the anti-alcohol movement has crossed the line. Their strategy is not one of empowering consumers to make informed choices. Their objective seems to be to eliminate the use of wine. One basic problem with this strategy is the question of whether we want to permit government to decide for us what we eat and drink.

Another problem is that the anti-alcohol strategy does not discriminate between use and abuse.

But the most important problem with the approach of the anti-alcohol movement is that it suppresses the truth about wine, and thereby harms rather than promotes public health, and also denies the public the enjoyment of a historic, traditional pleasure.

A good example comes from the field of health education in our schools. The anti-alcohol movement is having a chilling effect on what our schools are permitted to teach. By teaching that all alcohol is a sin and a drug, they are inviting *abuse* of the product, rather than responsible use or abstinence. They are setting alcohol up as a symbol of rebellion, and we all know that children progress through a period of rebellion. The result is that when children inevitably experiment with alcohol, they are not equipped to deal with it properly.

I compare this with the way my parents taught me to drink wine. Starting when I was about seven years old, I recall that a bottle of wine and a pitcher of water always stood on our dining room table. I remember my grandfather, and later my father, pouring a few drops of wine into my glass of water. As I grew older, more and more drops. This was the custom at the time. In that way, I learned how to drink and enjoy wine in moderation.

The neo-Prohibitionists would have people believe that a drink is a drink—and therefore bad. I'll bet that no one has ever gone into a bar and ordered a double-shot of Cabernet. Wine historically has been a beverage of moderation to be enjoyed with food.

It still is.

The dangers of alcoholism have been common knowledge for centuries. It is possible, however, that progress can still be made toward the prevention and cure of this disorder.

To that end, I established in 1982 the Ernest Gallo Clinic and Research Center at the University of California, San Francisco. The Center's approach is to apply state-of-the-art advances in biomedical research to determine how alcohol affects the brain. The Center's scientific advisory board is composed of leading physicians and medical researchers from universities across the country. These scientists use cutting-edge research tools derived from the revolution currently under way in gene biology. The hope is that these space-age techniques will help identify people with a genetic affinity for alcoholism and will lead to remedies for the disease.

The Ernest Gallo Center, which is affiliated with UCSF's Department of Neurology, has grown to include a staff of thirty-four. Headed by Dr. Ivan Diamond, it has five research programs directed by three medical doctors (two of whom also have PhDs) and two senior PhD scientists. Because of the success of the program, I have recently decided to finance major expansion of the Center and its resources.

Research performed at the Gallo Center has received widespread national and international recognition. As a result, the Center has obtained millions of dollars of federal grant support and has attracted many young scientists seeking advanced training. There are currently twenty-two postdoctrinal trainees and technicians at the Center, many of them preparing for careers in alcohol research.

THE WINE MARKET IS CHANGING and we must change with it. Consumers are increasingly interested in varietal wines, while the generic table-wine business continues to decline. We are now selling much more varietal wine than our nearest competitor.

As we approached the release of our estate wines, grown and produced in Sonoma County, I was advised to market them under a name other than Gallo. The advice from members of my own marketing team was pointed: "We can't sell a Chardonnay at thirty dollars or a Cabernet at sixty if we put the Gallo name on it."

The new line represented the culmination of many years of preparation, planning and development by Julio, me, and many others in the Production and Sales and Marketing departments. My brother and I agreed that it would not be any fun if we did not put our names on our finest wines. We released our estate Chardonnay in 1993, with our signatures on the front of the label.

For this 1991 vintage from our Laguna Ranch vineyard—average yield 2.3 tons per acre—no pressing was employed. Only free-run juice released from the weight of the grapes themselves was used. New 100 percent French oak barrels were used for the fermentation and aging of the wine. Barrel fermentation proceeded slowly over 10 to 12 days at a temperature range of 54 to 63 degrees. Aging time was determined barrel by barrel. Before bottling, the final blend was decided by Julio, incorporating only the "best of the best" barrels.

Our 1991 Estate Chardonnay was ranked among the top 10 wines by *Bon Appetit* magazine. In a blind tasting conducted by *Wine Spectator*, a leading industry publication, our estate wine was tasted against leading California Chardonnays and judged to be among "the best of the 1991 Chardonnays . . . elegant, rich and flavorful . . . This wine will change the way you think about Gallo." Priced at $30 a bottle, this wine marked our entry into the ultrapremium wine market.

We soon followed with an estate Cabernet Sauvignon. Julio and his winemakers produced it from a blend of three grape varieties: 79 percent Cabernet Sauvignon, 14 percent Merlot, and 7 percent Cabernet

Franc—a style traditionally used in Bordeaux red wines. Each varietal type was fermented separately. Blending took place prior to barrel aging, which again took place in 100 percent new French oak with aging time determined barrel to barrel. We priced it at $60 a bottle. *Wine Spectator* judged this 1990 vintage from our Frei Ranch in Dry Creek to be "outstanding . . . a wine of superior character and style."

One of the objectives in coming out with these exceptional wines was to enhance our image as fine-wine producers. There is no question that it has been effective. However, an unexpected problem developed: The displeasure of so many retailers and consumers when we could not supply the demand for our estate wines. The people that were saying that the public would not buy wines with a Gallo label that sold for $30 or $60 a bottle have been awfully quiet lately.

"My brother and I achieved nearly every goal we set for ourselves," I said at the time our estate wines were released. "There is one left, however: to create wines that would be recognized as among the world's best. It takes a tremendous investment of resources and a real passion to do that. We have been fortunate enough to have both. It's a matter of personal satisfaction."

I am hopeful that most, if not all, of my five grandchildren will one day join the winery. Their areas of interest are widespread.

David and his wife, Mary, have two children. Theresa, 22, is a student at Stanislaus State University. Her brother, Christopher, 20, is studying at UC Davis.

Joe's and his wife, Ofelia's, oldest child, Stephanie, 22, is a recent graduate of the University of Notre Dame. Her brother Ernest, 21, is a senior at Stanford University. Joseph, 18, is a freshman at the University of Notre Dame.

I am proud of my grandchildren.

I look forward to their coming into *their* winery.

EPILOGUE

Nob Hill, San Francisco

Ernest and Julio Gallo, in black tie and dinner jackets, waited at the head table in the ornate grand ballroom of the Fairmont Hotel. In the brothers' more than half century in the California wine business, it was the first time they had both been present to receive a major industry award. Indeed, they had spent their lives endeavoring to avoid such fanfare.

Though rich with memories of more than half a century in the wine industry they helped spawn, Ernest and Julio had shared little of their history with anyone outside their families. Occasionally, in the right mood and perhaps over an enjoyable meal, one or the other would regale an attentive son or grandchild with a colorful tale. Very private people, they have always believed that their wines speak for themselves. Even so, they have kept their names listed in the Modesto phone directory so that people will feel they are accessible. Though consistently ranked by *Forbes* as among the four hundred richest Americans, Ernest and Julio never had divulged their net worth and never would.

Ernest and Julio had aged and mellowed, it might be suggested, rather like fine red wine. None of their shared native gifts—astounding common sense, an inquisitive nature, irrepressible drive—had dimmed a single watt. Each brother still put in regular workdays, attending to startling small details having to do with his end of the business. They had always seen themselves as builders. Building something they could be proud of. Building something they could pass on to their children and grandchildren.

There was an air of expectancy as moderator Marvin R. Shanken, editor and publisher of the influential *Wine Spectator*, began his introduction of the guests of honor: "There is not a person sitting in this room who has not been touched by, or benefited from, the energies, pioneering courage and accomplishments of the two brothers being honored here tonight."

Summoned forward to collect their distinguished-service awards, Ernest and Julio both hesitated, genuinely caught off guard by the groundswell of applause filling the hall, as all around them leaders of their industry came to their feet.

Ernest and Julio came forward together.

Their togetherness had made them strong but their real secret was their separate-but-equal status; neither told the other how to ply his trade. Julio's long-professed goal was to make more wine than Ernest could sell, while Ernest strived to sell more wine than Julio could make. In truth, they both succeeded.

The brothers were presented with engraved plaques.

Julio expressed his thanks quickly, graciously, and slightly self-consciously.

Ernest stepped up, prepared to say more. "Julio and I view the accomplishments attributed to us in the following light: We are lucky to have had the parents that we had. We are lucky, as young men, to have been growing grapes at the repeal of Prohibition. We are lucky that we both felt that the production of wine was a natural outgrowth of raising grapes. We are lucky that we decided to go into the wine business."

Ernest sincerely believed that luck played a role. If they had not been California-born, or if their father had been in a business other than wine grapes, or if they'd been born a few years earlier or later and if their age of maturity had not dovetailed with the repeal of Prohibition, they might never have gone into the wine business.

They were lucky to have recognized, appreciated, and respected each other's aptitudes, Ernest continued. They were lucky that they both always felt that the future of the wine business depended upon quality. They were lucky to have attracted some of the most talented and dedicated employees and distributors in the country. "I am lucky to have two fine, talented sons, and my brother to have a fine, talented son and son-in-law—all of them working in the business."

Two silver-haired women, their faces glowing with pride, watched from the head table. The brothers were in agreement that their long and challenging road to the top would have been more difficult, perhaps even impassable, without the love and support of Amelia and Aileen.

"We are both lucky," Ernest now said, his voice catching slightly, "to have fine, remarkable wives."

Everyone in the house knew he meant it.

"You can understand therefore, because of all this luck, that Julio and I must accept these awards with some reservation."

In all, Ernest credited good fortune nine times.

If we were always so lucky, Julio wondered as he stood next to his brother and partner, *why did we have to work so damn hard?*

POSTSCRIPT

Ernest

Fortune has a way of favoring those in the right place at the right time, which is exactly where Julio and I were as young men in 1933.

We could easily have been discouraged by what we had heard from our elders and never started our winery. In hindsight, it would appear that we had no reasonable chance of surviving. The odds against us were formidable when we set out on our course. The country was in the depth of the Great Depression, and we were facing comparatively large, established, well-financed (and often government-financed) competitors. We didn't even know how to make wine commercially when we decided to start our winery. We were challenged by the hardships of our youth, by the Depression, and by the loss of our parents.

By nature we were never satisfied with doing anything less than well. Each of us was guided by one principle: to strive for perfection. We never achieved perfection, but we constantly kept trying.

We both knew when we started that we had to make quality products and sell them at fair and competitive prices if we were to succeed.

We believed then, and now, that there is an overriding imperative that private enterprise must provide real value to the consumer if it is to be rewarded with a legitimate, long-range profit.

When we introduced our varietal wines, there were no products better and few as good. We feel that this remains true today, when we make wines at every price level up to sixty dollars a bottle. We have given American wine consumers the greatest value—outstanding quality at reasonable prices—in every category in which we do business, and the consumers have responded accordingly.

From the beginning, Julio and I have been fortunate in finding employees and distributors who believe, as we do, that striving for perfection is a way of life.

With perfection as our goal, we have always tried to do our best—grape-growing, winemaking, production, marketing, salesmanship. It is still a goal for which we continue to strive in every aspect of our business.

Along with our colleagues in the wine business, we helped transform the small struggling industry we entered in 1933 into a consumer-responsive national and international business of world-class stature, and the best is yet to come. The wine industry has some great things going for it as we look to the twenty-first century:

- The weight of medical and scientific evidence regarding the health benefits of responsible wine consumption, from such prestigious medical schools as Harvard and the University of California (Davis), among others, is expanding to the point of irrefutability. As the consumer becomes increasingly aware of the unquestionable benefits of wine, consumption of wine will increase to the benefit of all.

- The program we initiated some years ago of long-term contracts to encourage growers to replant their vineyards with fine varietal grapes has significantly contributed to the great improvement of the types of grapes now available in California for the production of world-class wines.

•Advancing enological research and technology is resulting in new and better products.

After having lived a lifetime in the wine business, we continue to see infinite possibilities.

We feel that our industry provides and will continue to provide people with one of the great things in life—an enjoyable beverage with strong familial, communal, cultural, and even religious ties.

We wrote of our experiences in the hope that our story might serve as encouragement to others—particularly the young—that our country's system works for those with the commitment to succeed. There is a great need to preserve our system of free enterprise under which this was all possible.

A *final note*

I hope our story will be inspiring, particularly to the young, that if they have the will to work hard and make a strong commitment to succeed, the American system works for everyone. Not only for people of wealth, but also for sons of immigrants who have nothing.

—*Julio R. Gallo*

My brother Julio died on May 2, 1993, in a jeep accident on his son's ranch west of Modesto. He was eighty-three.

Julio was a great brother, a great partner, and a great human being. His passing is an enormous personal loss to me, and both of our families. There are no words to describe how much we miss him.

—*Ernest Gallo*

INDEX

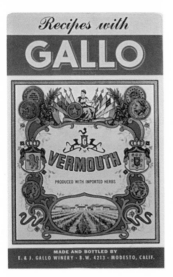

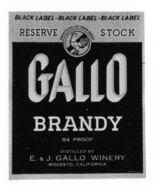